HOLT SCIENCE & TECHNOLOGY

Life Science

Interactive Textbook

HOLT, RINEHART AND WINSTON

A Harcourt Education Company

Orlando • Austin • New York • San Diego • London

Contents

CHAPTER 6 Genes and DNA

CHAPTER 7 The Evolution of Living Things

CHAPTER 8 The History of Life on Earth

CHAPTER 9 Classification

CHAPTER 10 Bacteria and Viruses

CHAPTER 11 Protists and Fungi

CHAPTER 12 Introduction to Plants

CHAPTER 13 Plant Processes

CHAPTER 14 Animals and Behavior

CHAPTER 15 Invertebrates

CHAPTER 16 Fishes, Amphibians, and Reptiles

CHAPTER 17 Birds and Mammals

CHAPTER 18 Interactions of Living Things

CHAPTER 19 Cycles in Nature

CHAPTER 20 The Earth's Ecosystems

CHAPTER 21 Environmental Problems and Solutions

CHAPTER 22 Body Organization and Structure

CHAPTER 23 Circulation and Respiration

CHAPTER 24 The Digestive and Urinary Systems

CHAPTER 25 Communication and Control

CHAPTER 26 Reproduction and Development

CHAPTER 27 Body Defenses and Diseases

CHAPTER 28 Staying Healthy

CHAPTER 2 It's Alive!! Or Is It?

SECTION
1 **Characteristics of Living Things**

14/15 on quizzia

National Science Education Standards
LS 1b, 1c, 1d, 2a, 2b, 2c, 3a, 3b, 3c

What Are All Living Things Made Of?

If you saw a bright yellow, slimy blob in the grass, would you think it was alive? How could you tell? All living things, or *organisms*, share several characteristics. What does a dog have in common with a bacterium? What do *you* have in common with a bright yellow slime mold?

All living things are made of one or more cells. A **cell** is the smallest unit that can carry out all the activities of life. Every cell is surrounded by a cell membrane. The *cell membrane* separates the cell from the outside environment.

Some organisms are made of trillions of cells. In these organisms, different kinds of cells do different jobs. For example, muscle cells are used for movement. Other organisms are made of only one cell. In these organisms, different parts of the cell have different jobs.

STUDY TIP

Organize As you read this section, make a list of the six characteristics of living things.

STANDARDS CHECK

LS 1b All organisms are composed of cells—the fundamental unit of life. Most organisms are single cells; other organisms, including humans, are multicellular.

1. Identify What are all living things made of?

_____

_____

Some organisms, such as the monkeys on the left, are made up of trillions of cells. The protists on the right are made up of one or a few cells. They are so small they can only be seen with a microscope.

How Do Living Things Respond to Change?

All organisms can sense changes in their environments. Each organism reacts differently to these changes. A change that affects how an organism acts is called a **stimulus** (plural, *stimuli*). Stimuli can be chemicals, light, sounds, hunger, or anything that causes an organism to react. ☑

READING CHECK

2. List Give three examples of stimuli.

_____

_____

_____

The touch of an insect is a stimulus for a Venus' flytrap. The stimulus causes the plant to close its leaves quickly.

TAKE A LOOK
3. Complete For a Venus' flytrap, the touch of an insect is a ___Stimulus___.

Critical Thinking

4. Predict What would happen if your body couldn't maintain homeostasis?

When you're hot, you would burn up, and when you're cold, you would freeze (get deseases from cold easier.

Even when things outside the body change, an organism must keep the conditions inside its body the same. The act of keeping a constant environment inside an organism is called **homeostasis**. When an organism maintains homeostasis, all the chemical reactions inside its body can work correctly.

RESPONDING TO EXTERNAL CHANGES

If it is hot outside, your body starts to sweat to cool down. If it is cold outside, your body starts to shiver to warm up. In each situation, your body reacts to the changes in the environment. It tries to return itself to normal.

Different kinds of organisms react to changes in the environment in different ways. For example, crocodiles lie in the sun to get warm. When they get too warm, they open their mouths wide to release heat.

How Do Organisms Have Offspring?

Every type of organism has *offspring*. The two ways organisms can produce offspring are by sexual or asexual reproduction. Generally, in **sexual reproduction**, two parents make offspring. The offspring get traits from both parents. In **asexual reproduction**, one parent makes offspring. The offspring are identical to the parent. ☑

Most plants and animals make offspring by sexual reproduction. However, most single-celled organisms and some multicellular organisms make offspring by asexual reproduction. For example, hydra make offspring by forming buds that break off and grow into new hydra.

 READING CHECK

5. Identify How many parents are generally needed to produce offspring by sexual reproduction?

_____

SECTION 1 Characteristics of Living Things *continued*

Like most animals, bears produce offspring by sexual reproduction. However, some animals, such as hydra, can reproduce asexually.

Why Do Offspring Look Like Their Parents?

All organisms are made of cells. Inside each cell, there is information about all of the organism's traits. This information is found in DNA (**d**eoxyribo**n**ucleic **a**cid). *DNA* carries instructions for the organism's traits. Offspring look like their parents because they get copies of parts of their parent's DNA. Passing traits from parent to offspring is called **heredity**. ☑

Why Do Organisms Need Energy?

All organisms need energy to live. Most organisms get their energy from the food they eat. Organisms use this energy to carry out all the activities that happen inside their bodies. For example, organisms need energy to break down food, to move materials in and out of cells, and to build cells.

An organism uses energy to keep up its metabolism. An organism's **metabolism** is all of the chemical reactions that take place in its body. Breaking down food for energy is one of these chemical reactions.

How Do Organisms Grow?

All organisms grow during some part of their lives. In a single-celled organism, the cell gets bigger and divides. This makes new organisms. An organism made of many cells gets bigger by making more cells. As these organisms grow, they get new traits. These traits often change how the organism looks. For example, as a tadpole grows into a frog, it develops legs and loses its tail. ☑

TAKE A LOOK
6. Identify How do most animals reproduce?

Animals mostly have sexual reproduc...

☑ **READING CHECK**
7. Define What is the function of DNA?

It has tha specific traits and is passed down when its organism reproduces

☑ **READING CHECK**
8. Compare How does growth differ in single-celled organisms and those made of many cells?

Organisms with many cells grow more cells and single-celled organisms grow their one cell.

Section 1 Review

NSES LS 1b 1c, 1d, 2a, 2b, 2c, 3a, 3b, 3c

SECTION VOCABULARY

asexual reproduction reproduction that does not involve the union of sex cells and in which one parent produces offspring that are genetically identical to the parent.	**homeostasis** the maintenance of a constant internal state in a changing environment
cell in biology, the smallest unit that can perform all life processes; cells are covered by a membrane and contain DNA and cytoplasm	**metabolism** the sum of all chemical processes that occur in an organism
	sexual reproduction reproduction in which the sex cells from two parents unite to produce offspring that share traits from both parents
heredity the passing of genetic traits from parent to offspring	**stimulus** anything that causes a reaction or change in an organism or any part of an organism

1. Summarize Complete the Spider Map to show the six characteristics of living things. Add lines to give details on each characteristic.

cellular organization

respond to their surroundings

contain similar chemicals

Characteristics of living things

grow and develope

reproduce

use energy

2. Compare How does sexual reproduction differ from asexual reproduction?

_____

_____

_____

3. Explain How do the buds of an organism such as hydra compare to the parent?

_____

_____

4. Identify Relationships How is a bear's fur related to homeostasis?

_____

_____

_____

CHAPTER 2 (It's Alive!! Or Is It?)

SECTION 2 | The Necessities of Life

BEFORE YOU READ

After you read this section, you should be able to answer these questions:

- What things do almost all organisms need?
- Why do living things need food?

What Do Living Things Need?

Would it surprise you to learn that you have the same basic needs as a tree, a frog, and a fly? Almost every organism has the same basic needs: water, air, a place to live, and food.

WATER

Your body is made mostly of water. The cells that make up your body are about 70% to 85% water. Cells need water to keep their inside environments stable. Most of the chemical reactions that happen in cells need water. Your body loses water as you breathe, sweat, or get rid of wastes, such as urine. Because of this, you must replace the water that you lose.

Organisms get water from the fluids they drink and the foods they eat. However, organisms need different amounts of water. You could survive only three days without water. A kangaroo rat never drinks. It lives in the desert and gets all the water it needs from its food.

AIR

Oxygen, nitrogen, and carbon dioxide are some of the gases in air. Most organisms use oxygen to help them break down food for energy. Other organisms, such as green plants, use carbon dioxide to make food.

National Science Education Standards

LS 1a, 1c, 2c, 3a, 3d, 4b, 4c, 4d

 STUDY TIP

Organize As you read, make a table of the basic needs of most organisms. Fill in examples of how different organisms meet those needs.

STANDARDS CHECK

LS 1c Cells carry out the many <u>functions</u> needed to sustain life. They grow and divide, thereby producing more cells. This requires that they take in nutrients, which they use to provide energy for the work that cells do and to make the materials that a cell or organism needs.

Word Help: <u>function</u> use or purpose

1. Explain Why do cells need water?

_____

_____

_____

_____

_____

_____

TAKE A LOOK

2. Infer Why do you think this diving spider surrounds itself with a bubble in the water?

_____

_____

_____

_____

SECTION 2 The Necessities of Life *continued*

A PLACE TO LIVE

Just as you do, all living things need a place to live. Organisms look for an area that has everything they need to survive. Often, many organisms live in the same area. They all must use the same resources, such as food and water. Many times, an organism will try to keep others out of its area. For example, some birds keep other birds away by singing.

FOOD

All organisms need food. Food gives organisms energy and nutrients to live and grow. However, not all organisms get food in the same way. There are three ways in which organisms can get food. ☑

Some organisms, such as plants, are producers. **Producers** make their own food using energy from their environment. For example, plants, and some bacteria and protists, use the sun's energy to make food from carbon dioxide and water. This process is called *photosynthesis*.

Many organisms are consumers. **Consumers** eat other organisms to get food. For example, a frog is a consumer because it eats insects. All animals are consumers.

A mushroom is a decomposer. Decomposers are a special kind of consumer. **Decomposers** break down dead organisms and animal wastes to get food. Although they are a kind of consumer, decomposers play a different role in an ecosystem than most other consumers. Without decomposers, dead organisms and wastes would pile up all over the Earth!

Consumer

Producer

decomposer

READING CHECK

3. Explain Why do living things need food?

Food give nutrients and energy needed to live and grow

Critical Thinking

4. Identify Are you a producer, consumer, or decomposer? Explain your answer.

Consumer. I eat other living things, and don't eat them until they die.

TAKE A LOOK

5. Label On the picture, label the producer, consumer, and decomposer.

What Do Organisms Get from Food?

As you just read, organisms can get their food in three different ways. However, all organisms must break down their food to use the nutrients.

Nutrients are molecules. *Molecules* are made of two or more atoms joined together. Most molecules in living things are combinations of carbon, nitrogen, oxygen, phosphorus, and sulfur. Proteins, nucleic acids, lipids, carbohydrates, and ATP are some of the molecules needed by living things.

PROTEINS

Proteins are used in many processes inside a cell. **Proteins** are large molecules made up of smaller molecules called *amino acids*. Living things break down the proteins in food and use the amino acids to make new proteins. ☑

An organism uses proteins in many different ways. Some proteins are used to build or fix parts of an organism's body. Some proteins stay on the outside of a cell, to protect it. Proteins called *enzymes* help to start or speed up reactions inside a cell.

Some proteins help cells do their jobs. For example, a protein called *hemoglobin* is found in our red blood cells. It picks up oxygen and delivers it through the body.

Spider webs, horns, and feathers are made from proteins.

 Say It

Discuss With a partner, name 10 organisms and describe what foods they eat. Discuss whether these organisms are producers, consumers, or decomposers.

☑ **READING CHECK**

6. Complete Proteins are made up of _amino_ _acids_ .

Math Focus

7. Calculate Each red blood cell carries about 250 million molecules of hemoglobin. If every hemoglobin molecule is attached to four oxygen molecules, how many oxygen molecules could one red blood cell carry?

1 billion

1 billion oxygen molecules

NUCLEIC ACIDS

When you bake a cake, you follow instructions to make sure the cake is made correctly. When cells make new molecules, such as proteins, they also follow a set of instructions. The instructions for making any part of an organism are stored in *DNA*.

DNA is a nucleic acid. **Nucleic acids** are molecules made of smaller molecules called *nucleotides*. The instructions carried by DNA tell a cell how to make proteins. The order of nucleotides in DNA tells cells which amino acids to use and which order to put them in.

LIPIDS

Lipids are molecules that cannot mix with water. They are a form of stored energy. When lipids are stored in an animal, they are usually solid. These are called *fats*. When lipids are stored in a plant, they are usually liquid. These are called *oils*. When an organism has used up other sources of energy, it can break down fats and oils for more energy.

Lipids also form cell membranes. Cell membranes surround and protect cells. They are made of special lipids called **phospholipids**. When phospholipids are in water, the tail ends of the molecules come together and the head ends face out. This is shown in the figure below.

Phospholipid Membranes

Critical Thinking

8. Identify Relationships What is the relationship between amino acids and nucleotides?

_____

_____

_____

_____

_____

_____

TAKE A LOOK

9. Describe Describe the structure of a phospholipid, and how it behaves in water.

_____

_____

_____

_____

_____

CARBOHYDRATES

Carbohydrates are molecules made of sugars. They provide and store energy for cells. An organism's cells break down carbohydrates to free energy. There are two types of carbohydrates: simple and complex. ☑

Simple carbohydrates are made of one or a few sugar molecules. Both table sugar and sugar in fruits are simple carbohydrates. The simple carbohydrate *glucose* is the most common source of energy for cells. The body breaks down simple carbohydrates more quickly than complex carbohydrates.

Complex carbohydrates are made of hundreds of sugar molecules linked together. When organisms such as plants have more sugar than they need, they can store the extra sugar as complex carbohydrates. For example, potatoes store extra sugar as starch. You can also find complex carbohydrates in foods such as whole-wheat bread, pasta, oatmeal, and brown rice.

Hw

10. Identify What are two types of carbohydrates?

Simple

complex

Type of carbohydrate	Structure	Example
Simple	made of one or a few sugar molecules	Table sugar
Complex	hundreds of sugar molecules	Potatoes

TAKE A LOOK
11. Complete Complete the table to explain the two types of carbohydrates.

ATP

After carbohydrates and fats have been broken down, how does their energy get to where it is needed? The cells use **a**denosine **t**riphos**p**hate, or ATP. **ATP** is a molecule that carries energy in cells. The energy released from carbohydrates and fats is passed to ATP molecules. ATP then carries the energy to where it is needed in the cell. ☑

12. Identify What molecule carries energy in cells?

ATP

It's Alive!! Or Is It?

Name _____ Class _____ Date _____

Section 2 Review

HW   *8/10 on quiz?*

NSES LS 1a, 1c, 2c, 3a, 3d, 4b, 4c, 4d

SECTION VOCABULARY

ATP adenosine triphosphate, a molecule that acts as the main energy source for cell processes

carbohydrate a class of energy-giving molecules that includes sugars, starches, and fiber; contains carbon, hydrogen, and oxygen

consumer an organism that eats other organisms or organic matter

decomposer an organism that gets energy by breaking down the remains of dead organisms or animal wastes and consuming or absorbing the nutrients

lipid a type of biochemical that does not dissolve in water; fats and steroids are lipids

nucleic acid a molecule made up of subunits called nucleotides

phospholipid a lipid that contains phosphorus and that is a structural component in cell membranes

producer an organism that can make its own food by using energy from its surroundings

protein a molecule that is made up of amino acids and that is needed to build and repair body structures and to regulate processes in the body

1. List Name four things that organisms need to survive.

Food, a home, oxygon, and water

2. Explain Why are decomposers also consumers?

It consumes the dead organism's nutrients.

3. Identify What two nutrients store energy?

ATP and Lipids

4. Describe Describe the structure of a cell membrane.

They are made of phospolipids

5. Compare Name two ways that simple carbohydrates differ from complex carbohydrates.

Simple carbs have way less molecules The body breaks down simple carbs les easier than complex ones.

6. Explain Why is ATP important to cells?

ATP is needed to carry the energy to the cell.

Copyright © by Holt, Rinehart and Winston. All rights reserved.
Interactive Textbook   32   It's Alive!! Or Is It?

CHAPTER 6 Genes and DNA

SECTION 1 What Does DNA Look Like?

Hw

BEFORE YOU READ

After you read this section, you should be able to answer these questions:

• What units make up DNA?

• What does DNA look like?

• How does DNA copy itself?

National Science Education Standards
LS 1a, 2d, 5a

What Is DNA?

Remember that *inherited traits* are traits that are passed from generation to generation. To understand how inherited traits are passed on, you must understand the structure of DNA. **DNA** (*deoxyribonucleic acid*) is the molecule that carries the instructions for inherited traits. In cells, DNA is wrapped around proteins to form *chromosomes*. Stretches of DNA that carry the information for inherited traits are called *genes*.

> **STUDY TIP**
> **Clarify Concepts** As you read the text, make a list of ideas that are confusing. Discuss these with a small group. Ask your teacher to explain things that your group is unsure about.

What Is DNA Made Of?

DNA is made up of smaller units called nucleotides. A *nucleotide* is made of three parts: a sugar, a phosphate, and a base. The sugar and the phosphate are the same for each nucleotide. However, different nucleotides may have different bases.

There are four different bases found in DNA nucleotides. They are *adenine, thymine, guanine,* and *cytosine.* Scientists often refer to a base by its first letter: *A* for adenine, *T* for thymine, *G* for guanine, and *C* for cytosine. Each base has a different shape.

The Four Nucleotides of DNA

TAKE A LOOK
1. Identify What are two things that are the same in all nucleotides?

They have
sugar and phospate

Hw

What Does DNA Look Like?

As you can see in the figure below, a strand of DNA looks like a twisted ladder. This spiral shape is called a *double helix*. The two sides of the ladder are made of the sugar and phosphate parts of nucleotides. The sugars and phosphates alternate along each side of the ladder. The rungs of the DNA ladder are made of pairs of bases. ☑

The bases in DNA can only fit together in certain ways, like puzzle pieces. Adenine on one side of a DNA strand always pairs with thymine on the other side. Guanine always pairs with cytosine. This means that adenine is *complementary* to thymine, and guanine is complementary to cytosine. Because the pairs of bases in DNA are complementary, the two sides of a strand of DNA are also complementary.

☑ **READING CHECK**

2. Identify What are the sides of the DNA "ladder" made of?

sugar
phasphate

Critical Thinking

3. Apply Concepts Imagine that you are a scientist studying DNA. You measure the number of cytosines and thymines in a small strand of DNA. There are 45 cytosines and 55 thymines. How many guanines are there in the strand? How many adenines are there?

45 guanines
55 adenines

TAKE A LOOK
4. Identify Give the ways that DNA bases can pair up.

Adenine ~ thymine
cytosine ~ guanine

Each side of a DNA molecule is complementary to the other side.

How Does DNA Copy Itself?

Before a cell divides, it makes a copy of its genetic information for the new cell. The pairing of bases allows the cell to *replicate*, or make copies of, DNA. Remember that bases are complementary and can only fit together in certain ways. Therefore, the order of bases on one side of the DNA strand controls the order of bases on the other side of the strand. For example, the base order CGAC can only fit with the order GCTG. ☑

When DNA replicates, the pairs of bases separate and the DNA splits into two strands. The bases on each side of the original strand are used as a pattern to build a new strand. As the bases on the original strands are exposed, the cell adds nucleotides to form a new strand.

Finally, two DNA strands are formed. Half of each of the two DNA strands comes from the original strand. The other half is built from new nucleotides.

The DNA molecule splits down the middle. Two identical DNA molecules form from the strands of the original molecule.

Old

New

New

Old

DNA is copied every time a cell divides. Each new cell gets a complete copy of the entire DNA strand. Proteins in the cell unwind, copy, and rewind the DNA.

Hw

✓ READING CHECK

5. Explain What happens to DNA before a cell divides?

It makes a copy of its genetic information for the new cell

TAKE A LOOK

6. Compare What is the difference between an "old" and a "new" strand of DNA?

An old strand has its bases, while the new strand has to create bases based on the old strand

Section 1 Review

HW 4/5 on quizziz

NSES LS 1a, 2d, 5a

SECTION VOCABULARY

DNA deoxyribonucleic acid, a molecule that is present in all living cells and that contains the information that determines the traits that a living thing inherits and needs to live	**nucleotide** in a nucleic-acid chain, a subunit that consists of a sugar, a phosphate, and a nitrogenous base

1. Identify Where are genes located? What do they do?

They are located in the
DNA and carry information

2. Compare How are the four kinds of DNA nucleotides different from each other?

They each have a different shape and not fit

3. Apply Concepts The diagram shows part of a strand of DNA. Using the order of bases given in the top of the strand, write the letters of the bases that belong on the bottom strand.

together like puzzle pieces

G A A T C C G A A T G G T

4. Describe How is DNA related to chromosomes?

Chromosomes are made of DNA and
protiens

5. Identify Relationships How are proteins involved in DNA replication?

They unwind, copy, and then rewind
the DNA

6. List What are three parts of a nucleotide?

sugar, phosphate, and a nitrogenous base

CHAPTER 6 Genes and DNA

SECTION 2 How DNA Works

Hw

National Science Education Standards
LS 1c, 1e, 1f, 2b, 2c, 2d, 2e, 5c

BEFORE YOU READ

After you read this section, you should be able to answer these questions:

• What does DNA look like in different cells?

• How does DNA help make proteins?

• What happens if a gene changes?

What Does DNA in Cells Look Like?

The human body contains trillions of cells, which carry out many different functions. Most cells are very small and can only be seen with a microscope. A typical skin cell, for example, has a diameter of about 0.0025 cm. However, almost every cell contains about 2 m of DNA. How can so much DNA fit into the nucleus of such a small cell? The DNA is bundled.

STUDY TIP

Compare After you read this section, make a table comparing chromatin, chromatids, and chromosomes.

Math Focus

1. Convert About how long is the DNA in a cell in inches?
1 in. = 2.54 cm

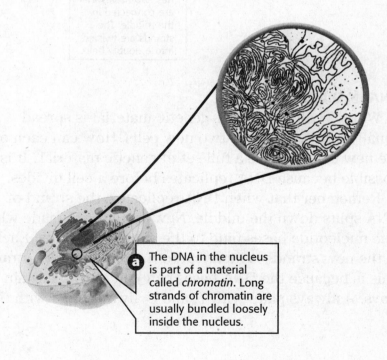

a The DNA in the nucleus is part of a material called *chromatin*. Long strands of chromatin are usually bundled loosely inside the nucleus.

TAKE A LOOK

2. Identify In what form is the DNA in the nucleus?

bundled

SECTION 2 How DNA Works *continued*

Hw

FITTING DNA INTO THE CELL

Large amounts of DNA can fit inside a cell because the DNA is tightly bundled by proteins. The proteins found with DNA help support the structure and function of DNA. Together, the DNA and the proteins it winds around make up a chromosome. ☑

DNA's structure allows it to hold a lot of information. Remember that a gene is made of a string of nucleotides. That is, it is part of the 2 m of DNA in a cell. Because there is an enormous amount of DNA, there can be a large variety of genes.

3. Identify What are two things that are found in a chromosome?

_____ DNA _____

_____ Protiens _____

TAKE A LOOK
4. Describe What is chromatin made of?

_____ DNA coiled _____

_____ around protiers _____

b A single strand of chromatin is made up of a long strand of DNA that is coiled around proteins.

Chromatin

Proteins   DNA

Nucleotide

c Each strand of DNA has two halves that are connected in the middle. The strands are twisted into a double helix.

Critical Thinking

5. Predict Consequences Imagine that DNA did not replicate before cell division. What would happen to the amount of DNA in each of the new cells formed during cell division?

_____ It would _____

_____ decrease by _____

_____ 50% _____

_____

_____

DNA IN DIVIDING CELLS

When a cell divides, its genetic material is spread equally into each of the two new cells. How can each of the new cells receive a full set of genetic material? It is possible because DNA replicates before a cell divides.

Remember that when DNA replicates, the strand of DNA splits down the middle. New strands are made when free nucleotide bases bind to the exposed strands. Each of the new strands is identical to the original DNA strand. This is because the DNA bases can join only in certain ways. *A* always pairs with *T*, and *C* always pairs with *G*.

SECTION 2 How DNA Works *continued*

When a cell is ready to divide, it has already copied its DNA. The copies stay attached as two chromatids. The two identical chromatids form a chromosome.

Chromatin

Chromatids

6. Identify Where is DNA found in a eukaryotic cell?

genes

How Does DNA Help Make Proteins?

Proteins are found throughout cells. They cause most of the differences that you can see among organisms. A single organism can have thousands of different proteins.

Proteins act as chemical messengers for many of the activities in cells, helping the cells to work together. They also affect traits, such as the color of your eyes and how tall you will grow.

Proteins are made from many subunits called *amino acids*. A long string of amino acids forms a protein.

The order of bases in DNA is a code. The code tells how to make proteins. A group of three DNA bases acts as a code for one amino acid. For example, the group of DNA bases CAA *codes for*, or stands for, the amino acid valine. A gene usually contains instructions for making one specific protein.

Math Focus
7. Calculate How many DNA bases are needed to code for five amino acids?

15

8. Identify What is one difference between RNA and DNA?

RNA has
Uracil instead
of Thymine

HELP FROM RNA

RNA, or *ribonucleic acid*, is a chemical that helps DNA make proteins. RNA is similar to DNA. It can act as a temporary copy of part of a DNA strand. One difference between DNA and RNA is that RNA contains the base *uracil* instead of thymine. Uracil is often represented by *U*. ☑

How Are Proteins Made in Cells?

The first step in making a protein is to copy one side of part of the DNA. This mirrorlike copy is made of RNA. It is called *messenger RNA* (mRNA). It moves out of the nucleus and into the cytoplasm of the cell.

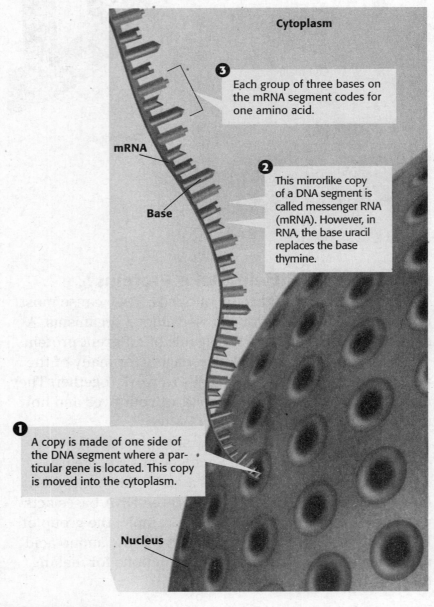

Cytoplasm

❸ Each group of three bases on the mRNA segment codes for one amino acid.

mRNA

Base

❷ This mirrorlike copy of a DNA segment is called messenger RNA (mRNA). However, in RNA, the base uracil replaces the base thymine.

❶ A copy is made of one side of the DNA segment where a particular gene is located. This copy is moved into the cytoplasm.

Nucleus

TAKE A LOOK

9. Compare How does the shape of RNA differ from the shape of DNA?

RNA only
has one side

SECTION 2 **How DNA Works** *continued*

RIBOSOMES

In the cytoplasm, the messenger RNA enters a protein assembly line. The "factory" that runs this assembly line is a ribosome. A **ribosome** is a cell organelle composed of RNA and protein. The mRNA moves through a ribosome as a protein is made.

Hw

Critical Thinking

10. Explain Proteins are made in the cytoplasm, but DNA never leaves the nucleus of a cell. How does DNA control how proteins are made?

DNA itself never leaves the nucleus but a copy of it (mRNA) does leave the cell.

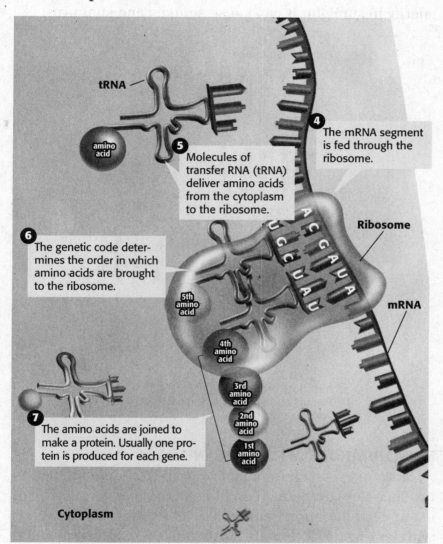

tRNA

amino acid

5 Molecules of transfer RNA (tRNA) deliver amino acids from the cytoplasm to the ribosome.

4 The mRNA segment is fed through the ribosome.

Ribosome

6 The genetic code determines the order in which amino acids are brought to the ribosome.

5th amino acid

4th amino acid

mRNA

3rd amino acid

2nd amino acid

7 The amino acids are joined to make a protein. Usually one protein is produced for each gene.

1st amino acid

Cytoplasm

TAKE A LOOK
11. Identify What does tRNA do?

It delivers amino acids to the ribosome

What Happens If Genes Change?

Read this sentence: "Put the book on the desk." Does it make sense? What about this sentence: "Rut the zook in the tesk."? Changing only a few letters in a sentence can change what the sentence means. It can even keep the sentence from making any sense at all! In a similar way, even small changes in a DNA sequence can affect the protein that the DNA codes for. A change in the nucleotide-base sequence of DNA is called a **mutation**.

READING CHECK
12. Define What is a mutation?

Mutation is a change in the base sequence of DNA

HOW MUTATIONS HAPPEN

Some mutations happen because of mistakes when DNA is copied. Other mutations happen when DNA is damaged. Things that can cause mutations are called *mutagens*. Examples of mutagens include X rays and ultraviolet radiation. Ultraviolet radiation is one type of energy in sunlight. It can cause suntans and sunburns.

Mutations can happen in different ways. A nucleotide may be replaced, added, or removed.

TAKE A LOOK

13. Compare What happens to one strand of DNA when there is a change in a base on the other strand?

The strand changes to stay complimentary with the base strand

Say It

Brainstorm Whether a mutation is helpful or harmful to an organism often depends on the organism's environment. In a group, discuss how the same mutation could be helpful in one environment but harmful in another.

HOW MUTATIONS AFFECT ORGANISMS

Mutations can cause changes in traits. Some mutations produce new traits that can help an organism survive. For example, a mutation might allow an organism to survive with less water. If there is a drought, the organism will be more likely to survive.

Many mutations produce traits that make an organism less likely to survive. For example, a mutation might make an animal a brighter color. This might make the animal easier for predators to find.

Some mutations are neither helpful nor harmful. If a mutation does not cause a change in a protein, then the mutation will not help or hurt the organism.

PASSING ON MUTATIONS

Cells make proteins that can find and fix many mutations. However, not all mutations can be fixed.

If a mutation happens in egg or sperm cells, the changed gene can be passed from one generation to the next. For example, sickle cell disease is caused by a genetic mutation that can be passed to future generations.

Sickle-cell disease is caused by a substitution mutation.

How Can We Use Genetic Knowledge?

Scientists use their knowledge of genetics in many ways. Most of these ways are helpful to people. However, other ways can cause ethical and scientific concerns.

GENETIC ENGINEERING

Scientists have learned how to change individual genes within organisms. This is called *genetic engineering*. In some cases, scientists transfer genes from one organism to another. For example, scientists can transfer genes from people into bacteria. The bacteria can then make proteins for people who are sick. ☑

GENETIC IDENTIFICATION

Your DNA is unique, so it can be used like a fingerprint to identify you. *DNA fingerprinting* identifies the unique patterns in a person's DNA. Scientists can use these genetic fingerprints as evidence in criminal cases. They can also use genetic information to determine whether people are related.

TAKE A LOOK
14. Identify What kind of mutation causes sickle cell disease: deletion, insertion, or substitution?

substitution (handwritten)

 READING CHECK

15. **Define** What is genetic engineering?

genetic engineering is when individual genes are changed (handwritten)

Section 2 Review

HW

NSES   LS 1c, 1e, 1f, 2b, 2c, 2d, 2e, 5c

*quizziz had questions not learned
26/29 right   in book*

SECTION VOCABULARY

mutation a change in the nucleotide-base sequence of a gene or DNA molecule **ribosome** a cell organelle composed of RNA and protein; the site of protein synthesis	**RNA** ribonucleic acid, a molecule that is present in all living cells and that plays a role in protein production

1. Identify What structures in cells contain DNA and proteins?

_____ *it   chromosome, nucleus, chromatin* _____

2. Calculate How many amino acids can a sequence of 24 DNA bases code for?

_____ *72* _____

3. Explain Fill in the flow chart below to show how the information in the DNA code becomes a protein.

DNA

makes a copy of itself called

mRNA

which moves into the cytoplasm to a

ribosome

where amino acids are joined to make a

Proteins

4. Draw Conclusions How can a mutation in a DNA base sequence cause a change in a gene and a trait? What determines whether the mutation is passed on to offspring?

*When   one   strand   is   changed, the   other
strand   also   changes   to   be   complimentary to
the   base   strand. Mutation   that   happen
in   egg   or   sperm   cells   are   passed   down   generations*

5. Identify Give two ways that genetic fingerprinting can be used.

*Genetic   fingerprinting   can   be
used   in   criminal   cases   or   finding   out
if   people   are   related.*

CHAPTER 9 Classification

SECTION
1 **Sorting It All Out**

National Science
Education Standards
LS 5a

BEFORE YOU READ

After you read this section, you should be able to answer these questions:

- What is classification?
- How do scientists classify organisms?
- How do scientists name groups of organisms?

Why Do We Classify Things?

Imagine that you lived in a tropical rain forest and had to get your own food, shelter, and clothing from the forest. What would you need to know to survive? You would need to know which plants were safe to eat and which were not. You would need to know which animals you could eat and which ones could eat you. In other words, you would need to study the organisms around you and put them into useful groups. You would *classify* them.

Biologists use a *classification* system to group the millions of different organisms on Earth. **Classification** is putting things into groups based on characteristics the things share. Classification helps scientists answer several important questions:

- What are the defining characteristics of each species?
- When did the characteristics of a species evolve?
- What are the relationships between different species?

How Do Scientists Classify Organisms?

What are some ways we can classify organisms? Perhaps we could group them by where they live or how they are useful to humans. Throughout history, people have classified organisms in many different ways.

In the 1700s, a Swedish scientist named Carolus Linnaeus created his own system. His system was based on the structure or characteristics of organisms. With his new system, Linnaeus founded modern taxonomy. **Taxonomy** is the science of describing, classifying, and naming organisms. ☑

STUDY TIP

Organize As you read, make a diagram to show the eight-level system of organization.

Say It

Discuss With a partner, describe some items at home that you have put into groups. Explain why you grouped them and what characteristics you used.

READING CHECK

1. Explain How did Linnaeus classify organisms?

_____

_____

_____

CLASSIFICATION TODAY

Taxonomists use an eight-level system to classify living things based on shared characteristics. Scientists also use shared characteristics to describe how closely related living things are.

The more characteristics organisms share, the more closely related they may be. For example, the platypus, brown bear, lion, and house cat are thought to be related because they share many characteristics. These animals all have hair and mammary glands, so they are grouped together as mammals. However, they can also be classified into more specific groups.

BRANCHING DIAGRAMS

Shared characteristics can be shown in a *branching diagram*. Each characteristic on the branching diagram is shared by only the animals above it. The characteristics found higher on the diagram evolved more recently than the characteristics below them.

In the diagram below, all of the animals have hair and mammary glands. However, only the brown bear, lion, and house cat give birth to live young. More recent organisms are at the ends of branches high on the diagram. For example, according to the diagram, the house cat evolved more recently than the platypus. ☑

Critical Thinking

2. Infer What is the main difference between organisms that share many characteristics and organisms that do not?

_____

_____

_____

_____

_____

✓ **READING CHECK**

3. Identify On a branching diagram, where would you see the characteristics that evolved most recently?

_____

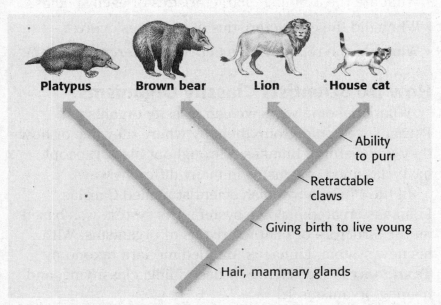

This branching diagram shows the similarities and differences between four kinds of mammals. The bottom of the diagram begins in the past, and the tips of the branches end in the present.

TAKE A LOOK

4. Identify According to the diagram, which organisms evolved before the lion? Circle these organisms.

What Are the Levels of Classification?

Scientists use shared characteristics to group organisms into eight levels of classification. At each level of classification, there are fewer organisms than in the level above. A domain is the largest, most general level of classification. Every living thing is classified into one of three domains.

Species is the smallest level of classification. A species is a group of organisms that can mate and produce fertile offspring. For example, dogs are all one species. They can mate with one another and have fertile offspring. The figure on the next page shows each of the eight levels of classification.

TWO-PART NAMES

We usually call organisms by common names. For example, "cat," "dog," and "human" are all common names. However, people who speak a language other than English have different names for a cat and dog. Sometimes, organisms are even called by different names in English. For example, cougar, mountain lion, and puma are three names for the same animal! ☑

Scientists need to be sure they are all talking about the same organism. They give organisms *scientific names*. Scientific names are the same in all languages. An organism has only one scientific name.

Scientific names are based on the system created by Linnaeus. He gave each kind of organism a two-part name. The first part of the name is the *genus*, and the second part is the *species*. All genus names begin with a capital letter. All species names begin with a lowercase letter. Both words in a scientific name are underlined or italicized. For example, the scientific name for the Asian elephant is *Elephas maximus.* ☑

READING CHECK

5. List What are two problems with common names?

_____

_____

_____

_____

READING CHECK

6. Identify What are the two parts of a scientific name?

_____

_____

```
┌─────────────┐
│  Two-part   │
│    name     │
└─────────────┘
```

```
┌──────────────┐        ┌──────────────┐
│ Genus:       │        │ species:     │
│ Elephas      │        │ maximus      │
└──────────────┘        └──────────────┘
```

Levels of Classification of the House Cat

Kingdom Animalia: All animals are in the kingdom Animalia.

Phylum Chordata: All animals in the phylum Chordata have a hollow nerve cord. Most have a backbone.

Class Mammalia: Animals in the class Mammalia have a backbone. They also nurse their young.

Order Carnivora: Animals in the order Carnivora have a backbone and nurse their young. They also have special teeth for tearing meat.

Family Felidae: Animals in the family Felidae are cats. They have a backbone, nurse their young, have special teeth for tearing meat, and have retractable claws.

TAKE A LOOK

7. Identify Which level contains organisms that are more closely related: a phylum or a class?

_____

_____

8. Describe How does the number of organisms change from the level of kingdom to the level of species?

_____

_____

_____

Genus *Felis*: Animals in the genus *Felis* share traits with other animals in the same family. However, these cats cannot roar; they can only purr.

Species *Felis catus*: The species *Felis catus* is the common house cat. The house cat shares traits with all of the organisms in the levels above the species level, but it also has unique traits.

What Is a Dichotomous Key?

What could you do if you found an organism that you did not recognize? You could use a special guide called a dichotomous key. A **dichotomous key** is set of paired statements that give descriptions of organisms. These statements let you rule out out certain species based on characteristics of your specimen. There are many dichotomous keys for many different kinds of organisms. You could even make your own!

In a dichotomous key, there are only two choices at each step. To use the key, you start with the first pair of statements. You choose the statement from the pair that describes the organism. At each step, the key may identify the organism or it may direct you to another pair of statements. By working through the statements in order, you can identify the organism.

Critical Thinking

9. Infer Why couldn't one single dichotomous key be used for all of the organisms on Earth?

_____

_____

_____

_____

Dichotomous Key to 10 Common Mammals in the Eastern United States

1. a. This mammal flies. Its "hand" forms a wing.	**little brown bat**
b. This mammal does not fly. It's "hand" does not form a wing.	**Go to step 2.**
2. a. This mammal has no hair on its tail.	**Go to step 3.**
b. This mammal has hair on its tail.	**Go to step 4.**
3. a. This mammal has a short, naked tail.	**eastern mole**
b. This mammal has a long, naked tail.	**Go to step 5.**
4. a. This mammal has a black mask across its face.	**raccoon**
b. This mammal does not have a black mask across its face.	**Go to step 6.**
5. a. This mammal has a tail that is flat and paddle shaped.	**beaver**
b. This mammal has a tail that is not flat or paddle shaped.	**opossum**
6. a. This mammal is brown and has a white underbelly.	**Go to step 7.**
b. This mammal is not brown and does not have a white underbelly.	**Go to step 8.**
7. a. This mammal has a long, furry tail that is black on the tip.	**longtail weasel**
b. This mammal has a long tail that has little fur.	**white-footed mouse**
8. a. This mammal is black and has a narrow white stripe on its forehead and broad white stripes on its back.	**striped skunk**
b. This mammal is not black and does not have white stripes.	**Go to step 9.**
9. a. This mammal has long ears and a short, cottony tail.	**eastern cottontail**
b. This mammal has short ears and a medium-length tail.	**woodchuck**

TAKE A LOOK
10. Identify Use this dichotomous key to identify the two animals shown.

_____

Section 1 Review

SECTION VOCABULARY

classification the division of organisms into groups, or classes, based on specific characteristics **dichotomous key** an aid that is used to identify organisms and that consists of the answers to a series of questions	**taxonomy** the science of describing, naming, and classifying organisms

1. List Give the eight levels of classification from the largest to the smallest.

_____

_____

2. Identify According to the branching diagram below, which characteristic do ferns have that mosses do not?

_____

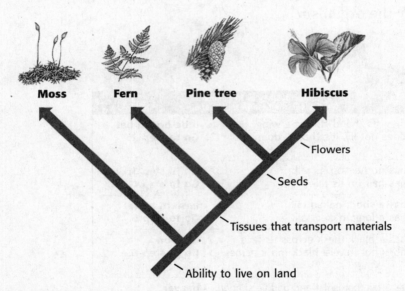

Moss   Fern   Pine tree   Hibiscus

Flowers

Seeds

Tissues that transport materials

Ability to live on land

3. Analyze Which species in the diagram above is most similar to the hibiscus? Which is the least similar?

_____

_____

4. Identify What are the two parts of a scientific name?

_____

5. Infer Could you use the dichotomous key in this section to identify a species of lizard? Explain your answer.

_____

_____

_____

CHAPTER 9 Classification

SECTION 2 # Domains and Kingdoms

National Science
Education Standards
LS 1f, 2a, 4b, 4c, 5b

BEFORE YOU READ

After you read this section, you should be able to answer these questions:

• How are prokaryotes classified?

• How are eukaryotes classified?

How Do Scientists Classify Organisms?

For hundreds of years, all organisms were classified as either plants or animals. However, as more organisms were discovered, scientists found some organisms that did not fit well into these two kingdoms. Some animals, for example, had characteristics of both plants and animals.

What would you call an organism that is green and makes its own food? Is it a plant? What if the organism moved and could also eat other organisms? Plants generally do neither of these things. Is the organism a plant or an animal?

Members of genus *Euglena* have
characteristics of both plants and animals.

The organism above belongs to genus *Euglena*. Its members show all of the characteristics just described. As scientists discovered organisms, such as *Euglena*, that didn't fit easily into existing groups, they created new ones. As they added kingdoms, scientists found that members of some kingdoms were closely related to members of other kingdoms. Today, scientists group kingdoms into *domains*.

All organisms on Earth are grouped into three domains. Two domains, Bacteria and Archaea, are made up of prokaryotes. The third domain, Eukarya, is made up of all the eukaryotes. Scientists are still working to describe the kingdoms in each of the three domains.

STUDY TIP

List As you read this section, make a list of the domains and kingdoms scientists use to classify organisms.

Critical Thinking

1. Apply Concepts In which domain would multicellular organisms be classified? Explain your answer.

_____

_____

_____

_____

How Are Prokaryotes Classified?

A prokaryote is a single-celled organism that does not have a nucleus. Prokaryotes are the oldest group of organisms on Earth. They make up two domains: Archaea and Bacteria.

DOMAIN ARCHAEA

Domain **Archaea** is made up of prokaryotes. The cell walls and cell membranes of archaea are made of different substances than those of other prokaryotes. Many archaea can live in extreme environments where other organisms could not survive. Some archaea can also be found in more moderate environments, such as the ocean. ☑

DOMAIN BACTERIA

All bacteria belong to domain **Bacteria**. Bacteria can be found in the air, in soil, in water, and even on and inside the human body!

We often think of bacteria as bad, but not all bacteria are harmful. One kind of bacterium changes milk into yogurt. *Escherichia coli* is a bacterium that lives in human intestines. It helps break down undigested food and produces vitamin K. Some bacteria do cause diseases, such as pneumonia. However, other bacteria make chemicals that can help us fight bacteria that cause disease. ☑

The Grand Prismatic Spring in Yellowstone National Park contains water that is about 90°C (190°F). Most organisms would die in such a hot environment.

✓ **READING CHECK**

2. Compare How are members of Archaea different from other prokaryotes?

_____
_____
_____
_____
_____

✓ **READING CHECK**

3. Explain Are all bacteria harmful? Explain your answer.

_____
_____
_____
_____

TAKE A LOOK

4. Apply Concepts What kind of prokaryotes do you think could live in this spring? Explain your answer.

_____
_____
_____
_____

How Are Eukaryotes Classified?

Organisms that have cells with membrane-bound organelles and a nucleus are called *eukaryotes*. All eukaryotes belong to domain **Eukarya**. Domain Eukarya includes the following kingdoms: Protista, Fungi, Plantae, and Animalia.

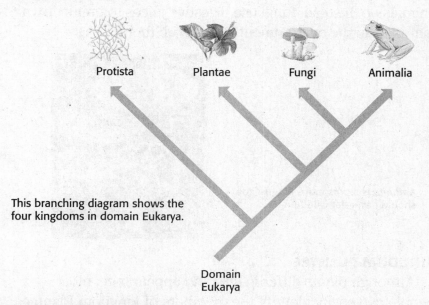

Protista   Plantae   Fungi   Animalia

This branching diagram shows the four kingdoms in domain Eukarya.

Domain Eukarya

STANDARDS CHECK

LS 5a Biological evolution accounts for the diversity of species developed through gradual processes over many generations. Species acquire many of their unique characteristics through biological adaptation, which involves the <u>selection</u> of naturally occurring <u>variations</u> in populations. Biological adaptations include changes in structures, behaviors, or physiology that enhance survival and reproductive success in a particular environment.

Word Help: <u>selection</u>
the process of choosing

Word Help: <u>variation</u>
a difference in the form or function

5. Identify Based on the branching diagram, which two kingdoms in Eukarya evolved most recently? How do you know?

_____

_____

_____

_____

_____

_____

KINGDOM PROTISTA

Members of kingdom **Protista** are either single-celled or simple multicellular organisms. They are commonly called *protists*. Scientists think that the first protists evolved from ancient bacteria about 2 billion years ago. Much later, plants, fungi, and animals evolved from ancient protists.

Kingdom Protista contains many different kinds of organisms. Some, such as *Paramecium*, resemble animals. They are called *protozoa*. Plantlike protists are called *algae*. Some algae, such as phytoplankton, are single cells. Others, such as kelp, are multicellular. Multicellular slime molds also belong to kingdom Protista.

Paramecium

KINGDOM FUNGI

Molds and mushrooms are members of kingdom **Fungi**. Some fungi (singular, *fungus*) are unicellular. That is, they are single-celled organisms. Yeast is unicellular. Most other fungi are multicellular. Unlike plants, fungi do not perform photosynthesis. However, they also do not eat food, as animals do. Instead, fungi use digestive juices to break down materials in the environment and absorb them. ☑

✓ **READING CHECK**

6. Describe How do fungi get food?

_____

_____

_____

_____

Amanita is a poisonous fungus. You should never eat wild fungi.

KINGDOM PLANTAE

Although plants differ in size and appearance, most people can easily identify the members of kingdom Plantae. Kingdom **Plantae** contains organisms that are eukaryotic, have cell walls, and make food by photosynthesis. Most plants need sunlight to carry out photosynthesis. Therefore, plants must live in places where light can reach.

The food that plants make is important for the plants and also for other organisms. Many animals, fungi, protists, and bacteria get nutrients from plants. When they digest the plant material, they get the energy stored by the plant. Plants also provide homes for other organisms.

Math Focus

7. Calculate The average student's arms extend about 1.3 m. How many students would have to join hands to form a human chain around a giant sequoia?

23

_____

The giant sequoia is one of the largest members of kingdom Plantae. A giant sequoia can measure 30 m around the base and grow more than 91 m tall!

SECTION 2 Domains and Kingdoms *continued*

KINGDOM ANIMALIA

Kingdom **Animalia** contains complex, multicellular organisms. Organisms in kingdom Animalia are commonly called *animals*. The following are some characteristics of animals:

• Their cells do not have cell walls.
• They are able to move from place to place.
• They have sense organs that help them react quickly to their environment.

TAKE A LOOK
8. Identify Which animal characteristic from above can be seen in this bald eagle?

_____

STRANGE ORGANISMS

Some organisms are not easy to classify. For example, some plants can eat other organisms to get nutrition as animals do. Some protists use photosynthesis as plants do but also move around as animals do.

Red Cup Sponge

Critical Thinking

9. Apply Concepts To get nutrients, a Venus' flytrap uses photosynthesis and traps and digests insects. Its cells have cell walls. Into which kingdom would you place this organism? Explain your answer.

_____
_____
_____
_____
_____

What kind of organism is this red cup sponge? It does not have sense organs and cannot move for most of its life. Because of this, scientists once classified sponges as plants. However, sponges cannot make their own food as plants do. They must eat other organisms to get nutrients. Today, scientists classify sponges as animals. Sponges are usually considered the simplest animals.

Section 2 Review

SECTION VOCABULARY

Animalia a kingdom made up of complex, multicellular organisms that lack cell walls, can usually move around, and quickly respond to their environment

Archaea in a modern taxonomic system, a domain made up of prokaryotes (most of which are known to live in extreme environments) that are distinguished from other prokaryotes by differences in their genetics and in the makeup of their cell wall; this domain aligns with the traditional kingdom Archaebacteria

Bacteria in a modern taxonomic system, a domain made up of prokaryotes that usually have a cell wall and that usually reproduce by cell division. This domain aligns with the traditional kingdom Eubacteria

Eukarya in a modern taxonomic system, a domain made up of all eukaryotes; this domain aligns with the traditional kingdoms Protista, Fungi, Plantae, and Animalia

Fungi a kingdom made up of nongreen, eukaryotic organisms that have no means of movement, reproduce by using spores, and get food by breaking down substances in their surroundings and absorbing the nutrients

Plantae a kingdom made up of complex, multicellular organisms that are usually green, have cell walls made of cellulose, cannot move around, and use the sun's energy to make sugar by photosynthesis

Protista a kingdom of mostly one-celled eukaryotic organisms that are different from plants, animals, bacteria, and fungi

1. **Compare** What is one major difference between domain Eukarya and domains Bacteria and Archaea?

_____

_____

2. **Explain** Why do scientists continue to add new kingdoms to their system of classification?

_____

_____

3. **Analyze Methods** Why do you think Linnaeus did not include classifications for archaea and bacteria?

_____

_____

_____

4. **Apply Concepts** Based on its characteristics described at the beginning of this section, in which kingdom would you classify *Euglena*?

_____

SECTION 1
Bacteria and Archaea

BEFORE YOU READ

After you read this section, you should be able to answer these questions:

- What are bacteria and archaea?
- What are the characteristics of bacteria?
- How do archaea and bacteria differ?

National Science Education Standards
LS 1b, 1c, 2a, 3a, 3b, 4b

What Are Bacteria and Archaea?

Organisms are grouped by traits they have in common. All living things can be grouped into one of three domains: Bacteria, Archaea, or Eukarya.

All organisms in domain Eukarya are eukaryotes. Each cell of a *eukaryote* has a nucleus and membrane-bound organelles. All organisms in domains Bacteria and Archaea are prokaryotes. A **prokaryote** is an organism that is single-celled and has no nucleus.

Although many prokaryotes live in groups, they are single organisms that can move, get food, and make copies of themselves. Most prokaryotes are very small and cannot be seen without a microscope. However, you can see some very large bacteria with your naked eye. ☑

STUDY TIP
Underline Use colored pencils to underline the characteristics of bacteria in red, characteristics of archaea in blue, and characteristics shared by both in green.

READING CHECK

1. Identify What are two characteristics of prokaryotes?

_____

_____

_____

Prokaryotes
- single-celled
- no nucleus
- no membrane-bound organelles

Eukaryotes
- single-celled or multicellular
- nucleus
- membrane-bound organelles

Domain Bacteria

Domain Archaea

Domain Eukarya

What Characteristics Do Archaea and Bacteria Share?

NO NUCLEUS

Prokaryotes do not store their DNA in a nucleus as eukaryotes do. Their DNA is stored as a circular loop inside the cell. ☑

READING CHECK

2. Describe What does the DNA of a prokaryote look like?

_____

_____

REPRODUCTION

Prokaryotes copy themselves, or reproduce, by a process called binary fission. **Binary fission** is reproduction in which a single-celled organism splits into two single-celled organisms. Before a prokaryote can reproduce, it must make a copy of its loop of DNA. After the cell splits, the two new cells are identical to the original cell. ☑

✓ **READING CHECK**

3. Identify How do prokaryotes reproduce?

_____

_____

Binary Fission

❶ The cell grows.

❷ The cell makes a copy of its DNA. Both copies attach to the cell membrane.

❸ The DNA and its copy separate as the cell grows larger.

❹ The cells separate. Each new cell has a copy of the DNA.

TAKE A LOOK

4. Describe After binary fission, how do the two cells compare to the original cell?

_____

_____

What Are Some Characteristics of Bacteria?

Most of the prokaryotes that scientists have found are bacteria. Domain Bacteria has more individual members than domains Archaea and Eukarya combined have. Bacteria can be found almost everywhere.

SECTION 1 Bacteria and Archaea *continued*

SHAPE

Most bacteria are one of three shapes: bacilli, cocci, and spirilla. *Bacilli* are rod-shaped. *Cocci* are spherical. *Spirilla* are long and spiral-shaped. Different shapes help bacteria survive. Most bacteria have a stiff cell wall that gives them their shape. ☑

Some bacteria have hairlike parts called *flagella* (singular, *flagellum*). A flagellum works like a tail to push a bacterium through fluids.

✓ **READING CHECK**

5. List What are three common shapes of bacteria?

_____

_____

_____

The Most Common Shapes of Bacteria

Bacilli are rod shaped. They have a large surface area, which helps them take in nutrients. However, a large surface area causes them to dry out quickly.

Cocci are spherical. They do not dry out as quickly as rod-shaped bacteria.

Spirilla are long and spiral-shaped. They have flagella at both ends. These tail-like structures help the bacteria move through fluids.

TAKE A LOOK

6. Compare What advantage do cocci have over bacilli?

_____

_____

7. Compare What advantage do bacilli have over cocci?

_____

_____

_____

_____

SECTION 1 Bacteria and Archaea *continued*

ENDOSPORES

Most bacteria do well in warm, moist places. Some species of bacteria die in dry and cold surroundings. However, some bacteria form endospores to survive these kinds of conditions. An **endospore** is a thick, protective covering that forms around the DNA of a bacterium. The endospore protects the DNA from changes in the environment. When conditions are good, the endospores break open, and the bacteria begin to grow.

CLASSIFICATION

Scientists can classify bacteria by the way the bacteria get food. There are three ways for bacteria to get food: consume it, decompose it, or produce it.

- *Consumers* eat other organisms.
- *Decomposers* eat dead organisms or waste.
- *Producers* make their own food. Some bacteria can make food using the energy from sunlight.

Decomposers, such as the ones helping to decay this leaf, return nutrients to the soil. This allows other living things to use those nutrients.

CYANOBACTERIA

Cyanobacteria are producers. These bacteria have a green pigment called *chlorophyll*. Chlorophyll traps the energy from the sun. The cell uses this energy to make food.

Some scientists think that billions of years ago, bacteria similar to cyanobacteria began to live inside larger cells. According to this hypothesis, the bacteria made food for itself and the larger cells. In return, the larger cells protected the bacteria. This relationship may have led to the first plant cells on Earth.

STANDARDS CHECK

LS 4b Populations of organisms can be <u>categorized</u> by the functions they serve in an ecosystem. Plants and some microorganisms are producers—they make their own food. All animals, including humans, are consumers, which obtain their food by eating other organisms. Decomposers, primarily bacteria and fungi, are consumers that use waste materials and dead organisms for food. Food webs identify the relationship among producers, consumers, and decomposers in an ecosystem.

Word Help: <u>categorized</u> to put into groups or classes

8. List Name three roles bacteria can play in an ecosystem.

_____

_____

_____

SECTION 1 Bacteria and Archaea *continued*

How Do Archaea Differ from Bacteria?

Like bacteria, archaea are prokaryotes. However, archaea are different from bacteria. For example, not all archaea have cell walls. When they do have them, the cell walls are made of different materials than the cell walls of bacteria. ☑

There are three types of archaea: heat lovers, salt lovers, and methane makers. *Heat lovers* live in hot ocean vents and hot springs. They usually live in water that is 60°C to 80°C. However, they have been found in living in water as hot as 250°C.

Salt lovers live where there are high levels of salt, such as the Dead Sea. *Methane makers* give off methane gas. Methane makers often live in swamps. They can also live inside animal intestines.

☑ **READING CHECK**

9. Identify What is one difference between archaea and bacteria?

_____

_____

_____

_____

_____

TAKE A LOOK
10. Identify What type of archaea do you think would live in this swamp?

_____

_____

HARSH ENVIRONMENTS

Although bacteria can be found almost anywhere, archaea can live in places where even bacteria cannot survive. For example, many archaea live in places with little or no oxygen. Many can also survive very high temperatures and pressures.

Scientists have found archaea in the hot springs at Yellowstone National Park and beneath 430 m of ice in Antarctica. Archaea have even been found 8 km below the surface of the Earth! Even though they can be found in harsh environments, many archaea also live in more moderate environments, such as the ocean.

Critical Thinking

11. Infer What kind of prokaryote would most likely be found near vents at the bottom of the ocean with extremely high temperatures? Explain your answer.

_____

_____

_____

_____

Section 1 Review

NSES   LS 1b, 1c, 2a, 3a, 3b, 4b

SECTION VOCABULARY

binary fission a form of asexual reproduction in single-celled organisms by which one cell divides into two cells of the same size **endospore** a thick-walled protective spore that forms inside a bacterial cell and resists harsh conditions	**prokaryote** an organism that consists of a single cell that does not have a nucleus

1. List What are the three domains that include all living things?

_____

2. Compare Fill in the Venn Diagram to compare bacteria and archaea.

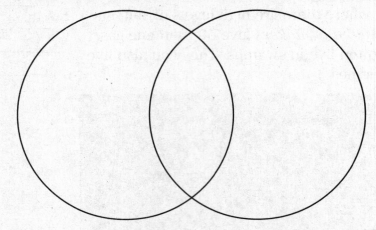

3. Describe How do some scientists think the first plants appeared on Earth?

_____

_____

_____

_____

4. List Name three kinds of archaea.

_____

_____

5. Infer Do you think it would be possible to find bacteria and archaea living in the same environment? Explain your answer.

_____

_____

_____

_____

CHAPTER 10 Bacteria and Viruses

SECTION 2 Bacteria's Role in the World

BEFORE YOU READ

After you read this section, you should be able to answer these questions:

- How are some bacteria helpful?
- How are some bacteria harmful?

National Science
Education Standards
LS 1f

Are All Bacteria Harmful?

Bacteria are everywhere. They live in our water, our food, and our bodies. Some bacteria cause disease. However, most of the types of bacteria are helpful to organisms and the environment. Some bacteria move nitrogen throughout the environment. Other bacteria help recycle dead animals and plants. Still other bacteria are used to help scientists make medicines. Bacteria help us every day.

STUDY TIP

Outline As you read, make an outline of this section. Use the header questions to help you make your outline.

How Are Bacteria Helpful to Plants?

Plants need nitrogen to live. Although nitrogen makes up about 78% of the air, plants cannot use this nitrogen directly. They need to take in a different form of nitrogen. Bacteria in the soil take nitrogen from the air and change it into a form that plants can use. This process is called *nitrogen fixation*.

Say It

Discuss Does it surprise you to learn that not all bacteria are harmful? What were some things you used to believe about bacteria? With a partner, talk about how your view of bacteria has changed.

Bacteria's Role in the Nitrogen Cycle

Most animals get the nitrogen they need by eating plants.

Nitrogen in the air enters the soil.

Bacteria are found in the soil and in nodules on the roots of plants. The bacteria change nitrogen into a form that plants can use.

TAKE A LOOK

1. Explain How do most animals get the nitrogen that they need?

_____

_____

_____

How Are Bacteria Helpful to the Environment?

Bacteria are useful for recycling nutrients and cleaning up pollution. In nature, bacteria break down dead plants and animals. Breaking down dead matter helps recycle the nutrients so they can be used by other organisms.

Some bacteria are used to fight pollution. This process is called bioremediation. **Bioremediation** means using microorganisms, such as bacteria, to clean up harmful chemicals. Bioremediation is used to clean up oil spills and waste from cities, farms, and industries.

Math Focus

2. Calculate An ounce (1 oz) is equal to about 28 g. If 1 g of soil contains 25 billion bacteria, how many bacteria are in 1 oz of soil?

_____700 billion____

How Are Bacteria Helpful to People?

MAKING FOOD

Many of the foods you eat are made with the help of bacteria. Bacteria are commonly used in dairy products. Every time you eat cheese, yogurt, buttermilk, or sour cream, you are also eating bacteria. These products are made using milk and bacteria. Bacteria change the sugar in milk, called *lactose*, into *lactic acid*. Lactic acid adds flavor to the food and preserves it.

Bacteria are used to make many kinds of food.

MAKING MEDICINES

What's the best way to fight bacteria that cause disease? Would you believe that the answer is to use other bacteria? An **antibiotic** is a medicine that can kill bacteria and other microorganisms. Many antibiotics are made by bacteria.

READING CHECK

3. Explain What does genetic engineering let scientists do?

_____

_____

_____

_____

GENETIC ENGINEERING

When scientists change an organism's DNA, it is called *genetic engineering*. For example, scientists have put genes from different organisms into bacteria. The added DNA gives the bacterium instructions for making different proteins. Genetic engineering lets scientists make products that are hard to find in nature. ☑

SECTION 2 Bacteria's Role in the World *continued*

Genes from the *Xenopus* frog were used to produce the first genetically engineered bacteria.

Scientists have used genetic engineering to produce insulin. The human body needs *insulin* to break down and use sugar. People who have a disease called *diabetes* cannot make enough insulin. In the 1970s, scientists found a way to put genes into bacteria so that the bacteria would produce human insulin.

How Can Bacteria Be Harmful?

Some bacteria can be harmful to people and other organisms. Bacteria that cause disease are called **pathogenic bacteria**. Pathogenic bacteria get inside a host organism and take nutrients from the organism's cells. Pathogenic bacteria can harm the organism. Today, people protect themselves from some bacterial diseases by vaccination. Many bacterial infections can be treated with antibiotics. ☑

Bacteria can cause disease in other organisms as well as people. Bacteria can rot or discolor a plant and its fruit. To stop this, plants are sometimes treated with antibiotics. Scientists also try to grow plants that have been genetically engineered to resist bacteria that cause disease.

Vaccines can protect you from bacterial diseases such as tetanus and diphtheria.

Critical Thinking

4. Infer Why do you think it is helpful to engineer bacteria to produce insulin?

_____

_____

_____

_____

 READING CHECK

5. Identify What can be used to treat bacterial infections?

_____

Section 2 Review

SECTION VOCABULARY

antibiotic medicine used to kill bacteria and other organisms	**pathogenic bacteria** bacteria that cause disease
bioremediation the biological treatment of hazardous waste by living organisms	

1. Define What is nitrogen fixation?

_____

_____

2. Complete Fill in the process chart for the nitrogen cycle. Be sure to describe what is happening during each step.

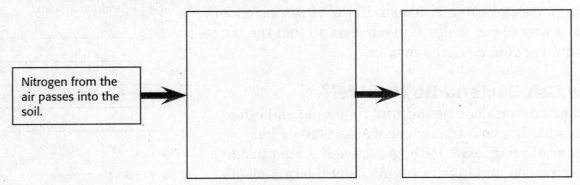

Nitrogen from the air passes into the soil.

3. Explain What are two ways that bacteria are helpful to other living things?

_____

_____

_____

4. Explain What is genetic engineering?

_____

_____

_____

_____

5. Explain How do pathogenic bacteria harm an organism?

_____

_____

_____

6. Identify Relationships Legumes, which include peanuts and beans, are good nitrogen-fixers. Legumes are also a good source of amino acids. What chemical element would you expect to find in amino acids?

_____

_____

CHAPTER 10 Bacteria and Viruses

SECTION 3 Viruses

National Science
Education Standards
LS 1f, 2a

BEFORE YOU READ

After you read this section, you should be able to answer these questions:

- What is a virus?
- How does a virus survive?
- How do viruses make more of themselves?

What Is a Virus?

Most people have either had chickenpox or seen someone with the disease. Chickenpox is caused by a virus. A **virus** is a tiny particle that gets inside a cell and usually kills it. Many viruses cause diseases, such as the common cold, the flu, and acquired immune deficiency syndrome (AIDS). Viruses are smaller than bacteria and can only be seen with a microscope. Viruses can also change quickly. These traits make it hard for scientists to fight viruses. ☑

Are Viruses Living?

Like living things, viruses have protein and genetic material. However, viruses are not alive. A virus cannot eat, grow, or reproduce like a living thing. For a virus to function, it needs to get inside a living cell. Viruses use cells as hosts. A **host** is a living thing that a virus lives on or in. A virus uses a host cell to make more viruses.

STUDY TIP

Compare As you read, make a Venn Diagram to compare viruses and bacteria.

READING CHECK

1. Explain Why is it difficult for scientists to fight viruses?

_____

_____

_____

STANDARDS CHECK

LS 2a Reproduction is a characteristic of all living systems; because no living organism lives forever, reproduction is essential to the continuation of every species. Some organisms reproduce asexually. Others reproduce sexually.

2. List Give three reasons that viruses are not considered living things.

_____

_____

_____

_____

_____

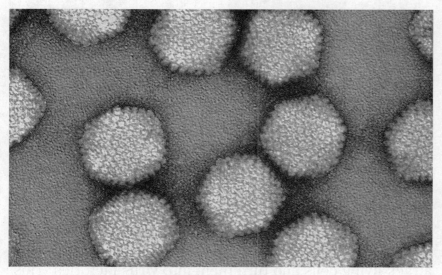

Viruses are not cells. They have genetic material, but they do not have cytoplasm or organelles.

What Is the Structure of a Virus?

Every virus is made up of genetic material inside a protein coat. The protein coat protects the genetic material and helps the virus enter a cell.

How Are Viruses Grouped?

Viruses can be grouped in several ways. These include shape and type of genetic material. The genetic material in viruses is either RNA or DNA. RNA is made of only one strand of nucleotides. DNA is made of two strands of nucleotides. The viruses that cause chickenpox and warts have DNA. The viruses that cause colds, flu, and AIDS have RNA. ☑

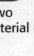

READING CHECK

3. Identify What two kinds of genetic material can viruses have?

_____

_____

The Basic Shapes of Viruses

Crystals
The polio virus is shaped like the crystals shown here.

Spheres
Influenza viruses look like spheres. HIV, the virus that causes AIDS, also has this structure.

Cylinders
The tobacco mosaic virus is shaped like a cylinder and attacks tobacco plants.

Spacecraft
One group of viruses attacks only bacteria. Many of these look almost like spacecraft.

TAKE A LOOK

4. Identify What shape are viruses that attack bacteria?

_____

_____

READING CHECK

5. Identify Name one way viruses are like living things.

_____

_____

_____

How Do Viruses Make More Viruses?

THE LYTIC CYCLE

Like living things, viruses make more of themselves. However, viruses cannot reproduce on their own. They attack living cells and turn them into virus factories. This process is called the *lytic cycle*. ☑

The Lytic Cycle

❶ The virus finds and joins itself to a host cell.

❷ The virus enters the cell, or the virus's genetic material is injected into the cell.

❸ Once the virus's genes are inside, they take control of the host cell and turn it into a virus factory.

❹ The host cell dies when the new viruses break out of it. The new viruses look for host cells, and the cycle continues.

Math Focus

6. Calculate If you enlarged an average virus 600,000 times, it would be about the size of a small pea. How tall would you be if you were enlarged 600,000 times?

_____

TAKE A LOOK

7. Explain What happens to a host cell when the new viruses are released?

_____

THE LYSOGENIC CYCLE

Some viruses don't go right into the lytic cycle. These viruses put their genetic material inside a host cell, but new viruses are not made. As the host cells divides, the genetic material of the virus is passed to the new cells. This is called the *lysogenic cycle*. The host cells can carry the genes of the virus for a long time. When the genes do become active, the lytic cycle begins.

How Can You Stop Viruses?

Antibiotics cannot destroy viruses. However, scientists have made some medicines called *antiviral medications*. These medicines stop viruses from reproducing in their host. Most diseases caused by viruses do not have cures. It is best to try to stop a virus from entering your body. Washing your hands helps you avoid some viruses. The vaccinations some children get also help to prevent viral infections.

Critical Thinking

8. Infer Why shouldn't you take antibiotics to treat a cold?

_____

_____

_____

_____

Section 3 Review

SECTION VOCABULARY

host an organism from which a parasite takes food or shelter	virus a microscopic particle that gets inside a cell and often destroys the cell

1. Compare How are viruses similar to living things?

_____

_____

2. Describe What is the structure of a virus?

_____

_____

3. List List four shapes that viruses may have.

_____

4. Summarize Complete the process chart to show the steps of the lytic cycle.

The virus attaches to a host cell.

↓

↓

↓

The new viruses break out of the host cell, and the host cell dies. The new viruses look for hosts.

5. Explain Why do viruses need hosts?

_____

_____

5. Compare How is the lysogenic cycle different from the lytic cycle?

_____

_____

_____

_____

6. List Name two ways to prevent a viral infection.

_____

_____

_____

CHAPTER 11 Protists and Fungi

SECTION 1 Protists

BEFORE YOU READ

After you read this section, you should be able to answer these questions:

• How are protists different from other organisms?

• How do protists get food?

• How do protists reproduce?

National Science Education Standards
LS 1b, 1c, 1f, 2a, 4b, 5a

What Are Protists?

Protists are members of the kingdom Protista. They are a very diverse group of organisms. Most are single-celled, but some have many cells. Some are single-celled but live in colonies. Members of the kingdom Protista have many different ways of getting food, reproducing, and moving.

Protists are very different from plants, animals, and fungi. They are also very different from each other. Scientists group protists together because they do not fit into any other kingdom. However, they do share a few characteristics:

• They are *eukaryotic* (each of their cells has a nucleus).

• They are less complex than other eukaryotic organisms.

• They do not have specialized tissues.

STUDY TIP

List As you read, make a table showing the ways different protists can obtain food and reproduce.

Critical Thinking

1. Infer Are protists prokaryotes or eukaryotes? Explain your answer.

_____

_____

_____

▼ Zooflagellate ▼ Pretzel slime mold
▼ Sea lettuce ▼ *Paramecium*

Protists have many different shapes.

How Do Protists Get Food?

Some protists can make their own food. Other protists need to get their food from other organisms or from the environment. Some protists use more than one method of getting food.

SECTION 1 Protists *continued*

AUTOTROPHS

Some protists are producers because they make their own food. The cells of these protists have structures called *chloroplasts*, which capture energy from the sun. Protists use this energy to produce food in a process called *photosynthesis*. Plants use the same process to make their own food. Producers are also known as *autotrophs*. *Autos* is Greek for "self." ☑

HETEROTROPHS

Some protists cannot make their own food. They are called **heterotrophs**. *Heteros* is Greek for "different." There are several ways that protist heterotrophs can obtain food.

- *Consumers* eat other organisms, such as bacteria, yeasts, or other protists.

- *Decomposers* break down dead organic matter.

- **Parasites** are organisms that feed on or invade other living things. The organism a parasite invades is called a **host**. Parasites usually harm their hosts. ☑

How Do Protists Reproduce?

Like all living things, protists reproduce. Some protists reproduce asexually, and some reproduce sexually. Some protists reproduce asexually at one stage in their life cycle and sexually at another stage.

ASEXUAL REPRODUCTION

Most protists reproduce asexually. In asexual reproduction, only one parent is needed to make offspring. These offspring are identical to the parent.

- In *binary fission,* a single-celled protist divides into two cells.

- In *multiple fission,* a single-celled protist divides into more than two cells. Each new cell is a single-celled protist.

READING CHECK

2. Define What is an autotroph?

_____

_____

READING CHECK

3. List What are the three kinds of protist heterotrophs?

_____

_____

_____

Math Focus

4. Calculate If seven individuals of genus Euglena reproduce at one time, how many individuals will result?

_____

Members of the genus *Euglena* reproduce by dividing lengthwise during fission.

SECTION 1 Protists *continued*

SEXUAL REPRODUCTION

Sexual reproduction requires two parents. The offspring have new combinations of genetic material. The two protists below are reproducing by conjugation. During *conjugation*, two organisms join and exchange genetic material. Then they divide to produce four new protists.

Protists of the genus *Paramecium* can reproduce by conjugation, a kind of sexual reproduction.

Some protists can reproduce both sexually and asexually. For example, some can reproduce asexually when environmental conditions are good. When conditions become difficult, such as when there is little food, the protists reproduce sexually. This allows the offspring to get new combinations of traits that might be helpful under difficult conditions.

What Is a Reproductive Cycle?

Some protists have complex reproductive cycles. These protists may change forms many times. For example, *Plasmodium vivax* is one of the protists that cause the disease malaria. *P. vivax* is a parasite. It needs both humans and mosquitoes to reproduce. Its reproductive cycle is shown below.

e In the mosquito, the *P. vivax* matures into its original form. The cycle then repeats.

a An infected mosquito bites a human and releases *Plasmodium vivax* into the bloodstream.

b *P. vivax* invades liver cells and reproduces. Then it enters the bloodstream again in a new form.

c *P. vivax* invades red blood cells and reproduces. When the red blood cells burst open, *P. vivax* enters the bloodstream in another new form.

d A mosquito bites a human and picks up *P. vivax*.

Critical Thinking

5. Apply Concepts Are the offspring produced by conjugation genetically identical to their parents? Explain your answer.

_____
_____
_____
_____
_____
_____

STANDARDS CHECK

LS 2a Reproduction is a characteristic of all living systems; because no living organism lives forever, reproduction is essential to the continuation of every species. Some organisms reproduce asexually. Others reproduce sexually.

6. Explain How does sexual reproduction during times of difficult conditions help protist offspring?

_____
_____
_____
_____
_____

TAKE A LOOK
7. Identify Inside the human body, where does *P. vivax* reproduce?

_____

Section 1 Review

SECTION VOCABULARY

heterotroph an organism that gets food by eating other organisms or their byproducts and that cannot make organic compounds from inorganic materials	**parasite** an organism that feeds on an organism of another species (the host) and that usually harms the host; the host never benefits from the presence of the parasite
host an organism from which a parasite takes food or shelter	**protist** an organism that belongs to the kingdom Protista

1. List Name three traits protists have in common.

_____

_____

_____

2. Identify What kind of reproduction results in offspring that are different from their parents? What kind of reproduction results in offspring that are identical to their parents?

_____

_____

3. Apply Concepts Why are mosquito control programs used to prevent the spread of malaria?

_____

_____

_____

4. List Name four ways protists obtain food.

_____

_____

_____

_____

5. Explain Some scientists think kingdom Protista should be divided into several kingdoms. What do you think is the reason for this?

_____

_____

_____

_____

CHAPTER 11 | Protists and Fungi

SECTION
2 **Kinds of Protists**

BEFORE YOU READ

After you read this section, you should be able to answer these questions:

- How are protists classified?
- What structures do protists use to move?

National Science Education Standards
LS 1a, 1b, 1f, 3a, 5a

How Do Scientists Classify Protists?

Protists are hard to classify, or group, because they are a very diverse group of organisms. Scientists are still learning how protists are related to each other. One way scientists classify protists is by their shared traits. Using this method, scientists classify protists into three groups: producers, heterotrophs that can move, and heterotrophs that cannot move. However, these groups do not show how protists are related to each other.

Which Protists Are Producers?

Protist producers are known as **algae** (singular, *alga*). Like plants, algae have chloroplasts. Recall that chloroplasts contain a green pigment called chlorophyll that captures energy from the sun. During photosynthesis, protists use this energy, carbon dioxide, and water to make food. Most algae also have other pigments that give them different colors. ☑

Almost all algae live in water. Some are single-celled, and some are made of many cells. Many-celled algae are called *seaweeds*. They usually live in shallow water and can grow to be many meters long.

Free-floating, single-celled algae are called **phytoplankton**. They are too small to be seen without a microscope. They usually float near the surface of the water. They provide food and oxygen for other organisms.

STUDY TIP

Organize As you read this section, make a table that describes each type of protist, how it gets food, and if and how it moves around.

READING CHECK

1. Identify What are protist producers called?

_____

Critical Thinking

2. Compare What is the difference between seaweeds and phytoplankton?

_____
_____
_____
_____
_____

Diatoms are a kind of plankton.

RED ALGAE

Most of the world's seaweeds are red algae. Their cells contain chlorophyll, but a red pigment gives them their color. Most red algae live in tropical oceans. They can thrive in very deep water. Their red pigment allows them to absorb the light that filters into deep water. ☑

READING CHECK

3. Explain What is the function of red pigment in red algae?

_____

_____

_____

GREEN ALGAE

Green algae are the most diverse group of protist producers. They are green because chlorophyll is their main pigment. Most live in water or moist soil, but they can also live in melting snow, on tree trunks, and inside other organisms. Many are single-celled. Some have many cells and can grow to be eight meters long. Some individual cells live in groups called *colonies*.

Volvox is a green alga that grows in round colonies.

TAKE A LOOK

4. Infer Is *Volvox* single-celled or multicellular? Explain your answer.

_____

_____

_____

BROWN ALGAE

Most of the seaweeds found in cool climates are brown algae. These algae have chlorophyll and a yellow-brown pigment. Brown algae live in oceans. They attach to rocks or form large floating groups called *beds*. ☑

Brown algae can grow to be very large. Some grow 60 m in just one season. That is about as long as 20 cars! Only a brown alga's top is exposed to sunlight. This part of the alga makes food through photosynthesis. The food is carried to parts of the algae that are too deep in the water to get sunlight.

READING CHECK

5. Identify In what type of climate are brown algae likely to be found?

_____

SECTION 2 Kinds of Protists *continued*

DIATOMS

Diatoms make up a large percentage of phytoplankton. Most are single-celled protists found in both salt water and fresh water. They get their energy from photosynthesis. Diatoms are enclosed in thin, two-part shells. The shell is made of a glass-like substance called *silica*. ☑

6. Identify What substance makes up the thin shells of diatoms?

_____

DINOFLAGELLATES

Most dinoflagellates are single-celled. They generally live in salt water, but a few species live in fresh water, or even in snow. Dinoflagellates spin through the water using whiplike structures called *flagella* (singular, *flagellum*). Most dinoflagellates get their energy from photosynthesis. However, a few are consumers, decomposers, or parasites.

EUGLENOIDS

Euglenoids are single-celled protists. They move through the water using flagella. Most have two flagella, one long and one short. They cannot see, but they have eyespots that sense light. A special structure called a *contractile vacuole* removes excess water from the cell.

Euglenoids do not fit well into any one protist group because they can get their food in several ways. Many euglenoids are producers. When there is not enough light to make food, they can be heterotrophs. Some euglenoids are full-time consumers or decomposers. ☑

✔ **READING CHECK**

7. Explain Why don't euglenoids fit well into any one group of protists?

_____

_____

_____

Structure of Euglenoids

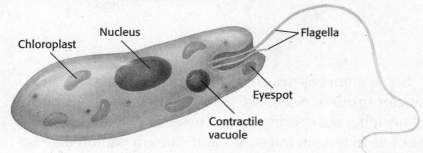

Chloroplast

Nucleus

Flagella

Eyespot

Contractile vacuole

Which Heterotrophs Can Move?

Heterotrophic protists that can move are sometimes called *protozoans*. They are usually single-celled consumers or parasites. They move using special structures, such as pseudopodia, flagella, or cilia. ☑

AMOEBAS

Amoebas are soft, jelly-like protozoans. Many amoebas are found in fresh water, salt water, and soil. Amoebas have contractile vacuoles to get rid of excess water. They move and catch food using pseudopodia (singular, *pseudopod*). *Pseudopodia* means "false feet." The figure below shows how an amoeba uses pseudopodia to move.

How Amoebas Move

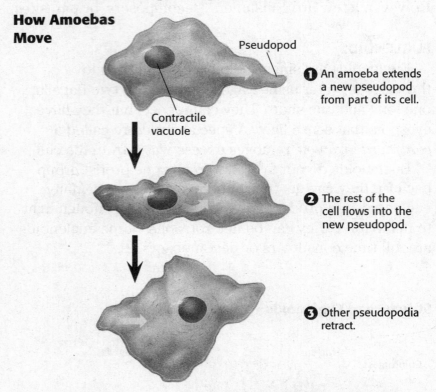

Pseudopod

Contractile vacuole

❶ An amoeba extends a new pseudopod from part of its cell.

❷ The rest of the cell flows into the new pseudopod.

❸ Other pseudopodia retract.

Some amoebas are consumers that eat bacteria and smaller protists. Some are parasites that get their food by invading other organisms. These include the amoebas that live in human intestines and cause a painful disease called *amoebic dysentery*.

Amoebas also use pseudopodia to catch food. When an amoeba senses food, it moves toward it using its pseudopodia. It surrounds the food with pseudopodia to form a *food vacuole*. Enzymes move into the vacuole to digest food. The digested food then passes into the amoeba.

Food
vacuole

An amoeba uses pseudopodia to catch food.

SHELLED AMOEBA-LIKE PROTISTS

Some amoeba-like protists have an outer shell. They move by poking pseudopodia out of pores in the shells. Some, such as *foraminiferans*, have snail-like shells. Others, such as *radiolarian*, look like glass ornaments. ☑

READING CHECK

10. Identify What are two kinds of shelled amoeba-like protists?

_____

_____

Radiolarians have shells.

ZOOFLAGELLATES

Zooflagellates are heterotrophic protists that move by waving flagella back and forth. Some live in water. Others live in the bodies of other organisms.

Some zooflagellates are parasites that cause disease. People who drink water containing the zooflagellate *Giardia lamblia* can get severe stomach cramps.

Some zooflagellates live in mutualism with other organisms. In *mutualism*, two different organisms live closely together and help each other survive. The zooflagellate shown on the next page lives in the gut of termites. The organisms help each other. The zooflagellate helps the termite digest wood, and the termite gives the protist food and a place to live. ☑

READING CHECK

11. Define What is mutualism?

_____

_____

_____

_____

Structure of Flagellates

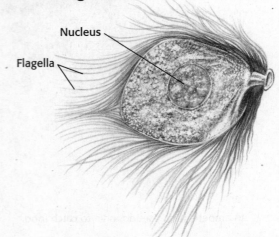

TAKE A LOOK
12. Apply Concepts Is this organism a prokaryote or a eukaryote? Explain your answer.

_____

_____

CILIATES

Ciliates are complex protists. They have hundreds of tiny, hairlike structures called *cilia*. The cilia beat back and forth very quickly to move the ciliate forward. Cilia also sweep food toward the ciliate's food passageway.

A *Paramecium* is a kind of ciliate. It has several important features:

- a large nucleus, called a *macronucleus*, that controls the cell's functions

- a smaller nucleus, called a *micronucleus*, that can pass genes to another *Paramecium* during sexual reproduction

- a food vacuole, where enzymes digest food

- an anal pore, where food waste is removed from the cell

- a contractile vacuole to remove excess water ☑

✓ READING CHECK
13. Identify What structure in a *Paramecium* is used to exchange genes with another *Paramecium* during sexual reproduction?

_____

Structure of Paramecium

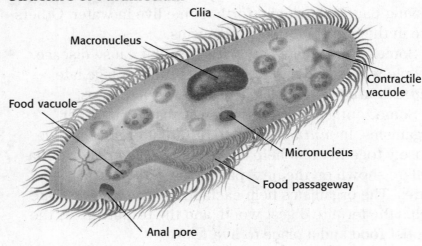

Which Heterotrophs Cannot Move?

Not all protist heterotrophs can move. Some of these are parasites. Others in this group only move at certain phases in their life cycles.

SPORE-FORMING PROTISTS

Many spore-forming protists are parasites. They absorb nutrients from their hosts. Spore-forming protists have complicated life cycles that usually include two or more hosts. For example, the spore-forming protists that cause malaria use mosquitoes and humans as hosts.

WATER MOLDS

Most water molds are small, single-celled protists. They live in water, moist soil, or other organisms. Some water molds are decomposers. Many water molds are parasites. Their hosts can be living plants, animals, algae, or fungi.

SLIME MOLDS

Slime molds live in cool, moist places. They look like colorful globs of slime. At certain phases of their life cycles, slime molds can move using pseudopodia. Some live as a giant cell with many nuclei at one stage of life. Some live as single-celled organisms. Slime molds eat bacteria and yeast. They also surround bits of rotting matter and digest them.

When water or nutrients are hard to find, slime molds grow stalk-like structures with round knobs on top. The knobs are called *sporangia*, and they contain spores. *Spores* are small reproductive cells covered by a thick cell wall. The spores can survive for a long time without water or nutrients. When conditions improve, the spores develop into new slime molds. ☑

Sporangia

The sporangia of a slime mold contain spores.

Critical Thinking

14. Identify What is one characteristic that slime molds, at certain phases of their life cycles, share with amoebas?

_____

_____

☑ **READING CHECK**

15. Explain How can spores help a species of slime mold survive difficult conditions?

_____

_____

_____

_____

Section 2 Review

NSES LS 1a, 1b, 1f, 3a, 5a

SECTION VOCABULARY

algae eukaryotic organisms that convert the sun's energy into food through photosynthesis but that do not have roots, stems, or leaves (singular, alga)	**phytoplankton** the microscopic, photosynthetic organisms that float near the surface of marine or fresh water

1. List Name three kinds of protists that use flagella to move.

_____

_____

2. Organize Fill in the Venn Diagram below to organize the different kinds of protists based on how they get food. Remember that some protists can get food in more than one way.

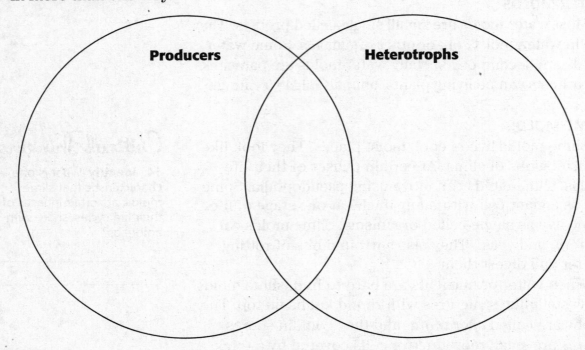

Producers   Heterotrophs

3. List Give two examples of each of the following: protist producers, heterotrophs that can move, and heterotrophs that cannot move.

_____

_____

_____

4. Identify What are two ways amoebas use pseudopodia?

_____

_____

_____

CHAPTER 11 Protists and Fungi

SECTION 3 Fungi

BEFORE YOU READ

After you read this section, you should be able to answer these questions:

• What are the characteristics of fungi?

• What are the four groups of fungi?

What Are Fungi?

Fungi (singular, *fungus*) are everywhere. The mushrooms on pizza are a type of fungus. The yeast used to make bread is also a fungus. If you have ever had athlete's foot, you can thank a fungus for that, too.

Fungi are so different from other organisms that they are placed in their own kingdom. There are many different shapes, sizes, and colors of fungi, but they have several characteristics in common.

• They are eukaryotic. (Their cells have nuclei.)

• They are heterotrophs. (They cannot make their own food.)

• Their cells have rigid cell walls.

• They have no chlorophyll.

• They produce reproductive cells called spores.

National Science Education Standards

LS 1a, 1b, 1d, 1f, 2a, 4b, 5a

STUDY TIP

Compare Make a chart showing how fungi in each group reproduce.

Critical Thinking

1. Compare What are two ways that fungi differ from plants?

_____

_____

_____

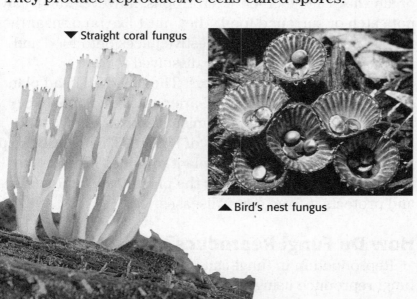

▼ Straight coral fungus

▲ Bird's nest fungus

Say It

Describe Where have you seen fungi before? What did they look like? With a partner, describe any fungi you have seen.

SECTION 3 Fungi *continued*

The mycelium of a fungus is underground. It is made up of hyphae.

Hyphae

Word Help: <u>categorize</u>
to put into groups or classes

Word Help: <u>function</u>
use or purpose

2. List What are three ways that fungi can get food?

_____

_____

_____

Some fungi are single cells, but most are made of many cells. Many-celled fungi are made up of chains of cells called *hyphae* (singular, *hypha*). A **hypha** is a thread-like filament. The cells in these filaments have openings in their cell walls. These openings allow cytoplasm to move between cells.

Most of the hyphae that make up a fungus grow together to form a twisted mass called the **mycelium**. The mycelium is generally the largest part of the fungus. It grows underground.

How Do Fungi Get Nutrients?

Fungi are heterotrophs, which means they feed on other organisms. Unlike other heterotrophs, however, fungi cannot catch or surround food. They must live on or near their food supply. They secrete digestive juices onto food and absorb the nutrients from the dissolved food.

Most fungi are decomposers. They feed on dead plant or animal matter. Some fungi are parasites. Some live in mutualism with other organisms. For example, some fungi grow on or in the roots of a plant. This relationship is called a *mycorrhiza*. The plant provides nutrients to the fungus. The fungus helps the plant absorb minerals and protects it from some diseases.

How Do Fungi Reproduce?

Reproduction in fungi can be asexual or sexual. Many fungi reproduce using spores. **Spores** are small reproductive cells or structures that can grow into a new fungus. They can be the formed by sexual or asexual reproduction. Many spores have thick cell walls that protect them from harsh environments.

ASEXUAL REPRODUCTION

Asexual reproduction can occur in several ways. Some fungi produce spores. The spores are light and easily spread by the wind. Asexual reproduction can also happen when hyphae break apart. Each new piece can become a new fungus. Single-celled fungi called yeasts reproduce through a process called *budding*. In budding, a new cell pinches off from an existing cell. ☑

SEXUAL REPRODUCTION

In sexual reproduction, special structures form to make sex cells. The sex cells join to produce sexual spores that grow into a new fungus.

This puffball is releasing sexual spores that can grow into new fungi.

READING CHECK

3. List What are three types of asexual reproduction in fungi?

_____

_____

_____

What Are the Four Kinds of Fungi?

Scientists classify fungi based on the shape of the fungi and the way they reproduce. There are four main groups of fungi: threadlike fungi, sac fungi, club fungi, and imperfect fungi.

THREADLIKE FUNGI

Have you ever seen fuzzy black mold growing on bread? A **mold** is a shapeless, fuzzy fungus. Most thread-like fungi live in the soil and are decomposers. However, some are parasites.

Threadlike fungi can reproduce asexually. Structures called *sporangia* (singular, *sporangium*) produce spores. When sporangia break open, they release the spores into the air. ☑

Threadlike fungi can also reproduce sexually. Hyphae from two different individuals can join together and grow into specialized sporangia. These sporangia can survive in the cold and with little water. When conditions improve, these specialized sporangia release spores that can grow into new fungi.

READING CHECK

4. Define What are sporangia?

_____

_____

_____

SECTION 3 Fungi *continued*

These groups of sporangia are magnified. Each tiny, round sporangium contains thousands of spores.

TAKE A LOOK
5. Circle On the figure, circle one sporangium.

 READING CHECK
6. Identify How do sac fungi usually reproduce?

_____

_____

SAC FUNGI
Sac fungi are the largest group of fungi. Members of this group include yeasts, mildew, truffles, and morels. Sac fungi can reproduce both asexually and sexually. Usually they use asexual reproduction. When they do reproduce sexually, they form a sac called an *ascus*. Sexual spores develop inside the ascus. ☑

Most sac fungi are multicellular. However, yeasts are single-celled sac fungi. When yeasts reproduce asexually, they use a process called budding. In budding, a new cell pinches off from an existing cell.

Yeasts are the only fungi that reproduce by budding.

Yeasts use sugar as food and produce carbon dioxide and alcohol as waste. Because of this, humans use yeasts to make products such as alcohol and bread. Bread dough rises because of trapped bubbles of waste carbon dioxide from the yeast.

 READING CHECK
7. List Name three ways humans use sac fungi.

_____

_____

_____

Some sac fungi are used to make vitamins and antibiotics. Others cause plant diseases. One of these diseases, Dutch elm disease, has killed millions of elm trees. Humans can use some sac fungi, such as morels and truffles, as food. ☑

SECTION 3 Fungi *continued*

Morels are only part of a larger sac fungus. They are the reproductive part of a fungus that lives under the soil.

CLUB FUNGI

Mushrooms are the most familiar club fungi. Other club fungi include bracket fungi, smuts, rusts, and puffballs. Bracket fungi grow on wood and form small shelves or brackets. Smuts and rusts are common plant parasites that can attack corn and wheat.

Bracket fungi look like shelves on trees. The underside of the bracket contains spores,

Club fungi reproduce sexually. They grow special hyphae that form clublike structures called *basidia* (singular, *basidium*). Sexual spores develop on the basidia. The spore-producing part of the organism is the only part of a mushroom that is above the ground. Most of the organism is underground. ☑

The most familiar mushrooms are called *gill fungi*. The basidia of these mushrooms develop in structures called *gills*, under the mushroom cap. Some gill fungi are the edible mushrooms sold in supermarket. However, other gill fungi are extremely poisonous.

Say It

Investigate Use your school's media center to research a bracket, rust, or smut club fungus. Learn about where the fungus lives and how it gets nutrients. Describe this fungus to your class.

READING CHECK

8. Identify What part of a mushroom grows above the ground?

_____

_____

SECTION 3 Fungi *continued*

TAKE A LOOK

9. Infer Does this picture show the largest part of the fungus? Explain your answer.

_____

_____

_____

Witch's hat fungus is a gill fungus.

IMPERFECT FUNGI

This group includes all of the fungi that do not fit into the other groups. Imperfect fungi do not reproduce sexually. This group includes some fungi that are harmful to humans and some that are useful.

Most imperfect fungi are parasites that cause diseases in plants and animals. One kind of imperfect fungus causes a skin disease called athlete's foot. Another kind of imperfect fungus produces aflatoxin. *Aflatoxin* is a poison that can cause cancer. Some imperfect fungi are used to make medicines, including the antibiotic penicillin. Other imperfect fungi are used to produce cheeses and soy sauce.

The fungus *Penicillium* produces a substance that kills certain bacteria.

STANDARDS CHECK

LS 1f Disease is the breakdown in structures or functions of an organism. Some diseases are the result of intrinsic failures of the system. Others are the result of damage by infection by other organisms.

10. Identify Name two diseases that can be caused by an imperfect fungus.

_____

_____

What Are Lichens?

A **lichen** is the combination of a fungus and an alga. The alga lives inside the cell walls of the fungus. This creates a mutualistic relationship. In a mututalistic relationship, both organisms benefit from living closely with another species. Even though lichens are made of two different organisms, scientists give lichens their own scientific names. This is because the two organisms together function like one organism. ☑

 READING CHECK

11. Identify What two kinds of organisms make up a lichen?

_____

_____

SECTION 3 Fungi *continued*

▲ Wolf lichen

▼ Christmas lichen

British soldier ▲ lichen

These are some of the many types of lichens.

Critical Thinking

12. Infer How do you think a fungus and an alga evolved to live together?

_____

_____

_____

_____

_____

The fungus and alga that make up a lichen benefit each other. Unlike fungi alone, lichens are producers. The algae in the lichens produce food through photosynthesis. Algae alone would quickly dry out in a dry environment. Fungi, however, have protective walls that keep moisture inside the lichen. This allows lichens to live in dry environments.

Lichens need only air, light, and minerals to grow. They can grow in very dry and very cold environments. They can even grow on rocks. Lichens are important to other organisms because they can help form soil. As they grow on a rock, lichens produce acid. The acid breaks down the rock. Soil forms from bits of rock and dead lichens. Once soil forms, plants can move into the area. Animals that eat the plants can also move into the area. ☑

Lichens are sensitive to air pollution. Because of this, they are good *ecological indicators*. This means that if lichens start to die off in an area, there may be something wrong in the environment.

✓ READING CHECK

13. Explain How do lichens make soil?

_____

_____

_____

_____

_____

Section 3 Review

NSES   LS 1a, 1b, 1d, 1f, 2a, 4b, 5a

SECTION VOCABULARY

fungus an organism whose cells have nuclei, rigid cell walls, and no chlorophyll and that belongs to the kingdom Fungi

hypha a nonreproductive filament of a fungus

lichen a mass of fungal and algal cells that grow together in a symbiotic relationship and that are usually found on rocks or trees

mold in biology, a fungus that looks like wool or cotton

mycelium the mass of fungal filaments, or hyphae, that forms the body of a fungus

spore a reproductive cell or multicellular structure that is resistant to stressful environmental conditions and that can develop into an adult without fusing with another cell

1. List What are the four groups of fungi?

_____

_____

2. Explain How does a mycorrhiza help both the plant and the fungus?

_____

_____

3. Identify Relationships How are a hypha and a mycelium related?

_____

4. Identify What part of a club fungus grows above the ground? What part grows below the ground?

_____

_____

5. Explain What is the function of sporangia?

_____

6. Compare How are lichens different from fungi?

_____

_____

_____

7. Compare What is the difference between a lichen and a mycorrhiza?

_____

_____

8. Identify Which group of fungi forms basidia during sexual reproduction?

_____

CHAPTER 12 | Introduction to Plants
SECTION
1 **What Is a Plant?**

HW   P 27

BEFORE YOU READ

After you read this section, you should be able to answer these questions:

• What characteristics do all plants share?

• What are two differences between plant cells and animal cells?

Natio...
Educa...

LS 1a, 2b, 4c, 5a

What Are the Characteristics of Plants?

A plant is an organism that uses sunlight to make food. Trees, grasses, ferns, cactuses, and dandelions are all types of plants. Plants can look very different, but they all share four characteristics.

STUDY TIP

Organize As you read, make a diagram to show the major groups of plants. Be sure to include the characteristics of each group.

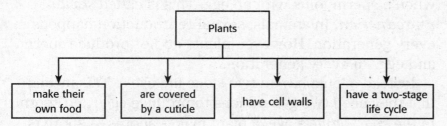

PHOTOSYNTHESIS

Plants make their own food from carbon dioxide, water, and energy from sunlight. This process is called *photosynthesis*. Photosynthesis takes place in special organelles called *chloroplasts*. Inside the chloroplasts, a green pigment called *chlorophyll* collects energy from the sun for photosynthesis. Chlorophyll is what makes most plants look green. Animal cells do not have chloroplasts. ☑

CUTICLES

Every plant has a cuticle that covers and protects it. A *cuticle* is a waxy layer that coats a plant's leaves and stem. The cuticle keeps plants from drying out by keeping water inside the plant.

CELL WALLS

How do plants stay upright? They do not have skeletons, as many animals do. Instead, each plant cell is surrounded by a stiff cell wall. The cell wall is outside the cell membrane. Cell walls support and protect the plant cell. Animal cells do not have cell walls.

READING CHECK

1. Define What is chlorophyll?

_____

_____

_____

_____

Structures in a Plant Cell

Large central vacuole
A vacuole stores water
and helps support
the cell.

Chloroplast Chloroplasts contain
chlorophyll. Chlorophyll captures
energy from the sun. Plants use this
energy to make food.

Cell membrane
The cell membrane sur-
rounds a plant cell and
lies under the cell wall.

Cell wall The cell wall
surrounds the cell mem-
brane. It supports and
protects the plant cell.

TAKE A LOOK
2. Identify What structure in
a plant cell stores water?

_____

_____

3. Identify Where is
chlorophyll found?

_____

TWO-STAGE LIFE CYCLE

Many organisms, including plants, produce offspring
when a sperm joins with an egg. This is called *sexual
reproduction*. In animals, sexual reproduction happens in
every generation. However, plants do not produce sperm
and eggs in every generation.

Instead, plants have a two-stage life cycle. This means
that they need two generations to produce eggs and sperm.
In the *sporophyte* stage, a plant makes spores. A spore is
a cell that can divide and grow into a new plant. This new
plant is called a *gametophyte*. In the gametophyte stage,
the plants produce sperm and eggs. The sperm and eggs
must join to produce a new sporophyte. ☑

READING CHECK
4. List What are the two
stages of the plant life cycle?

_____

_____

What Are the Main Groups of Plants?

There are two main groups of plants: vascular and
nonvascular. A **vascular plant** has specialized vascular
tissues. *Vascular tissues* move water and nutrients from
one part of a plant to another. A **nonvascular plant** does
not have vascular tissues to move water and nutrients.

The Main Groups of Plants

Nonvascular Plants	Vascular Plants		
Mosses, liverworts, and hornworts	Seedless plants	Seed plants	
	Ferns, horsetails, and club mosses	Nonflowering	Flowering
		Gymnosperms	Angiosperms

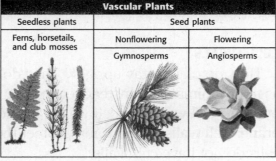

SECTION 1 What Is a Plant? *continued*

NONVASCULAR PLANTS

Nonvascular plants depend on diffusion to move water and nutrients through the plant. In *diffusion*, water and nutrients move through a cell membrane and into a cell. Each cell must get water and nutrients from the environment or a cell that is close by.

Nonvascular plants can rely on diffusion because they are small. If a nonvascular plant were large, not all of its cells would get enough water and nutrients. Most nonvascular plants live in damp areas, so each of their cells is close to water.

VASCULAR PLANTS

Many of the plants we see in gardens and forests are vascular plants. Vascular plants are divided into two groups: seedless plants and seed plants. Seed plants are divided into two more groups—flowing and nonflowering. Nonflowering seed plants, such as pine trees, are called **gymnosperms**. Flowering seed plants, such as magnolias, are called **angiosperms**.

How Did Plants Evolve?

What would you see if you traveled back in time about 440 million years? The Earth would be a strange, bare place. There would be no plants on land. Where did plants come from?

The green alga in the figure below may look like a plant, but it is not. However, it does share some characteristics with plants. Both algae and plants have the same kind of chlorophyll and make their food by photosynthesis. Like plants, algae also have a two-stage life cycle. Scientists think these similarities mean that plants evolved from a species of green algae millions of years ago.

Critical Thinking

5. Apply Concepts Do you think a sunflower is a gymnosperm or an angiosperm? Explain your answer.

_____

_____

_____

STANDARDS CHECK

LS 5a Millions of species of animals, plants, and microorganisms are alive today. Although different species might look dissimilar, the unity among organisms becomes apparent from an analysis of internal structures, the similarity of their chemical processes, and the <u>evidence</u> of common ancestry.

Word Help: <u>evidence</u> information showing whether an idea is true or valid

6. List Give three reasons scientists think plants evolved from an ancient green algae.

_____

_____

_____

_____

_____

_____

_____

_____

A modern green alga and plants, such as ferns, share several characteristics. Because of this, scientists think that both types of organisms shared an ancient ancestor.

Section 1 Review

SECTION VOCABULARY

angiosperm a flowering plant that produces seeds within a fruit **gymnosperm** a woody, vascular seed plant whose seeds are not enclosed by an ovary or fruit	**nonvascular plant** the three groups of plants (liverworts, hornworts, and mosses) that lack specialized conducting tissues and true roots, stems, and leaves **vascular plant** a plant that has specialized tissues that conduct materials from one part of the plant to another

1. Explain What are the two main differences between a plant cell and an animal cell?

_____

_____

_____

_____

2. Organize Fill in each box in the figure below with one of the main characteristics of plants.

3. Predict What would happen to a plant if its chloroplasts stopped working? Explain your answer.

_____

_____

_____

4. Compare What is the main difference between vascular and nonvascular plants?

_____

_____

_____

SECTION 2 | Seedless Plants

National Science
Education Standards
LS 1a, 1c, 2b, 5c

BEFORE YOU READ

After you read this section, you should be able to answer these questions:

- What are the differences between seedless vascular plants and nonvascular plants?
- How can plants reproduce without seeds?

What Are Seedless Plants?

When you think of plants, you probably think of plants that make seeds, such as flowers and trees. However, there are many plants that don't make seeds.

Remember that plants are divided into two main groups: nonvascular plants and vascular plants. All nonvascular plants are seedless, and some vascular plants are seedless, as well.

What Are the Features of Nonvascular Plants?

Mosses, liverworts, and hornworts are types of nonvascular plants. Remember that nonvascular plants do not have vascular tissue to deliver water and nutrients. Instead, each plant cell gets water and nutrients directly from the environment or from a nearby cell. Therefore, nonvascular plants usually live in places that are damp.

Nonvascular plants do not have true stems, roots, or leaves. However, they do have features that help them to get water and stay in place. For example, a **rhizoid** is a rootlike structure that holds some nonvascular plants in place. Rhizoids also help plants get water and nutrients. ☑

Nonvascular plants
• have no vascular tissue
• have no true roots, stems, leaves, or seeds
• are usually small
• live in damp places

REPRODUCTION IN NONVASCULAR PLANTS

Like all plants, nonvascular plants have a two-stage life cycle. They have a sporophyte generation, which produces spores, and a gametophyte generation, which produces eggs and sperm. Sperm from these plants need water so they can swim to the eggs. Nonvascular plants can also reproduce asexually, that is, without eggs and sperm.

STUDY TIP

Organize As you read this section, make a chart that compares vascular plants and nonvascular plants.

Critical Thinking

1. Apply Concepts Why wouldn't you expect to see nonvascular plants in the desert?

_____

_____

_____

_____

READING CHECK

2. List What are two functions of the rhizoid?

_____

_____

_____

Moss Life Cycle

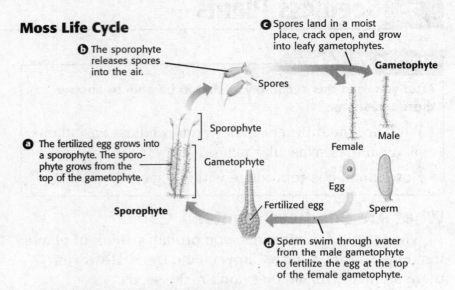

ⓑ The sporophyte releases spores into the air.

ⓒ Spores land in a moist place, crack open, and grow into leafy gametophytes.

Spores

Gametophyte

Sporophyte

Male

Female

ⓐ The fertilized egg grows into a sporophyte. The sporophyte grows from the top of the gametophyte.

Gametophyte

Egg

Sperm

Sporophyte

Fertilized egg

ⓓ Sperm swim through water from the male gametophyte to fertilize the egg at the top of the female gametophyte.

TAKE A LOOK

3. Identify Are the male and female gametophytes separate plants or part of the same plant?

_____

_____

Critical Thinking

4. Apply Concepts Why do you think nonvascular plants can be the first plants to grow in a new environment?

_____

_____

_____

_____

IMPORTANCE OF NONVASCULAR PLANTS

Nonvascular plants are usually the first plants to live in a new environment, such as newly exposed rock. When these plants die, they break down and help form a thin layer of soil. Then plants that need soil in order to grow can move into these areas.

Some nonvascular plants are important as food or nesting material for animals. A nonvascular plant called peat moss is important to humans. When it turns to peat, it can be burned as a fuel.

What Are the Features of Seedless Vascular Plants?

Vascular plants have specialized tissues that carry water and nutrients to all their cells. These tissues generally make seedless vascular plants larger than nonvascular plants. Because they have tissues to move water, vascular plants do not have to live in places that are damp. ☑

Many seedless vascular plants, such as ferns, have a structure called a rhizome. The **rhizome** is an underground stem that produces new leaves and roots.

☑ **READING CHECK**

5. Explain How do the cells of a seedless vascular plant get water?

_____

_____

_____

Leaf

Rhizome

REPRODUCTION IN SEEDLESS VASCULAR PLANTS

The life cycles of vascular plants and nonnvascular plants are similar. Sperm and eggs are produced in gametophytes. They join to form a sporophyte. The sporophyte produces spores. The spores are released. They grow into new gametophytes. ☑

Seedless vascular plants can also reproduce asexually in two ways. New plants can branch off from older plants. Pieces of a plant can fall off and begin to grow as new plants.

6. Identify What do spores grow into?

_____

_____

Fern Life Cycle

© Spores land on moist soil and grow into gametophytes.

Gametophyte

Spores

Sperm

Egg

Female

Male

ⓓ A sperm swims through water to fertilize an egg.

ⓑ The sporophyte releases spores into the air.

Sporophyte

Fertilized egg

ⓐ The fertilized egg grows into a sporophyte.

TAKE A LOOK

7. Apply Concepts Does this figure show sexual or asexual reproduction? Explain your answer.

_____

_____

_____

_____

IMPORTANCE OF SEEDLESS VASCULAR PLANTS

Did you know that seedless vascular plants that lived 300 million years ago are important to people today? After these ancient ferns, horsetails, and club mosses died, they formed coal and oil. Coal and oil are fossil fuels that people remove from Earth's crust to use for energy. They are called *fossil fuels* because they formed from plants (or animals) that lived long ago. ☑

Another way seedless vascular plants are important is they help make and preserve soil. Seedless vascular plants help form new soil when they die and break down. Their roots can make the soil deeper, which allows other plants to grow. Their roots also help prevent soil from washing away.

Many seedless vascular plants are used by humans. Ferns and some club mosses are popular houseplants. Horsetails are used in some shampoos and skincare products.

8. Explain Where does coal come from?

_____

_____

_____

_____

_____

Section 2 Review

SECTION VOCABULARY

rhizoid a rootlike structure in nonvascular plants that holds the plants in place and helps plants get water and nutrients	**rhizome** a horizontal underground stem that produces new leaves, shoots, and roots

1. Compare What are two differences between a rhizoid and a rhizome?

_____

_____

_____

_____

2. Explain In which generation does sexual reproduction occur? Explain your answer.

_____

_____

3. Compare Use a Venn Diagram to compare vascular and nonvascular plants.

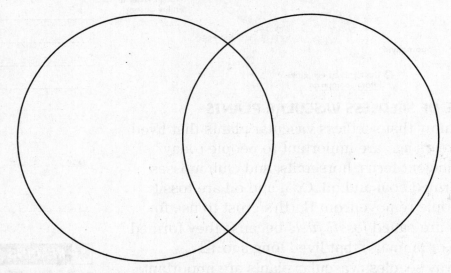

4. Describe What are two ways in which seedless nonvascular plants reproduce asexually?

_____

_____

5. Apply Concepts Nonvascular plants are usually very small. How does their structure limit their size?

_____

_____

_____

CHAPTER 12 Introduction to Plants

SECTION
3 **Seed Plants**   Hw   276-277

BEFORE YOU READ

After you read this section, you should be able to answer these questions:

• How are seed plants different from seedless plants?

• What are the parts of a seed?

• How do gymnosperms and angiosperms reproduce?

National Science Education Standards

LS 1a, 1d, 2b, 2c, 2d, 4b, 4c, 4d, 5b

What Are Seed Plants?

Think about the seed plants that you use during the day. You probably use dozens of seed plants, including the food you eat and the paper you write on. Seed plants include trees, such as oaks and pine trees, as well as flowers, such as roses and dandelions. Seed plants are one of the two main groups of vascular plants.

Like all plants, seed plants have a two-stage life cycle. However, seed plants differ from seedless plants, as shown below.

Seedless plants	Seed plants
They do not produce seeds.	They produce seeds.
The gametophyte grows as an independent plant.	The gametophyte lives inside the sporophyte.
Sperm need water to swim to the eggs.	Sperm are carried to the eggs by pollen.

Seed plants do not depend on moist habitats for reproduction, the way seedless plants do. Because of this, seed plants can live in many more places than seedless plants can. Seed plants are the most common plants on Earth today.

What Is a Seed?

A *seed* is a structure that feeds and protects a young plant. It forms after fertilization, when a sperm and an egg join. A seed has the following three main parts:

• a young plant, or sporophyte

• *cotyledons*, early leaves that provide food for the young plant

• a seed coat that covers and protects the young plant ☑

STUDY TIP

Organize As you read this section, make cards showing the parts of the life cycle of seed plants. Practice arranging the cards in the correct sequence.

TAKE A LOOK
1. Compare How do the gametophytes of seedless plants differ from those of seed plants?

In seedless plants, the gametophyte grows as an indepent plant. In seed plants, the gametophyte lives in the sporophyte.

READING CHECK

2. Identify What process must occur before a seed can develop?

Fertilization

SECTION 3 Seed Plants *continued*

hw

young plant

cotyledon

seed coat

A seed contains stored food and a young plant, or sporophyte. A seed is surrounded and protected by a seed coat.

TAKE A LOOK
3. Label Label the parts of a seed with these terms: young plant, seed coat, cotyledon.

LS 5b Biological evolution accounts for the <u>diversity</u> of species developed through gradual <u>processes</u> over many generations. Species acquire many of their unique characteristics through biological adaptation, which involves the selection of naturally occurring variations in populations. Biological adaptations include changes in structures, behaviors, or physiology that enhance <u>survival</u> and reproductive success in a particular environment.

Word Help: <u>diversity</u>
variety

Word Help: <u>process</u>
a set of steps, events, or changes

Word Help: <u>survival</u>
the continuing to live or exist

4. Identify What are two advantages seeds have over spores?

Seeds have stored food for the young plant and they can be spread by animals.

ADVANTAGES OF HAVING SEEDS

Seeds have some advantages over spores. For example, when the young plant inside a seed begins to grow, it uses the food stored in the seed. In contrast, the spores of seedless plants don't have stored food to help a new plant grow. Therefore, they will live only if they start growing when and where there are enough resources available.

Another advantage is that seeds can be spread by animals. The spores of seedless plants are usually spread by wind. Animals often spread seeds more efficiently than the wind spreads spores. Therefore, seeds that are spread by animals are more likely to find a good place to grow.

What Kinds of Plants Have Seeds?

Seed plants are divided into two main groups: gymnosperms and angiosperms. *Gymnosperms* are non-flowering plants, and *angiosperms* are flowering plants.

GYMNOSPERMS

Gymnosperms are seed plants that do not have flowers or fruits. They include plants such as pine trees and redwood trees. Many gymnosperms are evergreen, which means that they keep their leaves all year. Gymnosperm seeds usually develop in a cone, such as a pine cone.

Pine cone

Seeds

REPRODUCTION IN GYMNOSPERMS

The most well-known gymnosperms are the conifers. Conifers are evergreen trees and shrubs, such as pines, spruces, and firs, that make cones to reproduce. They have male cones and female cones. Spores in male cones develop into male gametophytes, and spores in female cones develop into female gametophytes. The gametophytes produce sperm and eggs.

A **pollen** grain contains the tiny male gametophyte. The wind carries pollen from the male cones to the female cones. This movement of pollen to the female cones is called **pollination**. Pollination is part of sexual reproduction in plants. ☑

After pollination, sperm fertilize the eggs in the female cones. A fertilized egg develops into a new sporophyte inside a seed. Eventually, the seeds fall from the cone. If the conditions are right, the seeds will grow into plants.

P284 - HW 285

☑ **READING CHECK**

5. Explain How is gymnosperm pollen carried from one plant to another?

The Wind

The Life Cycle of a Pine Tree

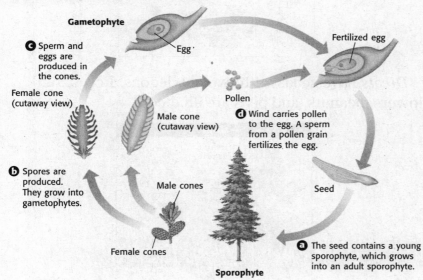

Gametophyte

c Sperm and eggs are produced in the cones.

Egg

Female cone (cutaway view)

Male cone (cutaway view)

Pollen

d Wind carries pollen to the egg. A sperm from a pollen grain fertilizes the egg.

Fertilized egg

b Spores are produced. They grow into gametophytes.

Male cones

Female cones

Sporophyte

Seed

a The seed contains a young sporophyte, which grows into an adult sporophyte.

TAKE A LOOK

6. Explain Does this picture show an example of sexual or asexual reproduction? Explain.

Sexual, as there is a male and female.

IMPORTANCE OF GYMNOSPERMS

Gymnosperms are used to make many products, such as medicines, building materials, and household products. Some conifers produce a drug used to fight cancer. Many trees are cut so that their wood can be used to build homes and furniture. Pine trees make a sticky substance called resin. Resin can be used to make soap, paint, and ink.

Hw

P 289

Math Focus

7. Calculate Percentages
More than 265,000 species of plants have been discovered. About 235,000 of those species are angiosperms. What percentage of plants are angiosperms?

_____

88.67

What Are Angiosperms?

Angiosperms are seed plants that produce flowers and fruit. Maple trees, daisies, and blackberries are all examples of angiosperms. There are more angiosperms on Earth than any other kind of plant. They can be found in almost every land ecosystem, including grasslands, deserts, and forests.

TWO KINDS OF ANGIOSPERMS

There are two kinds of angiosperms: monocots and dicots. These plants are grouped based on how many cotyledons, or seed leaves, the seeds have. *Monocots* have seeds with one cotyledon. Grasses, orchids, palms, and lilies are all monocots.

Dicots have seeds with two cotyledons. Roses, sunflowers, peanuts, and peas are all dicots.

TAKE A LOOK

8. Complete Fill in the table to show the differences between monocots and dicots.

Monocots	Dicots
flower parts in 3s	flower parts in fours or fives
leaves with parallel veins	Leaves with branching veins
one cotyledon	two cotyledons
bundles of vascular tissue scattered	bundles of vascular tissue in a ring.

SECTION 3 Seed Plants *continued*

REPRODUCTION IN ANGIOSPERMS

In angiosperms, pollination takes place in flowers.
Some angiosperms depend on the wind for pollination.
Others rely on animals such as bees and birds to carry
pollen from flower to flower.

Angiosperm seeds develop inside fruits. Some fruits
and seeds, like those of a dandelion, are made to help
the wind carry them. Other fruits, such as blackberries,
attract animals that eat them. The animals drop the seeds
in new places, where they can grow into plants. Some
fruits, such as burrs, travel by sticking to animal fur. ☑

290-291
Hw

Each of the fluffy structures on this dandelion is actually a fruit. Each of the
fruits contains a seed.

READING CHECK

9. Identify Where do
angiosperm seeds develop?

They develope
in fruits.

TAKE A LOOK
10. Identify How are the
fruits of this dandelion spread?

They are spread
by the wind

IMPORTANCE OF ANGIOSPERMS

Like many other plants, flowering plants provide food for
animals. A mouse that eats seeds and berries uses flowering
plants directly as food. An owl that eats a field mouse uses
flowering plants indirectly as food. Flowering plants can
also provide food for the animals that pollinate them.

People use flowering plants, too. Major food crops,
such as corn, wheat, and rice, come from flowering
plants. Many flowering trees, such as oak trees, can be
used for building materials. Plants such as cotton and
flax are used to make clothing and rope. Flowering plants
are also used to make medicines, rubber, and perfume oils.

Say It

Describe Think of all the
products you used today that
came from angiosperms.
Describe to the class five
items you used in some way
and what kind of angiosperm
they came from.

Section 3 Review

NSES LS 1a, 1d, 2b, 2c, 2d, 4b, 4c, 4d, 5b

SECTION VOCABULARY

pollen the tiny granules that contain the male gametophyte of seed plants	**pollination** the transfer of pollen from the male reproductive structures to the female reproductive structures of seed plants

1. Compare How are the gametophytes of seed plants different from the gameto-phytes of seedless plants?

_____

_____

_____

2. Describe What happens during pollination?

_____

_____

3. Compare Use a Venn Diagram to compare gymnosperms and angiosperms.

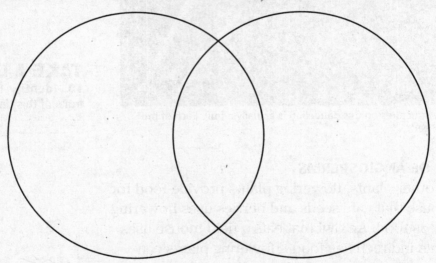

4. List What are the three main parts of a seed? What does each part do?

_____

_____

_____

5. Identify In what structure do gymnosperm seeds usually develop?

_____

6. Identify What two structures are unique to angiosperms?

_____

_____

CHAPTER 12 | Introduction to Plants

SECTION
4 **Structures of Seed Plants**

BEFORE YOU READ

After you read this section, you should be able to answer these questions:

• What are the functions of roots and stems?

• What is the function of leaves?

• What is the function of a flower?

National Science Education Standards
LS 1a, 1d, 2b, 3d, 4c, 5b

What Structures Are Found in a Seed Plant?

Remember that seed plants include trees, such as oaks and pine trees, as well as flowers, such as roses and dandelions. Seed plants are one of the two main groups of vascular plants.

You have different body systems that carry out many functions. Plants have systems too. Vascular plants have a root system, a shoot system, and a reproductive system. A plant's root and shoot systems help the plant to get water and nutrients. Roots are often found underground. Shoots include stems and leaves. They are usually found above ground. ☑

STUDY TIP

List As you read this section, make a chart listing the structures of seed plants and their functions.

READING CHECK

1. Identify What are the three main parts of a seed plant?

_____

_____

_____

Onion

Dandelion

Carrots

The roots of plants absorb and store water and nutrients.

VASCULAR TISSUE

Like all vascular plants, seed plants have specialized tissues that move water and nutrients through the plant. There are two kinds of vascular tissue: xylem and phloem. **Xylem** moves water and minerals from the roots to the shoots. **Phloem** moves food molecules to all parts of the plant. The vascular tissues in the roots and shoots are connected.

What Are Roots?

Roots are organs that have three main functions:

• to absorb water and nutrients from the soil

• to hold plants in the soil

• to store extra food made in the leaves

Roots have several structures that help them do these jobs. The *epidermis* is a layer of cells that covers the outside of the root, like skin. Some cells of the epidermis, called *root hairs*, stick out from the root. These hairs expose more cells to water and minerals in the soil. This helps the root absorb more of these materials.

Roots grow longer at their tips. A *root cap* is a group of cells found at the tip of a root. These cells produce a slimy substance. This helps the root push through the soil as it grows.

STANDARDS CHECK

LS 1a Living systems at all levels of organization demonstrate the complementary nature of structure and function. Important levels of organization for structure and function include cells, organs, tissues, organ systems, whole organisms, and ecosystems.

Word Help: structure
the way in which a whole is put together

Word Help: function
use or purpose

2. Describe What are the functions of xylem and phloem?

_____

_____

_____

_____

_____

Critical Thinking

3. Apply Concepts What do you think happens to water and minerals right after they are absorbed by roots?

_____

_____

_____

TAKE A LOOK
4. Identify Where is the vascular tissue located in this root?

_____

_____

The Parts of a Root

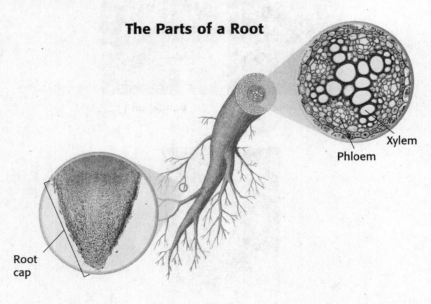

Xylem

Phloem

Root cap

Hw

TYPES OF ROOT SYSTEMS

There are two kinds of root systems: taproot systems and fibrous root systems. A *taproot system* has one main root, or taproot, that grows downward. Many smaller roots branch from the taproot. Taproots can reach water deep underground. Carrots are plants that have taproot systems.

A *fibrous root system* has several roots that spread out from the base of a plant's stem. The roots are usually the same size. Fibrous roots usually get water from near the soil surface. Many grasses have fibrous root systems.

What Are Stems?

27

A stem is an organ that connects a plant's roots to its leaves and reproductive structures. A stem does the following jobs: ☑

- Stems support the plant body. Leaves are arranged along stems so that each leaf can get sunlight.
- Stems hold up reproductive structures such as flowers. This helps bees and other pollinators find the flowers.
- Stems carry materials between the root system and the leaves and reproductive structures. Xylem carries water and minerals from the roots to the rest of the plant. Phloem carries the food made in the leaves to roots and other parts of the plant.
- Some stems store materials. For example, the stems of cactuses can store water.

✓ READING CHECK

5. Define What is a stem?

_____

_____

_____

HERBACEOUS STEMS

There are two different types of stems: herbaceous and woody. *Herbaceous* stems are thin, soft, and flexible. Flowers, such as daisies and clover, have herbaceous stems. Many crops, such as tomatoes, corn, and beans, also have herbaceous stems.

Phloem
Xylem
Herbaceous stems are thin and flexible

TAKE A LOOK
6. Compare Examine this figure and the pictures of woody stems on the next page. How are herbaceous and woody stems similar?

_____

_____

Critical Thinking

7. Infer How do you think growth rings can be used to tell how old a tree is?

_____

_____

_____

_____

_____

_____

_____

TAKE A LOOK

8. Compare How are herbaceous and woody stems different?

_____

_____

_____

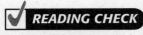

9. Identify What is the main function of a leaf?

_____

_____

WOODY STEMS

Other plants have woody stems. *Woody* stems are stiff and are often covered by bark. Trees and shrubs have woody stems. The trunk of a tree is actually its stem!

Trees or shrubs that live in areas with cold winters grow mostly during the spring and summer. During the winter, these plants are *dormant*. This means they are not growing or reproducing. Plants that live in areas with wet and dry seasons are dormant during the dry season.

When a growing season starts, the plant produces large xylem cells. These large cells appear as a light-colored ring when the plant stem is cut. In the fall, right before the dormant period, the plant produces smaller xylem cells. The smaller cells produce a dark ring in the stem. A ring of dark cells surrounding a ring of light cells makes up a *growth ring*. The number of growth rings can show how old the tree is.

Woody stems are usually thick and stiff.

What Are Leaves?

FUNCTION OF LEAVES

Leaves are organs, too. The main function of leaves is to make food for the plant. The leaves are where most photo-synthesis happens. Chloroplasts in the leaf cells trap energy from sunlight. The leaves also absorb carbon dioxide from the air. They use this energy, carbon dioxide, and water to make food. ☑

All leaf structures are related to the leaf's main job, pho-tosynthesis. A *cuticle* covers the surfaces of the leaf. It pre-vents the leaf from losing water. The *epidermis* is a single layer of cells beneath the cuticle. Tiny openings in the epi-dermis, called *stomata* (singular, *stoma*), let carbon dioxide enter the leaf. *Guard cells* open and close the stomata.

Structure of a Leaf

P278   Hw

LEAF LAYERS

Most photosynthesis takes place in the two layers in the middle of the leaf. The upper layer, called the *palisade layer*, contains many chloroplasts. Sunlight is captured in this layer. The lower layer, called the *spongy layer*, has spaces between the cells, where carbon dioxide can move. The spongy layer also has the vascular tissues that bring water to the leaves and move food away.

LEAF SHAPES

Different kinds of plants can have different shaped leaves. Leaves may be round, narrow, heart-shaped, or fan-shaped. Leaves can also be different sizes. The raffia palm has leaves that may be six times longer than you are tall! Duckweed is a tiny plant that lives in water. Its leaves are so small that several of them could fit on your fingernail. Some leaves, such as those of poison ivy below, can be made of several leaflets.

This is one poison ivy leaf. It is made up of three leaflets

TAKE A LOOK
10. Explain Is this plant vascular or nonvascular? Explain your answer.

_____
_____
_____

 Say It

Describe Some people are allergic to poison ivy. They can get a rash from touching its leaves. Some other plants can be poisonous to eat. Are there any other plants you know of that can be poisonous to touch or eat? Describe some of these plants to a partner.

SECTION 4 | Structures of Seed Plants *continued*

What Are Flowers?

All plants have reproductive structures. In angiosperms, or flowering plants, flowers are the reproductive structures. Flowers produce eggs and sperm for sexual reproduction. ☑

PARTS OF A FLOWER

There are four basic parts of a flower: sepals, petals, stamens, and one or more pistils. These parts are often arranged in rings, one inside the other. However, not all flowers have every part.

Different species of flowering plants can have different flower types. Flowers with all four parts are called *perfect flowers*. Flowers that have stamens but no pistils are male. Flowers that have pistils but no stamens are female.

11. Identify For which group of plants are flowers the reproductive structures?

_____

TAKE A LOOK

12. Label As you read, fill in the missing labels on the diagram.

13. Identify What two parts make up the stamen?

_____

_____

14. Identify What three parts make up the pistil?

_____

_____

_____

Parts of a Flower

Stamen ⎡Anther
       ⎣Filament

Stigma⎤
Style ⎥Pistil
Ovary ⎦

Ovule

SEPALS

Sepals are leaves that make up the outer ring of flower parts. They are often green like leaves, but they may have other colors. Sepals protect and cover the flower while it is still a bud. When the flower begins to open, the sepals fold back, so the petals can be seen.

PETALS

Petals are leaflike parts of a flower. They make up the next ring inside of the sepals. Petals are sometimes brightly colored, like the petals of poppy flowers or roses. Many plants need animals to help spread their pollen. These colors help attract insects and other animals.

SECTION 4 Structures of Seed Plants *continued*

STAMENS

A **stamen** is the male reproductive structure of a flower. Structures on the stamen called *anthers* produce pollen. Pollen contains the male gametophyte, which produces sperm. The anther rests on a thin stalk called a *filament*. ☑

PISTILS

A **pistil** is the female reproductive structure. The tip of the pistil is called the *stigma*. The long, thin part of the pistil is called the *style*. The rounded base of the pistil is called the **ovary**. The ovary contains one or more ovules. Each ovule contains an egg.

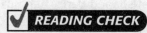

READING CHECK

15. Identify What is the male reproductive structure of a flower?

_____

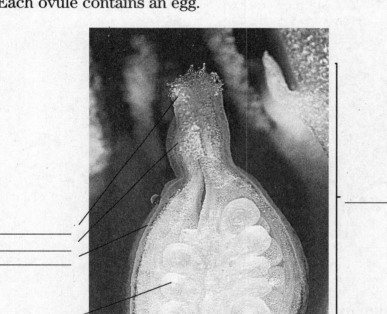

TAKE A LOOK

16. Label Label the female reproductive structures in this picture.

Pollinators brush pollen onto the style, and sperm from inside the pollen travel down the style to the ovary. One sperm can fertilize the egg of one ovule. After fertilization, an ovule develops into a seed. The ovary surrounding the ovule develops into a fruit.

IMPORTANCE OF FLOWERS

Flowers are important to plants because they help plants reproduce. They are also important to animals, such as insects and bats, that use parts of flowers for food. Humans also use flowers. Some flowers, such as broccoli and cauliflower, can be eaten. Others, such as chamomile, are used to make tea. Flowers are also used in perfumes, lotions, and shampoos.

Say It

Discuss What is your favorite flower? Have you ever seen any unusual flowers in nature? In groups of two or three, discuss your experiences with flowers.

Section 4 Review

NSES LS 1a, 1d, 2b, 3d, 4c, 5b

SECTION VOCABULARY

ovary in flowering plants, the lower part of a pistil that produces eggs in ovules	**sepal** in a flower, one of the outermost rings of modified leaves that protect the flower bud
petal one of the usually brightly colored, leaf-shaped parts that make up one of the rings of a flower	**stamen** the male reproductive structure of a flower that produces pollen and consists of an anther at the tip of a filament
phloem the tissue that conducts food in vascular plants	**xylem** the type of tissue in vascular plants that provides support and conducts water and nutrients from the roots
pistil the female reproductive part of a flower that produces seeds and consists of an ovary, style, and stigma	

1. Label Label the parts of this flower.

2. Compare How do taproot and fibrous root systems differ?

_____

_____

_____

3. Describe What are the three functions of a stem?

_____

_____

_____

4. List What are the four main organs of a flowering seed plant?

_____

_____

_____

CHAPTER 13 Plant Processes

SECTION 1 Photosynthesis

National Science Education Standards
LS 1a, 1c, 3c, 4c

BEFORE YOU READ

After you read this section, you should be able to answer these questions:

- How do plants make food?
- How do plants get energy from food?
- How do plants exchange gases with the environment?

What Is Photosynthesis?

Many organisms, including humans, have to eat to get energy. Plants, however, are able to make their own food. Plants make their food by a process called **photosynthesis**. During photosynthesis, plants use carbon dioxide, water, and energy from sunlight to make sugars.

How Do Plants Get Energy from Sunlight?

Plant cells have organelles called *chloroplasts*. Chloroplasts capture the energy from sunlight. Inside a chloroplast, membranes called *grana* contain chlorophyll. **Chlorophyll** is a green pigment that absorbs light energy. Many plants look green because chlorophyll reflects the green wavelengths of light. ☑

STUDY TIP

Outline As you read, outline the steps of photosynthesis. Use the questions in the section titles to help you make your outline.

READING CHECK

1. Define What is chlorophyll?

_____

_____

_____

The grana in chloroplasts contain chlorophyll. Chlorophyll is a pigment that absorbs sunlight.

Chloroplast

Plant cell

Chloroplasts

Grana

TAKE A LOOK

2. Identify Where is chlorophyll found in a plant cell?

_____

_____

_____

How Do Plants Make Sugar?

During photosynthesis, plants take in water and carbon dioxide and absorb light energy. Plants use the light energy captured by chlorophyll to help form glucose molecules. *Glucose* is the sugar that plants use for food. In addition to producing sugar, plants give off oxygen during photosynthesis. ☑

The following chemical equation summarizes photosynthesis:

READING CHECK

3. Identify What are two products of photosynthesis?

_____

_____

$$6CO_2 + 6H_2O \xrightarrow{\text{light energy}} C_6H_{12}O_6 + 6O_2$$

(carbon dioxide) (water) (glucose) (oxygen)

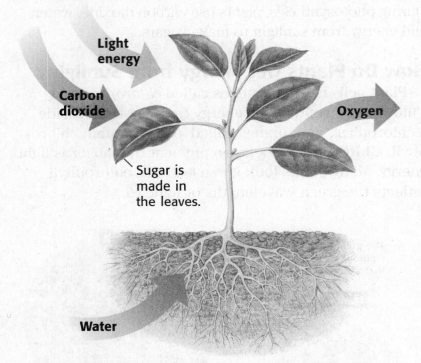

Light energy

Carbon dioxide

Oxygen

Sugar is made in the leaves.

Water

During photosynthesis, plants take in carbon dioxide and water and absorb light energy. They make sugar and release oxygen.

How Do Plants Get Energy from Sugar?

Glucose molecules store energy. To use this energy, a plant cell needs its mitochondria to break down the glucose. This process of breaking down food molecules to get energy is called **cellular respiration**. During cellular respiration, cells use oxygen to break down food molecules. Like all cells, plant cells then use the energy from food to do work.

STANDARDS CHECK

LS 1c Cells carry on the many functions needed to sustain life. They grow and divide, thereby producing more cells. This requires that they take in nutrients, which they use to provide energy for the work cells do and to make the materials that a cell or an organism needs.

4. Identify Which cell structures release the energy stored in sugar?

_____

How Does a Plant Take in the Gases It Needs?

Plants take in carbon dioxide and give off oxygen. These gases move into and out of the leaf through openings called **stomata** (singular, *stoma*). Stomata allow gases to move through the plant's *cuticle*, the waxy layer that prevents water loss. Each stoma is surrounded by two guard cells. The guard cells act like double doors by opening and closing a stoma.

Water vapor also moves out of the leaf through stomata. The loss of water from leaves is called **transpiration**. Stomata open to allow carbon dioxide to enter a leaf. They close to prevent too much water loss.

Critical Thinking

5. Predict What do you think would happen if a plant had no stomata?

_____

_____

_____

_____

Cuticle

Vascular tissue

Stoma

Cuticle

CO₂ enters through stoma.

H₂O and O₂ exit through stoma.

TAKE A LOOK

6. Identify Circle the guard cells in this picture. What is their function?

_____

_____

Why Is Photosynthesis Important?

Plants, along with many bacteria and protists that also use photosynthesis, form the bases of most food chains on Earth. During photosynthesis, plants store light energy as chemical energy. Animals get this energy when they eat plants. Other animals get energy from plants indirectly. They eat the animals that eat plants. Most organisms could not survive without photosynthetic organisms. ☑

Photosynthesis is also important because it produces oxygen. Recall that cellular respiration requires oxygen to break down food. Most organisms, including plants and animals, depend on cellular respiration to get energy from their food. Without the oxygen produced during photosynthesis, most organisms could not survive.

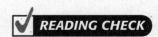 **Say It**

Describe Think of all the ways in which photosynthesis is important to you. Describe to the class three ways you depend on photosynthesis.

✓ READING CHECK

7. Complete During photosynthesis, plants store light energy as

_____

_____

Name _____ Class _____ Date _____

Section 1 Review

NSES LS 1a, 1c, 3c, 4c

SECTION VOCABULARY

cellular respiration the process by which cells use oxygen to produce energy from food **chlorophyll** a green pigment that captures light energy for photosynthesis **photosynthesis** the process by which plants, algae, and some bacteria use sunlight, carbon dioxide, and water to make food	**stoma** one of many openings in a leaf or a stem of a plant that enable gas exchange to occur (plural, *stomata*) **transpiration** the process by which plants release water vapor into the air through stomata; also the release of water vapor into the air by other organisms

1. Explain Why does chlorophyll look green?

_____

_____

2. Identify What is the role of mitochondria in plants? In what process do they take part?

_____

_____

3. Compare Complete the chart below to show the relationship between photosynthesis and cellular respiration.

Photosynthesis	Cellular respiration
	Cells break down food to provide energy.
Oxygen is produced.	

4. Identify What two structures in plant leaves help prevent the loss of water?

_____

5. Explain Why are photosynthetic organisms, such as plants, so important to life on Earth?

_____

_____

_____

6. Explain If plants need to take in carbon dioxide, why don't they keep their stomata open all the time?

_____

_____

CHAPTER 13 | Plant Processes

SECTION
2 **Reproduction of Flowering Plants**

National Science
Education Standards
LS 1a, 2a, 2b, 2d, 5b

BEFORE YOU READ

After you read this section, you should be able to answer
these questions:

• What are pollination and fertilization?

• How do seeds and fruits form?

• How can flowering plants reproduce asexually?

What Are Pollination and Fertilization?

Flowering plants are most noticeable to us when they
are in bloom. As flowers bloom, they surround us with
bright colors and sweet fragrances. However, flowers are
not just for us to enjoy. They are the structures for sexual
reproduction in flowering plants. Pollination and fertilization take place in flowers.

STUDY TIP

Summarize As you read,
write out or draw the steps of
pollination and fertilization.

Pollination and Fertilization

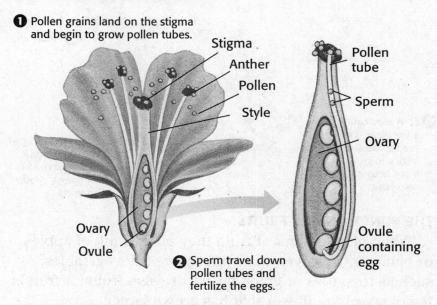

❶ Pollen grains land on the stigma
and begin to grow pollen tubes.

Stigma
Anther
Pollen
Style

Ovary
Ovule

❷ Sperm travel down
pollen tubes and
fertilize the eggs.

Pollen
tube
Sperm
Ovary
Ovule
containing
egg

TAKE A LOOK
1. Identify Circle the part of
the flower where pollination
occurs.

2. Identify Draw an arrow
to show where fertilization
will take place.

Sexual reproduction begins in flowers when wind
or animals move pollen from one flower to another.
Pollination occurs when pollen from an anther lands
on a stigma. Each pollen grain grows a tube through the
style to the ovary. The ovary has ovules, each of which
contains an egg. *Fertilization* occurs when a sperm joins
with the egg inside an ovule.

What Happens After Fertilization?

3. Explain Where do seeds and fruits come from?

_____

_____

_____

_____

_____

_____

a A mature plant produces a flower. Pollination and fertilization take place.

b After fertilization, each ovule within the ovary contains a fertilized egg.

Ovary

Ovule

c Petals and stamens fall away.

e Each seed contains a tiny plant. If a seed sprouts, or begins to grow, it can become a new plant.

d The ovary becomes the fruit, and each ovule becomes a seed. After the fruit ripens, seeds are dispersed.

TAKE A LOOK
4. Identify In step C, circle the structures that will become seeds.

5. List What are two functions of a fruit?

_____

_____

_____

THE FUNCTIONS OF FRUITS

When people think of fruit, they often think of apples or bananas. However, many things we call vegetables, such as tomatoes or green beans, are also fruits! A fruit is the ovary of the flower that has grown larger.

Fruits have two major functions. They protect seeds while the seeds develop. Fruits also help a plant spread its seeds to new environments. For example, an animal might eat a fruit and drop the seeds far from the parent plant. Fruits such as burrs spread when they get caught in an animal's fur. Other fruits are carried to new places by the wind or even by water. ☑

How Do Seeds Grow into New Plants?

The new plant inside a seed, called the *embryo*, stops growing once the seed is fully developed. However, the seed might not sprout right away. To sprout, most seeds need water, air, and warm temperatures. A seed might become **dormant**, or inactive, if the conditions are not right for a new plant to grow. For example, if the environment is too cold or too dry, a young plant will not survive. ☑

Dormant seeds often survive for long periods of time during droughts or freezing weather. Some seeds actually need extreme conditions, such as cold winters or forest fires, to *germinate*, or sprout.

☑ **READING CHECK**

6. Explain Why would a seed become dormant?

_____

_____

_____

Seeds grow into new plants. First, the roots begin to grow. Then, the shoots grow up through the soil.

TAKE A LOOK
7. Identify Which part of a new plant grows first?

_____

_____

How Else Can Flowering Plants Reproduce?

Flowering plants can also reproduce asexually, or without flowers. In asexual reproduction, sperm and eggs do not join. A new plant grows from a plant part such as a root or stem. These plant parts include plantlets, tubers, and runners.

Three Structures for Asexual Reproduction

Kalanchoe produces plantlets along the edges of their leaves. The plantlets will fall off and take root in the soil.

A potato is a tuber, or underground stem. The "eyes" of potatoes are buds that can grow into new plants.

The strawberry plant produces runners, or stems that grow along the ground. Buds along the runners take root and grow into new plants.

Critical Thinking

8. Infer When would asexual reproduction be important for the survival of a flowering plant?

_____

_____

_____

_____

_____

_____

Section 2 Review

NSES   LS 1a, 2a, 2b, 2d, 5b

SECTION VOCABULARY

dormant describes the inactive state of a seed or other plant part when conditions are unfavorable to growth	

1. **Apply Concepts** Is fertilization part of asexual reproduction or sexual reproduction? Explain your answer.

_____

_____

2. **Compare** What is the difference between pollination and fertilization?

_____

_____

3. **Summarize** Complete the Process Chart below to summarize how sexual reproduction produces new plants.

A mature plant produces flowers.

↓

↓

Eggs are fertilized.

↓

↓

4. **Identify** Name two environmental conditions that can cause a seed to become dormant.

_____

5. **List** What are three structures a flowering plant can use to reproduce asexually?

_____

6. **Infer** Why do you think roots are the first part of a plant to grow?

_____

_____

CHAPTER 13 Plant Processes

SECTION
3 **Plant Development and Responses**

National Science
Education Standards
LS 2b, 2c, 3a, 3c, 3d, 5b

BEFORE YOU READ

After you read this section, you should be able to answer
these questions:

• How do plants respond to the environment?

• Why do some trees lose their leaves?

How Do Plants Respond to the Environment?

What happens when you get cold? Do you shiver? Do
your teeth chatter? These are your responses to an environmental stimulus such as cold air. A *stimulus* (plural,
stimuli) is anything that causes a reaction in your body.
Plants also respond to environmental stimuli, but not to
the same ones we do and not in the same way. Plants
respond to stimuli such as light and the pull of gravity. ☑

Some plants respond to a stimulus, such as light, by
growing in a particular direction. Growth in response to a
stimulus is called a **tropism**. A tropism is either positive
or negative. Plant growth toward a stimulus is a positive
tropism. Plant growth away from a stimulus is a negative
tropism.

PLANT GROWTH IN RESPONSE TO LIGHT

Recall that plants need sunlight in order to make food.
What would happen to a plant that could get light from only
one direction, such as through a window? To get as much
light as possible, it would need to grow toward the light.
This growth in response to light is called *phototropism*.

STUDY TIP

Summarize With a partner,
take turns summarizing the
text under each header.

READING CHECK

1. Define What is a stimulus?

_____

_____

_____

TAKE A LOOK

2. Explain Place an **X** on the
picture to show where the
light must be coming from.
Explain your answer.

_____

_____

_____

PLANT GROWTH IN RESPONSE TO GRAVITY

Gravity can change the direction in which a plant's roots and shoots grow. Most shoot tips grow upward, away from the center of Earth. Most root tips grow downward, toward the center of Earth. If a plant is placed on its side or turned upside down, the roots and shoots will change direction. Shoots will turn to grow away from the Earth. Roots will turn to grow toward the Earth. This response is called *gravitropism*.

Critical Thinking

3. Apply Concepts Look at the plant on the left. Draw an arrow on the flower pot to show the direction the roots are probably growing.

TAKE A LOOK

4. Explain Look at the plant on the right. What do you think made its stem bend?

_____

_____

_____

_____

_____

Gravitropism

To grow away from the pull of gravity, this plant has grown upward.

What Happens to Plants When Seasons Change?

Have you ever noticed that some plants will drop their leaves in the fall even before the weather turns cool? How do the plants know that fall is coming? We often notice the changing seasons because the temperature changes. Plants, however, respond to change in the length of the day.

Math Focus

5. Calculate It must be dark for 70% of a 24-hour period before a certain plant will bloom. How many hours of daylight does this plant need to bloom?

_____

SHORT DAY AND LONG DAY PLANTS

Days are longer in summer and shorter in winter. The change in amount of daylight is a stimulus for many plants. Some plants that bloom in winter, such as poinsettias, need shorter periods of daylight to reproduce. They are called *short-day plants*. Others, such as clover, reproduce in spring or summer. They are called *long-day plants*.

SECTION 3 Plant Development and Responses *continued*

EFFECT OF SEASONS ON LEAF COLOR

The leaves of some trees may change color as seasons change. As the days shorten in fall, the chlorophyll in leaves breaks down. This makes the orange and yellow pigments in the leaves easier to see. During the summer, chlorophyll hides other pigments.

Amount of Leaf Pigment Based on Season

- ■ Chlorophyll
- ▨ Yellow pigment
- □ Orange pigment

TAKE A LOOK
6. Identify Which pigment's level decreases between summer and fall?

_____

7. Identify Which pigments' levels will stay the same between summer and fall?

_____

LOSS OF LEAVES

Every tree loses leaves throughout its life. Leaves are shed when they become old. For example, pine trees lose some of their leaves, or *needles*, year-round. Because leaves are lost and replaced throughout the year, the tree always has some leaves. These trees are called *evergreen*. A leaf of an evergreen tree is covered with a thick cuticle. The cuticle protects the leaf from cold and dry weather.

Deciduous trees lose all their leaves at about the same time each year. This generally happens as days shorten. The loss of leaves helps these plants survive cold or dry weather. In colder areas, deciduous trees usually lose their leaves before winter begins. In areas that have wet and dry seasons, deciduous trees lose their leaves before the dry season.

Describe What is your favorite kind of tree? Use the Internet or reference books to find out if the tree is evergreen or deciduous. Describe to the class what the tree looks like and where it lives.

Section 3 Review

SECTION VOCABULARY

tropism growth of all or part of an organism in response to an external stimulus, such as light	

1. Compare What is the difference between a negative tropism and a positive tropism?

_____

_____

_____

2. Explain What happens when a plant gets light from only one direction?

_____

_____

_____

3. Define What is gravitropism?

_____

_____

_____

4. Identify What stimulus causes seasonal changes in many plants?

_____

_____

5. Compare What is the difference between short-day plants and long-day plants?

_____

_____

_____

6. Explain Why do leaves look green during the summer even though they have orange and yellow pigments?

_____

_____

_____

7. Explain Many evergreen trees live in areas with long, cold winters. How can they keep their leaves all year?

_____

_____

_____

CHAPTER 14 Animals and Behavior
SECTION
1 **What Is an Animal?**

National Science
Education Standards
LS 1a, 1b, 1d, 2a, 2b, 4b, 5a

BEFORE YOU READ

After you read this section, you should be able to answer
these questions:

• What do all animals have in common?

• What are vertebrates and invertebrates?

What Are Animals?

What do you think of when you hear the word animal?
You may think of a dog or cat. You may think of giraffes
or grizzly bears. Would you think of a sponge?

How many kinds of animals are in the picture below?
You may be surprised to learn that feather stars and coral
are animals. Some animals have four legs and fur. Other
animals have wings and feathers. Some animals are so
small that they can only be seen with a microscope. Other
animals are bigger than a bus. Scientists have named more
than 1 million species of animals. However, there are still
millions of species that have not been named.

Although the feather star and coral look like plants, they
are actually animals.

CHARACTERISTICS OF ANIMALS

Animals may look very different from one another, but
they all have some things in common. While other organisms
have some of these characteristics, only animals have all five:

1. They are multicellular.

2. Almost all can reproduce sexually.

3. They have specialized parts.

4. They can move.

5. They eat other organisms.

STUDY TIP

Outline As you read, make
an outline descrbing the
characteristics of animals. Be
sure to include examples of
each characteristic.

Critical Thinking

1. Infer Why do you think
there are many species of
animals that have not been
named?

_____

_____

_____

_____

Say It

Describe Choose your
favorite animal. Describe to
the class how this animal
shows the five characteristics
of animals.

MULTICELLULAR

All animals are *multicellular*. This means they are made of more than one cell. Your own body is made of trillions of cells. Animal cells are *eukaryotic*, which means they have a nucleus. Plants are also multicellular. However, plant cells have cell walls and animal cells do not. Animal cells are surrounded only by cell membranes. ☑

READING CHECK

2. Define What does multicellular mean?

_____

_____

_____

REPRODUCTION

Most animals can reproduce sexually. They make sex cells called eggs and sperm. When an egg and sperm join, they form a new cell. This cell grows and divides to form an embryo. An **embryo** is the early stage of development of an organism. A few animals can reproduce asexually. For example, flatworms called *Planaria* break off part of their bodies to form offspring.

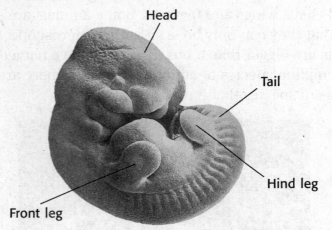

Head
Tail
Hind leg
Front leg

Cells in the mouse embryo will differentiate as the mouse develops. These cells will produce skin, muscles, nerves, and all the other parts of the mouse's body.

TAKE A LOOK

3. Explain What happens to the cells in an embryo as the embryo develops?

_____

_____

CELL SPECIALIZATION

As a fertilized egg develops, it divides into many cells. As the organism develops, its cells *differentiate*. When cells differentiate, they develop different structures so they can perform different functions. Some cells become skin cells, while others become muscle or bone cells. Groups of similar cells form *tissues*. For example, muscle cells form muscle tissue. ☑

Tissues can group together to form *organs*. An organ is a group of tissues that carry out a special job in the body. Your heart, lung, and kidneys are all organs. Each organ in an animal's body does different jobs. The figure on the next page shows some of the organs in a shark's body.

READING CHECK

4. Explain What happens when cells differentiate?

_____

_____

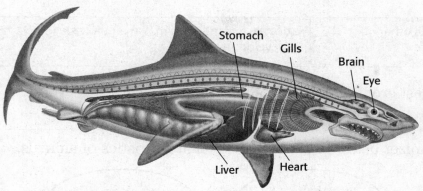

Like most animals, sharks have organs for digestion, circulation, and sensing the environment.

MOVEMENT

Most animals can move from place to place. They can fly, run, swim, or jump. Some animals use movements to find food, shelter, and mates. However, not all animals can move their entire lives. For example, young sea anemones swim to find their food. As adults, sea anemones attach to rocks or the ocean floor and wait for food to drift by.

EATING

Unlike plants, animals cannot make their own food. They are consumers. A **consumer** must eat other organisms to survive. Some animals eat plants or parts of plants. Some animals eat other animals.

What Are the Two Main Groups of Animals?

VERTEBRATES

Most animals don't look like humans. However, humans are part of a group of animals called vertebrates. A *vertebrate* is an animal that has a backbone or spine. Vertebrates include fishes, amphibians, reptiles, birds, and mammals. Humans are a kind of mammal.

INVERTEBRATES

Although you are probably more familiar with vertebrates, most animals are actually invertebrates. *Invertebrates* are animals without a backbone. Insects, snails, jellyfish, and worms are examples of invertebrates. More than 95% of all animals are invertebrates. In fact, beetles make up more then 30% of all animal species! ☑

STANDARDS CHECK

LS 4b Populations of organisms can be <u>categorized</u> by the <u>functions</u> they serve in an ecosystem. Plants and some microorganisms are producers—they make their own food. All animals, including humans, are consumers, which obtain their food by eating other organisms. Decomposers, primarily bacteria and fungi, are consumers that use waste materials and dead organisms for food. Food webs identify the relationship among producers, consumers, and decomposers in an ecosystem.

Word Help: <u>categorize</u>
to put in groups or classes

Word Help: <u>function</u>
use or purpose

5. Explain Are animals producers or consumers? Explain your answer.

_____
_____
_____
_____
_____

☑ **READING CHECK**

6. Complete Most animals on Earth are _____

_____

Section 1 Review

NSES 1a, 1b, 1d, 2a, 2b, 4b, 5a

SECTION VOCABULARY

consumer an organism that eats other organisms or organic matter	**embryo** a plant or animal at an early stage of development

1. Identify What is the largest group of invertebrates on Earth?

_____

2. Summarize Use the organizer below to show the five characteristics of animals.

Characteristics of Animals

3. Apply Concepts Like animals, plants are multicellular and have specialized parts. Why are these considered characteristics of animals?

_____

_____

_____

4. Explain An adult sea anemone cannot move. Why is it considered an animal?

_____

_____

5. Compare What is the main difference between vertebrates and invertebrates? Give an example of each kind of animal.

_____

_____

_____

CHAPTER 14 Animals and Behavior

SECTION
2
Animal Behavior

BEFORE YOU READ

After you read this section, you should be able to answer these questions:

- How do learned and innate behaviors differ?
- What types of behaviors do animals use to survive?

National Science Education Standards

LS 1a, 3a, 3b, 3c, 3d, 5b

What Is Behavior?

Suppose you look out a window and see a bird flying away from a tree. Is the bird leaving a nest to look for food? Is it escaping from danger?

An animal may run or hide from an enemy. It may also search for food and look for a safe place to build its home. All of these activities are called *behaviors*. Behavior is the way an organism acts in different situations. Animals can be born with some behaviors. They may also learn other behaviors as they grow.

✏️ **STUDY TIP**

Summarize Make combination notes describing different survival behaviors and examples of each.

What Are The Two Main Types of Behavior?

Innate behaviors are behaviors that an animal does automatically. Animals are born with innate behaviors. For example, puppies like to chew and bees know how to fly. Some innate behaviors begin when the animal is born. Newborn whales, for example, can swim. Other innate behaviors begin months or years after an animal is born.

Animals can also learn a behavior. A **learned behavior** is a behavior that develops with experience or from watching other animals. For example, humans are born with an ability to speak. However, we must learn a language in order to speak. Humans are not the only animals that can learn.

STANDARDS CHECK

LS 3c Behavior is one kind of response an organism can make to an internal or environmental stimulus. A behavioral response requires coordination and communication at many levels, including cells, organ systems, and whole organisms. Behavioral response is a set of actions determined in part by heredity and in part from experience.

1. Compare How do innate behaviors and learned behaviors differ?

_____

_____

_____

_____

_____

_____

A male bowerbird collects colorful objects for its nest. These objects attract a female bowerbird.

TAKE A LOOK
2. Identify If this bowerbird collected objects for its nest without ever doing it before or seeing another bird do it, what type of behavior is the bird showing?

_____

SECTION 2 Animal Behavior *continued*

What Are Some Survival Behaviors?

Animals use their behaviors to survive. To stay alive and pass on its genes, an animal has to do many things. It must find food and a place to live. It also must protect itself against predators. Animals also find mates so that they can have off-spring. Some survival behaviors are described below.

FINDING FOOD

Different kinds of animals use different behaviors to find food. Some animals, such as koalas, climb trees to get their food. Other animals, such as tigers, chase prey.

Animals that eat other animals are called *predators*. The animal being eaten is called the *prey*. So, if a frog eats an insect, the frog is the predator and the insect is the prey. If the frog is then eaten by a snake, the snake becomes the predator and the frog is the prey. ☑

3. Complete An animal eaten by another animal is called _____.

Chimpanzees make and use tools to get food out of hard-to-reach places.

CLAIMING TERRITORY

Sometimes, members of the same species must compete for the same resources. These include food, mates, and places to live. Since resources are often limited, animals must often fight for them. To avoid competing for resources in one area, some animals claim territories. ☑

A **territory** is an area where one animal or a group of animals live. These animals do not let any other members of their species live there. For example, birds will often sing to warn other birds not to enter their area. Animals use their territories for mating, raising young, and finding food.

4. List What are three resources animals of the same species may compete for?

_____

_____

_____

PROTECTING THEMSELVES

Animals often have to protect their mates and offspring. They also have to protect their resources, such as food and mates. For example, a dog may growl when another animal enters its territory. Male lions fight to defend mates. Some birds, such as killdeer, will pretend to be hurt. This distracts a predator so that it will not attack the bird's young.

Animals often use their defensive behaviors to protect themselves from being eaten. Rabbits will freeze to blend into the background so that predators do not see them. If a predator does see them, they will run. Some animals, such as bees and wasps, will sting their attackers.

FINDING A MATE

For an individual's genes to survive, the individual must reproduce. For an animal to have offspring, it must first find a mate. Some animals have special behaviors that help them find mates. These behaviors are called *courtship*. Some birds and fish build nests to attract a mate. Other animals use special movements or sounds. ☑

RAISING OFFSPRING

Following a courtship behavior and mating, offspring are usually born. Some animals, such as caterpillars, can take care of themselves as soon as they are born. However, many young animals depend on their parents for survival.

Different animals take care of their young for different amounts of time. Some adult birds bring food to their young only until they can fly and get their own food. Other animals, such as killer whales, spend years teaching their young how to hunt for food.

Adult killer whales teach their young how to hunt in the first years of life.

READING CHECK

5. Identify What is the name for behaviors that an animal uses to find a mate?

_____

_____

TAKE A LOOK

6. Apply Concepts Is hunting in killer whales a learned or innate behavior?

_____

_____

What Do Animals Do As Seasons Change?

When seasons change, humans wear different clothes and do different activities. Animals also act differently during different seasons. During winter in some parts of the world, animals need to protect themselves from the cold. For example, frogs burrow into mud to stay warm. Some animals, such as squirrels, store food to use in winter. Different behaviors in different seasons help animals adjust to the environment. ☑

MIGRATION

Many animals avoid cold weather by traveling to warmer places. When animals travel from one place to another it is called *migration*. Animals migrate to find food, water, and safe places to have offspring. Whales, salmon, bats, and butterflies all migrate. When animals migrate, they use *landmarks* to find their way. Landmarks are fixed objects, such as mountain ranges, rivers, and stars, that animals use to find their way. ☑

HIBERNATION

During winter, some animals hibernate. During **hibernation**, an animal lowers its body temperature and is inactive. When they are hibernating, animals will not look for food or mates. Hibernating animals get nutrients from stored body fat. Most hibernating animals, such as mice, lower their heart rate and breathing. This lets their bodies use less energy. Their body temperature also lowers to just above freezing.

✔ READING CHECK

7. Explain Why do many animals have different behaviors in different seasons?

_____

_____

_____

_____

✔ READING CHECK

8. List Give three reasons animals migrate.

_____

_____

_____

_____

TAKE A LOOK

9. Explain Do bears hibernate? Explain your answer.

_____

_____

_____

_____

_____

Bears do not actually hibernate. They slow their bodies down for the winter, but their body temperatures do not drop as low as hibernating animals. They also sleep for shorter periods of time.

ESTIVATION

Some animals slow down their bodies when it is hot. Desert squirrels and mice slow down their bodies during the hottest part of summer. This lets them survive when there is little food or water. Reduced activity in the summer or during hot periods is called **estivation**.

How Do Animals Know When to Do Certain Behaviors?

Animals need to keep track of time so that they know when to store food or to migrate. An animal's natural cycles are called its *biological clock*. The biological clock is a control inside animals' bodies. Animals often use the length of the day and the temperature to set their biological clocks.

SHORT CYCLES

Some biological clocks keep track of daily cycles. These daily cycles are called **circadian rhythms**. Most animals, including humans, wake up and get sleepy at about the same time each day and night. This is an example of a circadian rhythm.

LONG CYCLES

Biological clocks can also control long cycles. Almost all animals have seasonal cycles, or cycles that change with the seasons. For example, many animals hibernate in one season and have offspring in another season. The start of migration is also controlled by seasonal changes.

Biological clocks can also control changes inside an animal. For example, insects such as treehoppers go through several changes during their lives. They start as eggs, hatch as nymphs, and then develop into adults.

The treehopper's biological clock tells the animal when to shed, or get rid of, its skin.

Critical Thinking

10. Compare How is hibernation different from estivation?

_____
_____
_____
_____
_____

Math Focus

11. Calculate Suppose that an animal's circadian rhythms tell it to eat a meal every 4 hours. How many meals will that animal eat in a day?

_____

Section 2 Review

SECTION VOCABULARY

circadian rhythm a biological daily cycle **estivation** a period of inactivity and lowered body temperature that some animals undergo in summer as a protection against hot weather and lack of food **hibernation** a period of inactivity and lowered body temperature that some animals undergo in winter as a protection against cold weather and lack of food	**innate behavior** an inherited behavior that does not depend on the environment or experience **learned behavior** a behavior that has been learned from experience **territory** an area that is occupied by one animal or a group of animals that do not allow other members of the species to enter

1. Explain If humans are born with the ability to speak, why isn't talking an innate behavior?

_____

_____

2. List Name five survival behaviors.

_____

_____

3. Infer Can an animal be both a predator and prey? Explain your answer.

_____

_____

4. Explain When animals migrate, how do they find their way?

_____

_____

5. Apply Concepts People who travel to different time zones often suffer from *jet lag*. Jet lag makes it hard for people to wake up or go to sleep at the right time. Why do you think people get jet lag?

_____

_____

_____

6. Identify Name two clues animals use to set their biological clocks.

_____

7. Identify Give an example of a seasonal cycle controlled by a biological clock.

_____

 Animals and Behavior

CHAPTER 14 | Animals and Behavior

SECTION 3 | Social Relationships

BEFORE YOU READ

After you read this section, you should be able to answer these questions:

- How do animals communicate?
- Why do some animals live in groups?

What Is Social Behavior?

Animals often interact with each other—in groups and one on one. They may work together or compete. Maybe you have seen two dogs barking at each other. We may not know exactly why they behave this way, but it is clear that they are interacting. These interactions are called social behavior. **Social behavior** is the interaction among animals that are the same species. Animals use communication for their social interactions. ☑

How Do Animals Communicate?

Imagine what life would be like if people could not read or talk. There would be no telephones, no books, no Internet, and no radios. Language is an important way for people to communicate. In **communication**, a signal is sent from one animal to another animal. The animal that receives the signal then answers back. Humans are the only animals that use complex words and grammar. However, other animals do communicate.

Animals, including humans, can communicate by using sound, touch, smells, and sight. Communication helps animals survive. Many animals, such as wolves, communicate to defend a territory or to identify family members. Animals also communicate to find food, to warn others of danger, to frighten predators, and to find mates.

STUDY TIP

Organize As you read, make a chart of the different ways animals communicate. List an example from the text and add another example of your own.

READING CHECK

1. Define What is social behavior?

_____

_____

_____

TAKE A LOOK

2. Apply Concepts Give two possible reasons these wolves could be howling.

_____

_____

_____

SECTION 3 | Social Relationships *continued*

SOUND

Many animals communicate by making noises. Wolves howl. Dolphins use whistles and make clicking noises. Male birds often sing to attract mates or defend their territories.

Sound can travel over large distances. Animals such as humpback whales and elephants use sounds to let others know where they are. Elephants make some sounds that are too low for humans to hear. Although humans cannot hear them, elephants that are kilometers away can.

Elephants communicate using low-pitched sounds. When an elephant makes these sounds, the skin on its forehead flutters.

TOUCH

Animals may also touch to communicate. For example, chimpanzees will groom each other. *Grooming* is when one animal picks dirt out of another animal's fur. Chimpanzees use grooming to calm and comfort each other. With touch, animals can also communicate friendship and support.

SMELL

Some animals, including humans, make chemicals called pheromones. A **pheromone** is a chemical that an animal uses to communicate with other members of its species. Ants and other insects make several pheromones. Some pheromones warn other ants of danger. Other pheromones are used by insects to find mates. Some insects that live in colonies, such as fire ants, use pheromones to control which colony members can reproduce. ☑

SIGHT

When you smile at a friend, you are using *body language*. Body language is the movements made by an animal that communicate an idea to another animal.

Critical Thinking

3. Infer Why do you think sound is a good way to communicate for animals that live in large areas?

_____
_____
_____
_____
_____

☑ **READING CHECK**

4. Define What are pheromones?

_____
_____
_____
_____

SECTION 3 Social Relationships *continued*

When dogs want to play, they drop down on their forelegs.

To scare others, an animal may ruffle its feathers, try to look bigger, or show its teeth. Animals can also use body language to show that they are friendly. The figure above shows how a dog behaves when it wants to play. Visual displays are also used in courtship. For example, fireflies blink signals to attract each other.

Why Do Some Animals Live In Groups?

Some animals live in groups because it can be safer than living alone. Group members can warn each other of danger. These animals work together to defend the entire group. By hunting in groups, animals can kill larger animals than they could by themselves.

However, there are some problems caused by living in a group. All the animals in a group must compete for the same food, shelter, and mates. Sometimes groups of animals must move around to find enough food to feed the group. Large groups of animals usually attract more predators. Sickness and disease can also spread quickly through a group.

Say It

Discuss Like many other animals, humans also live in groups. With your classmates, discuss ways that living in groups is helpful to humans. Then, discuss ways that living in groups can cause problems.

A ground squirrel whistles a loud alarm to alert the other ground squirrels that danger is near.

TAKE A LOOK
5. Identify Which advantage of living in a group does this figure show?

_____

_____

_____

Section 3 Review

NSES LS 1a, 3c, 3d, 4a

SECTION VOCABULARY

communication a transfer of a signal or message from one animal to another that results in some type of response	**pheromone** a substance that is released by the body and that causes another individual of the same species to react in a predictable way **social behavior** the interaction between animals of the same species

1. **Analyze** In parts of Africa, lions and crocodiles may fight over prey. Why is this *not* an example of social behavior?

_____

_____

_____

2. **List** Name six reasons animals communicate.

_____

_____

_____

3. **Summarize** Use the chart below to summarize the advantages and disadvantages of living in a group.

Advantages of living in a group	Disadvantages of living in a group

4. **Analyze** Imagine you are on a safari. You see a group of six lions feeding on a dead zebra. As another animal moves closer, the lions stand up and growl. Name some types of behaviors the lions are showing.

_____

_____

_____

5. **List** What are the four ways animals communicate?

_____

CHAPTER 15 | Invertebrates

SECTION
1 **Simple Invertebrates**

BEFORE YOU READ

After you read this section, you should be able to answer these questions:

• What are the characteristics of invertebrates?

• What are the four groups of simple invertebrates?

National Science Education Standards
LS 1d, 1f, 2a, 3a, 3c, 5a

What Are Invertebrates?

About 96% of all animal species are invertebrates. An **invertebrate** is an animal that does not have a backbone. Worms, jellyfish, octopuses, and butterflies are some examples of invertebrates. More than 1 million invertebrates have already been named. Scientists think there are millions of invertebrates that have not been found or named.

STUDY TIP

Outline As you read, make an outline of this section. Use the header questions to help you make your outline.

BODY PLANS

Invertebrates have three basic body plans: bilateral, radial, or asymmetrical. Most animals have bilateral symmetry. The three basic body plans are decribed below.

Animal Body Plans

Bilateral Symmetry

This ant has **bilateral symmetry**. The two sides of its body mirror each other. On each side of its body, the ant has one eye, one antenna, and three legs.

Radial Symmetry

This sea star has **radial symmetry**. Its body is organized around the center, like spokes on a wheel.

Asymmetry

This sponge is **asymmetrical**. You cannot draw a straight line to divide its body into equal parts. Its body is not organized around a center.

TAKE A LOOK

1. Describe What is bilateral symmetry?

_____

_____

_____

2. Apply Concepts What kind of symmetry does a butterfly have?

_____

NEURONS AND GANGLIA

All animals, except sponges, have special tissues that allow them to sense their environment. These tissues make fibers called *neurons*. Neurons carry messages around the body to control the animal's actions. Simple invertebrates have nerve cords. *Nerve cords* are bundles of neurons that carry messages along a single path.

Some invertebrates have nerve cells called ganglia (singular, *ganglion*). A **ganglion** is a mass of nerve cells grouped together. Each ganglion controls a different part of the body. The ganglia are connected by nerve cords. In complex invertebrates, a brain controls the ganglia and nerves throughout the body. ☑

GUTS

Most animals digest food in a gut. A **gut** is a hollow space lined with cells. The cells make chemicals to break down food into small particles. The cells then absorb the food particles.

In complex animals, the gut is inside a coelom. A **coelom** is a body cavity that surrounds the gut. The coelum keeps other organs, such as the heart, separated from the gut. That way, movements in the gut do not disturb the actions of other organs. In simple invertebrates, the gut is not surrounded by a coelom.

READING CHECK

3. Identify In an invertebrate's body, what connects all the ganglia?

_____

_____

Coelom   Gut

Earthworms have a coelom filled with fluid. The gut is inside the coelom.

TAKE A LOOK

4. Identify What is the name of the body cavity that surrounds the gut?

_____

_____

What Are Sponges?

Sponges are the simplest invertebrates. They are asymmetrical. They have no tissues, gut, or neurons. Adult sponges may move only a few millimeters each day or not all.

Scientists once thought sponges were plants. However, because sponges cannot make their own food, they are classified as animals.

SECTION 1 Simple Invertebrates *continued*

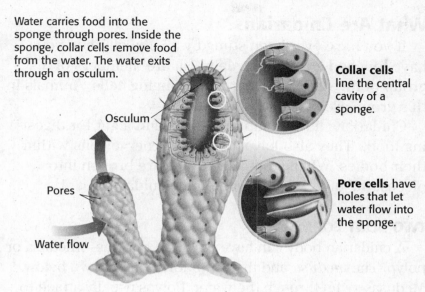

Water carries food into the sponge through pores. Inside the sponge, collar cells remove food from the water. The water exits through an osculum.

Osculum

Pores

Water flow

Collar cells line the central cavity of a sponge.

Pore cells have holes that let water flow into the sponge.

TAKE A LOOK
5. Identify What is the function of collar cells?

_____

_____

6. Identify Through what structure does water leave a sponge?

_____

HOW SPONGES FEED

As shown above, a sponge has a special way of getting food. Water flows into the body of a sponge through pores. *Pores* are holes on the outside of a sponge. The water flows into a cavity in the middle of the sponge. *Collar cells* line this cavity. Collar cells take in tiny plants and animals from the water and digest them. Water leaves through a hole at the top of the sponge. This is called the *osculum*.

REGENERATION

Sponges have some unusual abilities. If a sponge is forced through a strainer, the cells can come back together to re-form a new sponge. If part of a sponge is broken off, the missing part can grow back. This ability is called *regeneration*. A part of the sponge that is broken off can also grow into a new sponge. This means sponges can use regeneration as a way to reproduce.

SUPPORT IN A SPONGE BODY

Most sponges have skeletons that support their bodies and protect them from predators. This skeleton is not made of bones, however. It is made of small, hard fibers called *spicules*. Some spicules are straight, some are curved, and some are star-shaped.

STANDARDS CHECK

LS 2a Reproduction is a characteristic of all living systems; because no living organism lives forever, reproduction is essential to the continuation of every species. Some organisms reproduce asexually. Others reproduce sexually.

7. Apply Concepts When a new sponge grows from a piece of sponge that has broken off, is this asexual or sexual reproduction? Explain your answer.

_____

_____

_____

_____

SECTION 1 Simple Invertebrates *continued*

What Are Cnidarians?

If you have ever been stung by a jellyfish, then you have touched a cnidarian. Jellyfish are members of a group of invertebrates that have stinging cells. Animals in this group are called *cnidarians*. ☑

Cnidarians have complex tissues and a gut for digesting food. They also have a system of nerve cells within their bodies. When some cnidarians are broken into pieces, the pieces can become new cnidarians.

TWO BODY FORMS

A cnidarian body can have one of two forms—medusa or polyp. The *medusa* and the *polyp* forms are shown below. Medusas swim through the water. Polyps usually attach to a surface. Some cnidarians change forms during their lives. However, many cnidarians are polyps for their whole lives.

Medusa   Polyp

Both the medusa and the polyp forms of a jellyfish have radial symmetry

STINGING CELLS

All cnidarians have tentacles covered with stinging cells. The touch from another organism activates these stinging cells. Each stinging cell shoots a tiny spear into the organism. Each spear carries poison. Cnidarians use stinging cells to protect themselves and to catch food.

A tiny barbed spear is coiled inside each stinging cell.

When the tiny spear is fired, the long barbed strand is shot into the prey.

READING CHECK

8. Identify What do all cnidarians have in common?

_____

_____

TAKE A LOOK

9. Identify What kind of symmetry do jellyfish have?

_____

_____

TAKE A LOOK

10. List Name two reasons cnidarians use stinging cells.

_____

_____

_____

KINDS OF CNIDARIANS

There are three classes of cnidarians: hydrozoans, jellyfish, and sea anemones and corals. The figure below shows each type of cnidarian.

◄Hydrozoan

◄Jellyfish

Sea anemone ►

◄Coral

TAKE A LOOK
11. Apply Concepts Which of the cnidarians in this figure have the polyp body form?

_____

_____

_____

Hydrozoans live in both freshwater and saltwater. Most hydrozoans live as polyps their entire lives. Jellyfish use their tentacles to catch fish and other invertebrates. They spend most of their lives as medusas. Sea anemones and corals spend their lives as polyps. Corals can build large and colorful reefs.

What Are Flatworms?

When you think of worms, you probably think of earthworms. However, there are many other kinds of worms. Many of them are too small to see without a microscope. The simplest worms are the flatworms. ☑

Flatworms are divided into three classes: planarians, flukes, and tapeworms. All flatworms have bilateral symmetry. Most flatworms have a head and two eyespots. Some flatworms have a bump on each side of their heads. These are called sensory lobes. The flatworm uses sensory lobes to find food.

☑ READING CHECK
12. Identify What are the simplest worms?

_____

_____

SECTION 1 Simple Invertebrates *continued*

PLANARIANS

Planarians are flatworms that live in fresh water or damp places. As shown below, they have a head, eyespots, and sensory lobes. Most planarians are predators. They eat other animals or parts of animals and digest the food in a gut. Planarians use their sensory lobes to find food. Planarians also have a nervous system with a brain. ☑

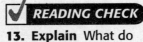

READING CHECK

13. Explain What do planarians use their sensory lobe for?

_____

_____

Eyespot   Sensory lobe

Planarians are often about 15 mm long.

FLUKES

Flukes are parasites. A *parasite* is an organism that feeds on another living thing. This organism is called the *host*.

Most flukes live and reproduce inside a host animal. The fertilized eggs of a fluke pass out of the animal's body with its waste products. If these eggs infect water or food, animals may eat them. These eggs would then grow into new flukes inside these animals. Flukes have no eyespots or sensory lobes. They use suckers to attach to their hosts.

Flukes use suckers to attach to their hosts. Most flukes are just a few millimeters long.

TAKE A LOOK

14. Identify What structures do flukes use to attach to a host?

_____

_____

TAPEWORMS

Tapeworms are also parasites. Like flukes, tapeworms live, feed, and reproduce inside a host. They have no eyespots, sensory lobes, or gut. Tapeworms simply attach to the intestines of their hosts and absorb nutrients. Nutrients move directly through the tapeworm's tissues. Some tapeworms can live in humans.

Tapeworms can grow very long. Some are longer than a bus!

What Are Roundworms?

Roundworms have bodies that are long, slim, and round, like short pieces of spaghetti. Like other worms, they have bilateral symmetry. Roundworms have a simple nervous system and brain. ☑

Most species of roundworms are very small. A single rotten apple could contain 100,000 roundworms! These tiny worms get nutrients by breaking down the tissues of dead plants and animals. This process helps put some nutrients back into the soil.

Some roundworms are parasites. Several roundworms, such as pinworms and hookworms, can infect humans. Humans can become infected with roundworms by eating meat that has not been fully cooked. In humans, roundworms can cause fever, tiredness, and digestive problems.

Critical Thinking

15. Compare How does the size of a tapeworm compare to the size of a planarian?

_____

_____

_____

_____

_____

READING CHECK

16. Describe Describe the body of a roundworm.

_____

_____

_____

This hookworm is a tiny larva. Even as an adult, it will be less than 15 mm.

Section 1 Review

SECTION VOCABULARY

coelom a body cavity that contains the internal organs **ganglion** a mass of nerve cells	**gut** the digestive tract **invertebrate** an animal that does not have a backbone

1. Identify What do all invertebrates have in common?

_____

2. List What are the four groups of simple invertebrates?

_____

3. Explain How does the gut of a complex animal differ from that of a simple animal?

_____

4. List Give two ways sponges use regeneration.

_____

5. Identify What are the two cnidarian body forms?

_____

6. Infer Why do you think it would be important to a parasite that its host survive?

_____

_____

_____

7. Compare Complete the chart below to compare the different types of flatworms.

Type of flatworm	Parasitic or nonparasitic?	Features
Planarians		head, eyespots, sensory lobes, brain

8. Explain Are all roundworms parasites? Explain your answer.

_____

_____

_____

Mollusks and Annelid Worms

National Science
Education Standards
LS 1a, 1d, 3a, 5a

BEFORE YOU READ

After you read this section, you should be able to answer
these questions:

- What are the four features of mollusks?
- What are the three kinds of annelid worms?

What Are Mollusks and Annelid Worms?

Have you ever eaten clams? Have you ever seen earthworms on the sidewalk after it rains? If so, then you have
already seen mollusks and annelid worms. These invertebrates are more complex than the simple invertebrates.
For example, mollusks and annelid worms have circulatory systems that carry materials throughout their bodies.

What Are Mollusks?

Snails, slugs, clams, oysters, squids, and octopuses are
all mollusks. Most mollusks live in the ocean. However,
some live in fresh water and some live on land.

There are three classes of mollusks: gastropods, bivalves,
and cephalopods. The *gastropods* include snails and slugs.
The *bivalves* include shellfish with two shells, such as clams
and oysters. *Cephalopods* include squids and octopuses. ☑

HOW MOLLUSKS EAT

Each kind of mollusk has its own way of eating. As shown
below, snails and slugs eat with a special organ called the
radula. The radula is a tongue covered with curved teeth.
It lets the animal scrape food off rocks, seaweed, or plants.
Clams and oysters use gills to filter tiny organisms from the
water. Squids and octopuses use tentacles to grab their food
and place it in their jaws.

The rows of teeth on a
slug's radula help scrape
food from surfaces. This
radula has been magnified
2,000 times.

STUDY TIP

Underline As you read, use
colored pencils to underline
the characteristics of mollusks
and annelid worms. Use one
color for mollusks and another
for annelid worms.

READING CHECK

1. Identify Which class of
mollusks do snails belong to?

_____

_____

TAKE A LOOK

2. Identify What is the
function of the radula?

_____

_____

_____

GANGLIA AND BRAINS

All mollusks have complex ganglia. They have special ganglia to control breathing, movement, and digestion. Cephalopods have the most advanced nervous system of all invertebrates. An octopus, for example, has a large brain that connects all of its ganglia. Cephalopods are thought to be the smartest invertebrates. ☑

PUMPING BLOOD

Unlike simple invertebrates, mollusks have a circulatory system. The circulatory system moves materials through the body in blood. Most mollusks have open circulatory systems. In an **open circulatory system**, a heart pumps blood through blood vessels that empty into spaces in the animal's body. These spaces are called *sinuses*.

Squids and octopuses have closed circulatory systems. In a **closed circulatory system**, a heart pumps blood through a network of blood vessels that form a loop.

MOLLUSK BODIES

Although mollusks can look quite different from one another, their bodies have similar parts. The body parts of mollusks are described below.

Body Parts of Mollusks

Mollusks have a broad, muscular **foot**. The foot helps the animals move. In gastropods, the foot makes mucus that the animal slides along.

The gills, gut, and other organs form the **visceral mass**. It lies in the center of the mollusk's body.

A layer of tissue called the **mantle** covers the visceral mass. The mantle protects the bodies of mollusks that do not have a shell.

In most mollusks, the outside of the mantle makes a **shell**. The shell protects the mollusks from predators. It also keeps land mollusks from drying out.

Snail

Clam

Squid

KEY		
▮ Foot		▮ Mantle
▮ Visceral mass		▯ Shell

READING CHECK

3. Identify Which group of invertebrates has the most advanced nervous systems?

_____

_____

Critical Thinking

4. Infer What kind of circulatory system do you have?

_____

_____

TAKE A LOOK

5. Identify Which mollusk does not have an obvious shell?

_____

_____

6. List What are two functions of a mollusk's shell?

_____

_____

_____

_____

What Are Annelid Worms?

The bodies of annelid worms are segmented. Annelid worms are sometimes called *segmented worms*. A **segment** is an identical, or almost identical, repeating body part.

Annelid worms are more complex than other worms. They have a closed circulatory system. They also have a complex nervous system with a brain. A nerve cord connects the brain to a ganglion in each segment.

Annelid worms live in salt water, fresh water, or on land. There are three kinds of annelid worms: earthworms, marine worms, and leeches. ☑

EARTHWORMS

Earthworms are the most familiar annelid worms. An earthworm has between 100 and 175 segments. Most segments look the same. However, some segments have special jobs, such as eating and reproduction.

As they feed, earthworms break down plant and animal matter in soil. They leave behind wastes called *castings*. Castings make soil richer by adding nutrients near the surface. Earthworms also improve soil by digging tunnels. These tunnels let air and water reach down into the soil. ☑

Except for the head, tail, and reproductive segments, all of the segments of an earthworm are the same.

Head

Reproductive segments

Tail

MARINE WORMS

Some worms live in the ocean. These marine worms are called *polychaetes*. They are covered with hairlike bristles and come in many bright colors. Marine worms eat small animals and mollusks. Some also filter food from the water.

LEECHES

Many people think of leeches as parasites that suck other animals' blood. This is true of some leeches. However, not all leeches are parasites. Some feed on dead animals. Others eat insects, slugs, and snails.

✔ **READING CHECK**

7. List What are the three kinds of annelid worms?

_____

_____

_____

✔ **READING CHECK**

8. Define What are castings?

_____

_____

_____

_____

Section 2 Review

NSES LS 1a, 1d, 3a, 5a

SECTION VOCABULARY

closed circulatory system a circulatory system in which the heart circulates blood through a network of blood vessels that form a closed loop	**segment** any part of a larger structure, such as the body of an organism, that is set off by natural or arbitrary boundaries
open circulatory system a circulatory system in which the circulatory fluid is not contained entirely within vessels	

1. Compare What is the difference between on open circulatory system and a closed circulatory system?

_____

_____

_____

2. List What are the four body parts that all mollusks have?

_____

3. Summarize Complete the organizer below to show the classes of mollusks.

4. Describe Describe two ways earthworms improve soil.

_____

_____

7. Explain Are all leeches parasites? Explain your answer.

_____

_____

CHAPTER 15 Invertebrates
SECTION
3 Arthropods

BEFORE YOU READ

After you read this section, you should be able to answer these questions:

• What are the four main characteristics of arthropods?

• What are two types of metamorphosis in insects?

National Science Education Standards
LS 1a, 1d, 1f, 5a

What Are the Characteristics of Arthropods?

How many animals do you think can live in one acre of land? If you could find all the arthropods in that acre, you would count more than a million animals!

Arthropods are the largest group of animals on Earth. Around 75% of all animal species are arthropods. Insects, spiders, crabs, and centipedes are all arthropods. ☑

Arthropods share four characteristics:

1. a segmented body with specialized parts
2. jointed limbs
3. an exoskeleton
4. a well-developed nervous system.

STUDY TIP

Organize As you read, make a chart listing the different kinds of arthropods, their characteristics, and examples of each.

✓ READING CHECK

1. Identify What percentage of all animals are arthropods?

_____
_____

SEGMENTED AND SPECIALIZED PARTS

Like annelid worms, arthropods are segmented. Some arthropods, such as centipedes, have segments that are mostly the same. Only the head and tail segments are different. However, most arthropods have segments with specialized structures. These specialized structures can be wings, antennae, gills, pinchers, and claws. As an arthropod develops, some of its segments grow together. This forms three main body parts: head, thorax, and abdomen.

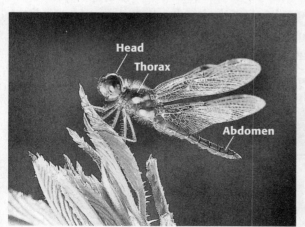
Head
Thorax
Abdomen

Like most arthropods, this dragonfly has a head, a thorax, and an abdomen.

TAKE A LOOK
2. Identify What are the three main body parts of an arthropod?

_____
_____

JOINTED LIMBS

Jointed limbs give arthropods their name. In Greek, *arthro* means "joint" and *pod* means "foot." Jointed limbs are legs or other body parts that bend at the joints. Having jointed limbs makes it easier for arthropods to move.

AN EXTERNAL SKELETON

Arthropods have an exoskeleton. An **exoskeleton** is a hard outer layer that covers the body. It is made of protein and a substance called *chitin*. An exoskeleton does some of the same things that an internal skeleton does. It supports the body and allows the animal to move. ☑

An exoskeleton also does things that an internal skeleton cannot do. It can protect the animal's body like a suit of armor. By keeping water inside the body, the exoskeleton helps keep the animal from drying out.

READING CHECK
3. Identify What is an exoskeleton made of?

_____

_____

The jointed limbs of a ghost crab let it move quickly across the sand. The exoskeleton protects the crab's body from drying out on land.

SENSING SURROUNDINGS

All arthropods have a head and a well-developed brain and nerve cord. The nervous system receives information from sense organs such as eyes and bristles. For example, tarantulas use bristles to detect movement and vibration. Some arthropods have simple eyes that only allow them to see light. Most arthropods have compound eyes. A **compound eye** is an eye made of many identical light sensors. ☑

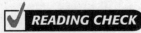
READING CHECK
4. Identify What kind of eyes do most arthropods have?

_____

_____

Compound eyes are made of many light-sensitive units that work together.

SECTION 3 Arthropods *continued*

What Are the Different Kinds of Arthropods?

Arthropods are grouped by the kinds of body parts they have. You can tell the difference between kinds of arthropods by looking at how many legs, eyes, and antennae they have. Arthropods include centipedes and millipedes, crustaceans, arachnids, and insects.

CENTIPEDES AND MILLIPEDES

Centipedes and millipedes have many segments. Centipedes have two legs on each segment and millipedes have four.

Centipedes and millipedes also have hard heads with one pair of antennae. An **antenna** is a feeler that senses touch, taste, or smell. Centipedes and millipedes also have one pair of mandibles. *Mandibles* are mouthparts that can stab and chew food.

Centipede

Millipede

Centipedes eat other animals.
Millipedes eat plants.

CRUSTACEANS

Shrimp, barnacles, crabs, and lobsters are *crustaceans*. Most crustaceans live in water. They have gills for breathing, mandibles for eating, and two compound eyes. Each eye is at the end of an eyestalk. Unlike other arthropods, crustaceans have two pairs of antennae. ☑

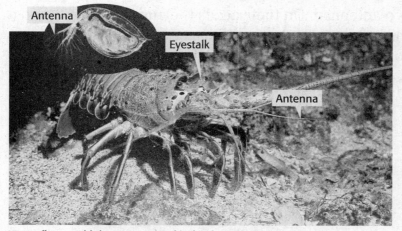
Antenna
Eyestalk
Antenna

Water fleas and lobsters are two kinds of crustaceans.

Math Focus

5. Calculate If a millipede has 752 legs, how many segments does it have? If a centipede has 354 legs, how many segments does it have?

_____

_____

✓ READING CHECK

6. Identify What is one difference between crustaceans and other arthropods?

_____

_____

ARACHNIDS

Spiders, scorpions, mites, and ticks are arachnids. *Arachnids* have two main body parts: the cephalothorax and the abdomen. The *cephalothorax* is made of a head and thorax. Most arachnids have eight legs and two simple eyes. They also have claw-like mouthparts called *chelicerae*. Spiders use their chelicerae to catch insects. ☑

Spiders can be helpful to humans becasue they kill many insect pests. Though some people are afraid of spiders, most spiders are not harmful. The mouthparts of most spiders are too small to bite humans. However, some spider bites do need medical treatment.

Ticks are parasites that feed on a host's blood. These animals are just a few millimeters long. They live in forests, brushy areas, and even lawns. Some ticks carry diseases, such as Lyme disease.

Arachnids have two main body parts. They have special mouthparts called chelicerae.

INSECTS

Insects make up the largest group of arthropods. The only place on Earth where insects do not live is in the oceans. Although some insects are pests, many insects are helpful. Many flowering plants need insects to carry pollen. Farmers depend on insects to pollinate fruit crops.

All insects have three main body parts, six legs, and two antennae. On their heads they have antennae and a pair of compound eyes. They use mandibles for eating. Some insects have wings on their thorax.

READING CHECK

7. Identify What are the two main body parts of an arachnid?

_____

_____

TAKE A LOOK

8. Identify What are the mouthparts of an archnid called?

_____

Say It

Investigate Choose an insect to research. Find out where it lives, what it eats, and whether it is considered helpful or harmful to humans. Present your findings to the class.

SECTION 3 Arthropods *continued*

METAMORPHOSIS

As an insect develops, it changes form. This process is called **metamorphosis**. Most insects, including butterflies, beetles, flies, wasps, and ants, go through complete metamorphosis. Complete metamorphosis has four stages, as shown below.

Stages of Complete Metamorphosis

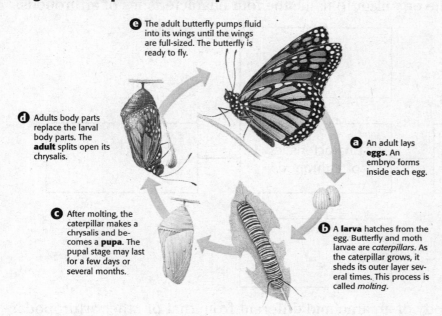

e The adult butterfly pumps fluid into its wings until the wings are full-sized. The butterfly is ready to fly.

d Adults body parts replace the larval body parts. The **adult** splits open its chrysalis.

c After molting, the caterpillar makes a chrysalis and becomes a **pupa**. The pupal stage may last for a few days or several months.

a An adult lays **eggs**. An embryo forms inside each egg.

b A **larva** hatches from the egg. Butterfly and moth larvae are *caterpillars*. As the caterpillar grows, it sheds its outer layer several times. This process is called *molting*.

TAKE A LOOK
9. List What are the four stages of complete metamorphosis?

_____

_____

Some insects, such as grasshoppers and cockroaches, go through incomplete metamorphosis. *Incomplete metamorphosis* has three stages: egg, nymph, and adult. Nymphs look like small adults. However, nymphs do not have wings.

Stages of Incomplete Metamorphosis

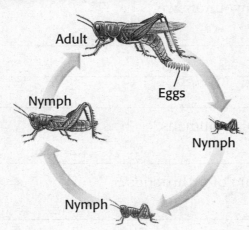

Adult

Eggs

Nymph

Nymph

Nymph

Critical Thinking

10. Compare How is incomplete metamorphosis different from complete metamorphosis?

_____

_____

_____

_____

_____

_____

_____

_____

Section 3 Review

NSES LS 1a, 1d, 1f, 5a

SECTION VOCABULARY

antenna a feeler that is on the head of an invertebrate, such as a crustacean or an insect, that senses touch, taste, or smell **compound eye** an eye composed of many light detectors	**exoskeleton** a hard, external, supporting structure **metamorphosis** a phase in the life cycle of many animals during which a rapid change from the immature form of an organism to the adult form takes place

1. Summarize Complete the organizer to name the four characteristics of arthropods.

2. Compare How is the body of an arachnid different from that of other arthropods?

_____

_____

_____

3. Apply Concepts Scientists have discovered a new organism. They know it is an arthropod because it has jointed legs and an exoskeleton. The organism also has mandibles and two pairs of antennae. Should they classify this organism as an insect or a crustacean? Explain your answer.

_____

_____

_____

_____

4. Explain How are spiders helpful to humans?

_____

5. Identify What is the largest group of arthropods?

_____

CHAPTER 15 Invertebrates

SECTION 4 Echinoderms

BEFORE YOU READ

After you read this section, you should be able to answer these questions:

• What are the characteristics of echinoderms?

• What are the five classes of echinoderms?

What Are Echinoderms?

Sea stars, sea urchins, and sand dollars are all echinoderms. Echinoderms are marine animals. They live on the sea floor in all parts of the world's oceans. Some echinoderms eat shellfish, some eat dead plants and animals, and others eat algae.

STUDY TIP

Organize As you read this section, make a Spider Map that shows the different kinds of echinoderms.

SPINY SKINNED

Echinoderms have spines. In Greek, the name echinoderm means "spiny skinned." The spines of an echinoderm are found on its skeleton. Echinoderms have an **endoskeleton**, which is found inside their bodies. The spines grow from the endoskeleton. The animal's skin then covers the spines.

SYMMETRY

As echinoderms grow, their body symmetry changes. When they are larvae, they have bilateral symmetry. However, as adults, they have radial symmetry.

Larva   Adult

The sea urchin larva has bilateral symmetry. The adult sea urchin has radial symmetry.

READING CHECK

1. Identify What kind of body symmetry does an adult echinoderm have?

_____

_____

NERVOUS SYSTEM

Echinoderms have a simple nervous system. Around the mouth is a circle of nerve fibers called the *nerve ring*. In sea stars, a *radial nerve* runs along each arm to the nerve ring. The radial nerves let a sea star move its arms. Sea stars have a simple eye at the tip of each arm. These eyes sense light. Other cells that cover the sea star's body sense touch and chemical signals in the water.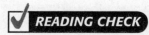

READING CHECK

2. Explain What do the radial nerves allow a sea star to do?

_____

_____

SECTION 4 Echinoderms *continued*

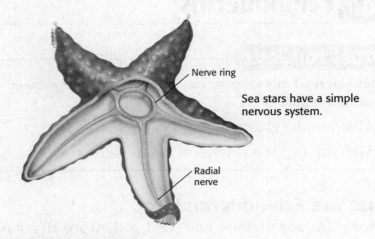

Nerve ring

Sea stars have a simple nervous system.

Radial nerve

TAKE A LOOK
3. Circle On the diagram, circle the areas where the eyespots of a sea star are found.

WATER VASCULAR SYSTEM

Only echinoderms have a water vascular system. A **water vascular system** is a system of tubes filled with fluid. Echinoderms use the water pressure in these tubes to move, eat, breathe, and sense their environment.

Water Vascular System

a Water enters through holes in a flat plate on top of the sea star. This plate is called the **sieve plate**.

b The water flows through a tube to the **ring canal** around the mouth.

e Each tube foot connects to an **ampulla**. The ampulla controls the water pressure in the tube foot. Changing pressure makes a tube foot extend and retract.

c From the ring canal, the water flows into radial canals in the arms.

d The radial canals connect to many suckers called **tube feet**. Sea stars use tube feet to move and to grip food. Oxygen enters and wastes leave through the thin walls of the tube feet.

TAKE A LOOK
4. Identify Through what structure does water enter the water vascular system?

_____

5. Explain What does a sea star use its tube feet for?

_____

_____

What Are the Different Kinds of Echinoderms?

There are five main classes of echinoderms. Sea stars are probably the most familiar class. The other classes are brittle stars and basket stars, sea urchins and sand dollars, sea lilies and feather stars, and sea cucumbers. Sea stars, brittle stars, basket stars, and feather stars can all grow back lost arms.

BRITTLE STARS AND BASKET STARS

Brittle stars and basket stars look like their close relatives, sea stars. However, their arms are longer, thinner, and smaller than those of sea stars.

◄ Basket star

▲ Brittle star

Basket stars and brittle stars move around more than other echinoderms do.

SEA URCHINS AND SAND DOLLARS

Sea urchins and sand dollars are round animals and have no arms. Like sea stars, they use tube feet to move. Sea urchins and sand dollars have shell-like endoskeletons. Sea urchins feed on algae they scrape from rocks. Sand dollars eat tiny particles they find in sand.

Sea urchin

Sand dollars

Sea urchins and sand dollars use their spines to protect themselves and to move.

SEA LILIES AND FEATHER STARS

Sea lilies and feather stars have 5 to 200 feathery arms. They use these arms to catch pieces of food in the water. A sea lily's arms sit on top of a stalk, making the animal look like a flower.

SEA CUCUMBERS

Unlike other echinoderms, sea cucumbers are long and shaped like fat worms. They have soft, leathery bodies and no arms. Like other echinoderms, sea cucumbers move with tube feet.

feather star

Sea Cucumber

Critical Thinking

6. Infer Suppose you found a brittle star that had four long arms and one short one. How could you explain this?

_____

_____

_____

_____

_____

_____

TAKE A LOOK
7. Identify What are the functions of spines on sea urchins and sand dollars?

_____

_____

TAKE A LOOK
8. Compare How are sea cucumbers, sand dollars, and sea urchins similar?

_____

_____

Section 4 Review

SECTION VOCABULARY

endoskeleton an internal skeleton made of bone or cartilage	**water vascular system** a system of canals filled with a watery fluid that circulates throughout the body of an echinoderm

1. Describe How does the body symmetry of an echinoderm change as the larva develops into an adult?

_____

_____

2. List What are the four main features of a sea star's nervous system?

_____

_____

3. List What are the five classes of echinoderms?

_____

_____

4. Compare How are sea cucumbers different from other echinoderms?

_____

5. Explain How does a sea star get oxygen from the water?

_____

6. Summarize Complete the Process Chart below to show how water moves through the water vascular system.

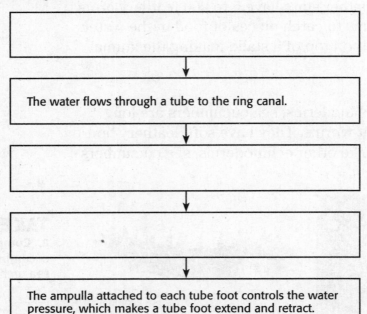

The water flows through a tube to the ring canal.

The ampulla attached to each tube foot controls the water pressure, which makes a tube foot extend and retract.

CHAPTER 16 Fishes, Amphibians, and Reptiles
SECTION 1
Fishes: The First Vertebrates

BEFORE YOU READ

After you read this section, you should be able to answer these questions:

• What are the two main characteristics of vertebrates?

• What is the difference between an ectotherm and an endotherm?

• What are the three classes of living fishes?

National Science Education Standards
LS 1a, 1d, 2a, 3a, 3b, 3c, 5a, 5c

What Are Chordates?

Many of the animals you are most familiar with, including fishes, reptiles, and mammals, belong to phylum Chordata. Members of this phylum are called *chordates*. Some chordates may be less familiar to you. Lancelets and tunicates are simple chordates.

STUDY TIP
Compare After you read this section, make a Concept Map using the vocabulary words from this section.

Tunicates

Lancelet

All chordates show four characteristics at some time in their lives. Sometimes the characteristic is found only in embryos.

• a tail
• a stiff flexible rod called the *notocord* that supports the body
• a hollow nerve cord, called a *spinal cord* in vertebrates
• structures called *pharyngeal pouches*, found in embryos that later become gills or other body parts ☑

Chordate Body Parts

Tail
Notochord
Hollow nerve cord
Pharyngeal pouches

✓ READING CHECK

1. List What are the four characteristics shared by chordates?

_____

_____

_____

_____

What Are Vertebrates?

The largest group of chordates is the vertebrates. **Vertebrates** are animals that have backbones. Fishes, amphibians, reptiles, birds, and mammals are vertebrates.

Vertebrates have two characteristics that lancelets and tunicates do not have—backbones and heads protected by skulls. A backbone is a strong, flexible column of bones called *vertebrae* (singular *vertebra*). It protects the spinal cord and helps support the rest of the body. The backbone replaces the notocord in most vertebrates.

In vertebrate embryos, the backbone, the skull, and the rest of the skeleton are made of cartilage. *Cartilage* is the tough material that makes up the flexible parts of our ears and nose. As most vertebrates grow, the cartilage is replaced by bone. Bone is much harder than cartilage. ☑

Because bone is so hard, it can be fossilized easily. Scientists have discovered many fossils of vertebrates. The fossils give scientists clues about how organisms are related to one another and when some organisms evolved.

The skull protects the head.

Vertebrae of the backbone protect the spinal cord.

☑ **READING CHECK**

2. Identify What material makes up the skeleton of vertebrate embryos?

_____

STANDARDS CHECK

LS 3b Regulation of an organism's internal environment involves sensing the internal environment and changing physiological activities to keep conditions within the range required to survive.

Word Help: environment the surrounding natural conditions that affect an organism

3. Infer If an ectotherm's body temperature became too high, what would it need to do? Explain your answer.

_____
_____
_____
_____
_____
_____

How Do Vertebrates Keep Their Bodies at the Right Temperature?

If an animal's body is too hot or too cold, its cells cannot work properly. Vertebrates control their body temperatures in two ways.

Ectotherms depend on their surroundings to stay warm. Their body temperatures change as the temperature of the environment changes. Most fish, and almost all amphibians and reptiles, are ectotherms. They are sometimes called *cold-blooded animals*.

Most fishes, including this leafy sea dragon, are ectotherms.

Endotherms generally have stable body temperatures, even when the temperature of the environment changes. They heat their bodies with energy from the chemical reactions in their cells. Birds and mammals are endotherms. They are sometimes called *warm-blooded animals.* ☑

What Are the Characteristics of Fishes?

Fossil evidence shows that fish evolved about 500 million years ago. They were the first vertebrates on Earth.

There are more than 25,000 species of fishes, and they come in many shapes, sizes, and colors. All fishes share several characteristics.

- a strong body for swimming, with muscles attached to the backbone
- fan-shaped structures called *fins* that help fishes swim, steer, stop, and balance
- scales to cover and protect the body
- gills
- senses of vision, hearing, and smell, including a lateral line system

The **lateral line** is a row of tiny sense organs along each side of the body. It detects water vibrations, such as those caused by other fish swimming by. ☑

Fish use **gills** to breathe. Water passes over the thin gill membranes. Oxygen moves from the water to the blood. Carbon dioxide moves from the blood to the water.

☑ **READING CHECK**

4. Explain How do endotherms heat their bodies?

_____

_____

_____

☑ **READING CHECK**

5. Identify What is the function of the lateral line system?

_____

_____

Fishes are many shapes and sizes, but all fish have gills, fins, and a tail.

TAKE A LOOK
6. Complete Fill in the missing labels on the diagram.

How Do Fishes Reproduce?

Most fishes reproduce by *external fertilization*. The female lays unfertilized eggs in the water, and the male drops sperm on them.

Some fishes use *internal fertilization*. The male deposits sperm inside the female. Usually, the female lays fertilized eggs that have embryos inside. In some species, the embryos develop inside the female.

What Are the Three Classes of Living Fishes?

There were once five classes of fishes, but two of them are now extinct. The three classes of fishes living today are *jawless fishes*, *cartilaginous fishes*, and *bony fishes*.

JAWLESS FISHES

The first fishes were probably jawless fishes. Today, the two kinds of jawless fishes are hagfish and lampreys. Hagfish and lampreys look like eels and have round mouths without jaws. They do not need jaws because they do not bite or chew. Instead, they attach to other animals and suck their blood and flesh. ☑

Jawless fishes share the following characteristics:

READING CHECK
7. Explain How do jawless fishes eat?

_____

_____

_____

• no jaws
• a notocord
• a skeleton made of cartilage

SECTION 1 Fishes: The First Vertebrates *continued*

Jawless Fishes

Hagfish can tie their flexible bodies into knots. They slide the knot from their tails to their heads to remove slime from their skin or to escape predators.

Lampreys can live in salt water or fresh water, but they must reproduce in fresh water.

CARTILAGINOUS FISHES

In most vertebrates, soft cartilage in the embryo is slowly replaced by bone. The skeletons of sharks, skates, and rays, however, are cartilage, and never change to bone. They are called *cartilaginous fishes*.

Cartilaginous fishes share the following characteristics:
- jaws
- a backbone
- a skeleton made of cartilage

Cartilaginous fishes store a lot of oil in their livers. Oil is less dense than water and this helps cartilaginous fishes float. However, they will sink if they stop swimming. Some cartilaginous fishes must also keep swimming to move water over their gills. Others can lie on the ocean floor and pump water across their gills. ☑

Cartilaginous Fish

Skates lay eggs. They move their fins up and down to swim.

Rays give birth to live young. Rays also use their fins to swim They feed on organisms from the sea floor, such as crabs and worms.

Sharks, such as this hammerhead shark, rarely prey on humans. They usually eat other fish.

TAKE A LOOK
8. Identify Give two reasons hagfish tie themselves in knots.

_____
_____
_____

☑ **READING CHECK**
9. Explain Do all cartilaginous fishes need to keep swimming in order to breathe? Explain your answer.

_____
_____
_____
_____

SECTION 1 Fishes: The First Vertebrates *continued*

Critical Thinking

10. Compare Give two differences between cartilaginous fishes and bony fishes.

_____
_____
_____
_____
_____
_____
_____

BONY FISHES

Ninety-five percent of all fishes are bony fishes. This group includes goldfish, tuna, trout, and catfish. Bony fishes have the following characteristics:

- jaws
- a backbone
- a skeleton made of bone
- a swim bladder

A **swim bladder** is a balloon-like organ filled with gases. It is also called a *gas bladder*. The swim bladder keeps bony fish from sinking. This lets them rest in one place without swimming.

What Are the Two Main Groups of Bony Fishes?

There are two main groups of bony fishes: *ray-finned fishes* and *lobe-finned fishes*.

Almost all bony fishes are ray-finned fishes. Their fins are supported by thin rays of bone. Eels, herrings, trout, minnows, and perch are all ray-finned fishes.

Lobe-finned fishes have thick, muscular fins. There are only seven species of lobe-finned fishes. Six of these species are lungfishes. Lungfishes are lobe-finned fishes with air sacs that can fill with air, like lungs. Scientists think that one group of lobe-finned fishes were the ancestors of amphibians. ☑

Bony Fishes

Lungfishes live in shallow waters that often dry up in the summer.

Pikes are fast predators. They move in quick bursts of speed to catch fish and invertebrates.

Masked butterfly fish live in warm waters around coral reefs.

✔ **READING CHECK**

11. Identify What group of fishes do scientists think were the ancestors of amphibians?

_____
_____

SECTION 1 Fishes: The First Vertebrates *continued*

How Are Fishes Related to Other Vertebrates?

The Concept Map below shows how fishes are related to each other and to other vertebrates and chordates. Vertebrates are the largest group of chordates. Bony fishes are the largest group of fishes. Ray-finned fishes are the largest group of bony fishes. ☑

 READING CHECK

12. Identify What is the largest group of fishes?

_____

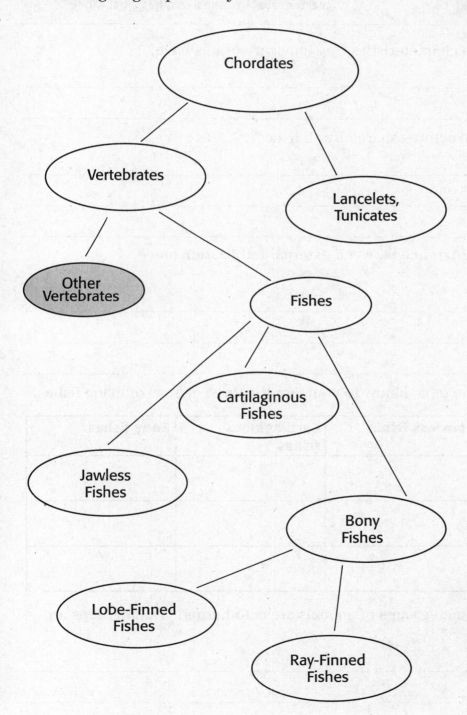

TAKE A LOOK
13. Identify Relationships Are lobe-finned fishes more closely related to jawless fishes or lancelets?

_____

_____

Section 1 Review

NSES   LS 1a, 1d, 2a, 3a, 3b, 3c, 5a, 5c

SECTION VOCABULARY

ectotherm an organism that needs sources of heat outside of itself

endotherm an animal that can use body heat from chemical reactions in the body's cells to maintain a constant body temperature

gill a respiratory organ in which oxygen from the water is exchanged with carbon dioxide from the blood

lateral line a faint line visible on both sides of a fish's body that runs the length of the body and marks the location of sense organs that detect vibrations in water

swim bladder in bony fishes, a gas-filled sac that is used to control buoyancy; also known as a gas bladder

vertebrate an animal that has a backbone

1. Identify What are two characteristics that only vertebrates have?

_____

_____

2. List What are three structures shared by all fishes?

_____

_____

_____

3. Explain What is the difference between external fertilization and internal fertilization?

_____

_____

_____

4. Compare Complete the table below to compare the three classes of living fishes.

Characteristic	Jawless fishes	Cartilaginous fishes	Bony fishes
Jaws (yes or no?)			
Structure for support (notocord or backbone?)			
Skeleton (cartilage or bone?)			

5. Identify In general, which groups of animals are ectotherms? Which groups are endotherms?

_____

_____

CHAPTER 16 | Fishes, Amphibians, and Reptiles

SECTION 2 Amphibians

National Science
Education Standards
LS 1a, 2a, 3a, 3c, 3d, 5a, 5b

BEFORE YOU READ

After you read this section, you should be able to answer these questions:

- How do amphibians breathe?
- What are the three groups of amphibians?
- What is metamorphosis ?

What Are Amphibians?

Amphibians are animals that have lungs and legs and can live in water. A **lung** is a saclike organ that delivers oxygen from the air to the blood.

Scientists think amphibians evolved from ancient lobe-finned fishes. These fishes developed lungs that could take oxygen from the air. They also had strong fins that could have evolved into legs. Fossils show that the first amphibians looked like a cross between a fish and a salamander. ☑

What Are the Characteristics of Amphibians?

Most amphibians must spend part of their lives in or near water. Most amphibians live in the water after hatching and later develop into adults that can live on land.

THIN SKIN

Amphibians have thin, smooth, moist skin. They can absorb water through their skin instead of drinking. However, they can also lose water through their skin. Because of this, they must live in water or in wet habitats. Some amphibians can breathe through their skin. The skin of some amphibians contains poison glands to protect the animals from predators.

STUDY TIP
Organize As you read this section, make combination notes to describe the different groups of amphibians.

✓ READING CHECK
1. Describe What type of animals do scientists think amphibians evolved from?

_____

_____

Critical Thinking
2. Analyze Ideas The word *amphibian* means "double life." Explain why this is a good description for amphibians.

_____

_____

_____

_____

METAMORPHOSIS

Most amphibians don't just get bigger as they grow into adults. They change form, or shape, as they grow. **Metamorphosis** is the change from an immature form to a different adult form. For example, a **tadpole** is an immature frog or toad. As it grows, it changes form. It loses its gills and develops structures such as lungs and legs that the adult will need to live on land.

Amphibian Metamorphosis

Adult frog

Fertilized eggs

1. The newly hatched tadpole has gills and a tail.

2. The tadpole begins to grow legs.

3. The tail and gills disappear and the the lungs begin to work.

A few types of amphibians do not go through full metamorphosis. Their young look like tiny adults when they hatch, but they have gills.

EGGS WITHOUT SHELLS

Most of the eggs you are probably familiar with are bird eggs, such as chicken, or duck. Unlike bird eggs, however, amphibian eggs do not have shells or membranes. Without shells, amphibian eggs dry out very easily. Because of this, amphibian embryos must develop in wet environments. ☑

BODY TEMPERATURE

Amphibians are ectotherms. Their body temperature depends on the temperature of the environment.

TAKE A LOOK
3. Compare How does breathing differ in tadpoles and adult frogs?

_____

_____

_____

✓ **READING CHECK**

4. Explain Why do amphibian embryos need to develop in wet environments?

_____

_____

_____

SECTION 2 Amphibians *continued*

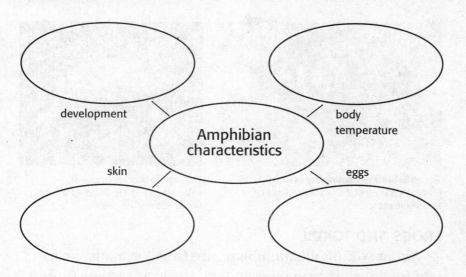

- development
- Amphibian characteristics
- body temperature
- skin
- eggs

TAKE A LOOK
5. Describe Complete the Spider Map to describe the characteristics of amphibians.

What Are the Three Groups of Amphibians?

More than 5,400 species of amphibians are alive today. They belong to three groups: caecilians, salamanders, and frogs and toads.

CAECILIANS

Most people are not familiar with caecilians. However, scientists have discovered more than 160 species. Caecilians live in warm climates in Asia, Africa, and South America. They have thin, moist skin like other amphibians. However, unlike other amphibians, some have bony scales in their skin. Caecilians also have no legs. They look like earthworms or snakes. ☑

✓ READING CHECK

6. Identify Name two ways caecilians are different from most amphibians.

_____

_____

_____

Caecilian

SALAMANDERS

There are about 500 known species of salamanders. Most adult salamanders live under stones and logs in the woods of North America. Salamanders have long tails and four strong legs. Some look like tadpoles when they hatch, others look like small adults. Most salamanders lose their gills and grow lungs as they develop. Some never lose their gills.

TAKE A LOOK

7. Compare What is one major difference between these two salamander species?

_____

_____

_____

The **marbled salamander** lives in damp places, such as under rocks or logs or among leaves.

This **axolotl** is an unusual salamander. It keeps its gills and never leaves the water.

Math Focus

8. Calculate Percentages A certain toad species spends two months of its life as a tadpole and three years as an adult. What percentage of its life is spent in the water?

_____

FROGS AND TOADS

About 90% of all amphibians are frogs or toads. Frogs and toads are very similar. In fact, toads are a type of frog. Frogs tend to have smooth, moist skin. Toads spend less time in the water and have drier, bumpier skin. Frogs and toads share the following characteristics:

- strong leg muscles for jumping
- well-developed ears for hearing
- a long sticky tongue for catching insects
- vocal cords

Frogs, such as this **bullfrog**, have smooth, moist skin.

Toads, such as this **Fowler's toad**, spend less time in water than frogs do. Their skin is drier and bumpier.

Critical Thinking

9. Infer Why do you think a frog needs a vocal sac to make its song louder?

_____

_____

_____

How Do Frogs Sing?

Frogs are well known for singing, or croaking, at night, However, many frogs sing during the daytime, too. Like we do, frogs make sounds by forcing air across their vocal cords. They have a sac of skin, called the vocal sac around their vocal cords. When a frog sings, its *vocal sac*, fills with air. The sac makes the song louder. Frogs sing to attract mates and to mark territory.

SECTION 2 Amphibians *continued*

Most frogs that sing are males.

What Can Amphibians Tell Us About the Environment?

Unhealthy amphibians can be an early sign of changes in an ecosystem. Because of this, they are called *ecological indicators*. Amphibians are very sensitive to changes in the environment, such as chemicals in the air or water. Climate change may also affect amphibians. When large numbers of amphibians grow abnormally or die, there may be a problem with the environment. ☑

How Are Amphibians Related to Other Vertebrates?

The Concept Map below shows how amphibians are related to each other and to other vertebrates and chordates. Vertebrates are the largest group of chordates. Frogs and toads are the largest group of amphibians.

☑ **READING CHECK**

10. Define What is an ecological indicator?

_____

_____

_____

_____

```
                    Chordates
                   /         \
         Vertebrates          Other
         /    |    \          chordates
   Other      |     \
   Vertebrates Amphibians    Fishes
              /    |    \
      Caecilians   |     Frogs and
              Salamanders   Toads
```

Section 2 Review

NSES LS 1a, 2a, 3a, 3c, 3d, 5a, 5b

SECTION VOCABULARY

lung a respiratory organ in which oxygen from the air is exchanged with carbon dioxide from the blood	**metamorphosis** a phase in the life cycle of many animals during which a rapid change from the immature form of an organism to the adult form takes place
	tadpole the aquatic, fish-shaped larva of a frog or toad

1. Explain Why do amphibians need to live in moist environments?

_____

_____

_____

2. Explain Why do frogs sing?

_____

_____

_____

3. Identify What body parts do tadpoles lose when they go through metamorphosis? What body parts do they gain?

_____

_____

4. List What are three organs amphibians can use to breathe?

_____

5. Compare Fill in the Venn Diagram to compare salamanders and frogs.

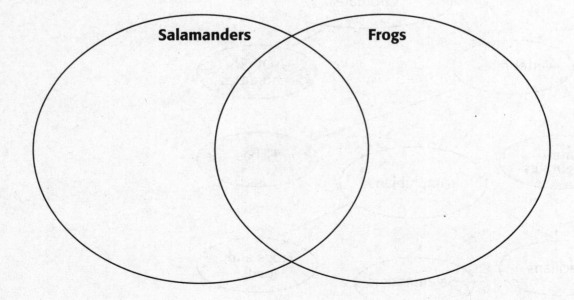

Salamanders   Frogs

SECTION 3 Reptiles

BEFORE YOU READ

After you read this section, you should be able to answer these questions:

- What characteristics of reptiles allow them to live on land?
- What is an amniotic egg?
- What are the four groups of living reptiles?

How Did Reptiles Evolve?

After amphibians moved onto land, some of them began to change. They grew thick, dry skin. Their legs changed and grew stronger. They also laid eggs that did not dry out. They had become reptiles, the first animals to live out of the water their whole lives.

Many reptiles are now extinct. Dinosaurs that lived on land are the most well-known prehistoric reptiles. However, there were many other ancient reptiles. Some could swim, some could fly, and many were similar to reptiles alive today.

What Are the Characteristics of Reptiles?

Reptiles are well-adapted for life on land. Unlike amphibians, most reptiles can spend their whole lives on land.

LUNGS

All reptiles—even reptiles that live in water—have lungs to breathe air. Most reptiles cannot breathe through their skin and get oxygen only from their lungs.

THICK SKIN

Thick, dry skin is a very important adaptation for life on land. This skin forms a watertight layer that keeps cells from losing too much water by evaporation. ☑

Reptiles, such as this crocodile, have thick skin.

STUDY TIP

Organize As you read, make a chart comparing the four different groups of reptiles.

Say It

Investigate Use your school's media center to learn about a prehistoric reptile that was not a dinosaur. Describe this reptile to the class.

✓ READING CHECK

1. Explain How is thick skin important for reptiles?

_____

_____

_____

SECTION 3 Reptiles *continued*

2. Infer How did the amniotic egg allow reptiles to live on land?

_____

_____

_____

_____

_____

BODY TEMPERATURE

Nearly all reptiles are ectotherms. They cannot keep their bodies at a stable temperature. They must use their surroundings to control their temperature. They are active when it is warm outside, and they slow down when it is cool. A few reptiles can get some heat from their own body cells.

AMNIOTIC EGG

The most important adaptation to life on land is the amniotic egg. An **amniotic egg** has membranes and a shell that protect the embryo. A reptile's amniotic egg can be laid under rocks, in the ground, or even in the desert.

What Are the Parts of the Amniotic Egg?

The parts of the amniotic egg protect the embryo from predators, infections, and water loss.

The **shell** protects the egg from damage and keeps it from drying out. It has small pores to let oxygen into the egg and to let carbon dioxide out.

The **albumen** provides water and protein to the embryo.

The **amniotic sac** is filled with fluid. It surrounds and protects the embryo.

The **yolk** supplies food to the embryo.

The **allantois** stores the embryo's wastes.

TAKE A LOOK

3. Compare Name one thing you can see in this picture that reptile eggs have but the amphibian eggs do not.

_____

_____

Amphibian eggs

Reptile eggs

The reptile eggs are amniotic but the amphibian eggs are not.

How Do Reptiles Reproduce?

Reptiles usually reproduce by internal fertilization. The egg is fertilized inside the female. Then a shell forms, and the female lays the egg. A few reptiles do not lay eggs. In this case, the embryos develop inside the mother and the young are born live. ☑

Unlike amphibians, reptiles do not go through metamorphosis. The embryo develops into a young reptile that looks like a tiny adult. ⌐

READING CHECK

4. Identify Which type of fertilization do reptiles use?

_____

_____

What Are the Four Kinds of Living Reptiles?

Many reptiles, including dinosaurs, are now extinct. Today, about 8,000 species of reptiles are known to exist. These species make up four main groups of reptiles.

TURTLES AND TORTOISES

In general, tortoises live on land and turtles spend all or much of their lives in water. Even if they live in the sea, turtles leave the water to lay their eggs on land.

Turtles and tortoises are unique because of their shells. Shells make turtles and tortoises slow, so they cannot run away from predators. However, many of these reptiles can pull their heads and limbs into their shells. The shells protect them like suits of armor.

Green sea turtle

Texas tortoise

Math Focus

5. Calculate Suppose a sea turtle laid 104 eggs. After the young hatch, 50% reach the ocean alive. Of those survivors, 25% grow to be adults. How many adults resulted from the eggs?

_____

_____

CROCODILES AND ALLIGATORS

Crocodiles and alligators spend most of their time in the water. Their eyes and nostrils are on the top of their flat heads. This lets them hide under water and watch their surroundings. They eat invertebrates, fishes, turtles, birds, and mammals. The figure on the next page shows some differences between crocodiles and alligators.

TAKE A LOOK

6. Describe How can you tell the difference between an alligator and a crocodile?

_____

_____

_____

_____

_____

A crocodile, such as this **American crocodile**, has a narrow head and pointed snout.

An alligator, such as this **American alligator**, has a broad head and a rounded snout.

Critical Thinking

7. Analyze Ideas
Rattlesnakes do not see very well. However, they can sense changes in temperature as small as 3/1000 of a degree Celsius. How could this ability be useful to snakes?

_____

_____

_____

SNAKES AND LIZARDS

Snakes and lizards are the most common reptiles alive today. Snakes are *carnivores*, or meat-eaters. They use a special organ in their mouths to smell prey. When a snake flicks out its tongue, molecules in the air stick to it and are brought back to the organ in the mouth. Snakes can open their mouths very wide. This lets them swallow animals and eggs whole. Some snakes squeeze prey to suffocate it. Others use fangs to inject venom into prey to kill it.

Cape Cobra

Frilled lizard

Most lizards eat insects and worms, but some eat plants. One giant lizard—the komodo dragon—eats deer, pigs, and goats! Lizards have loosely connected lower jaws. This lets them open their jaws wide. However, lizards do not swallow large prey whole. Many lizards can escape predators by breaking off their tails. They can grow back new tails.

SECTION 3 Reptiles *continued*

TUATARAS

Tuataras live only on a few islands off the coast of New Zealand. Tuataras look like lizards but are different from lizards in the following ways. Tuataras do not have visible ear openings on the outside of their bodies. Tuataras are most active when the temperature is low. They rest during the day and search for food at night. ☑

✓ **READING CHECK**

8. Describe When are tuataras most active?

_____

_____

_____

Tuataras have survived without changing for about 150 million years.

How Are Reptiles Related to Other Vertebrates?

Vertebrates are the largest group of chordates. Snakes and lizards are the most common reptiles alive today.

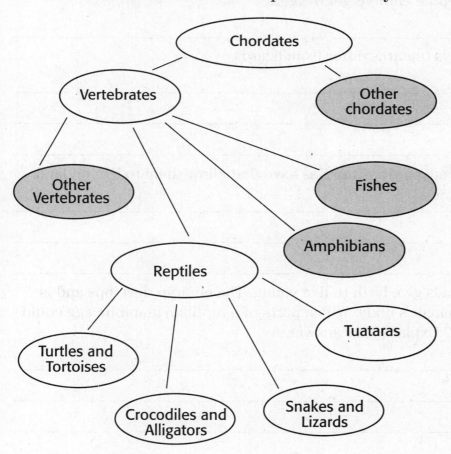

Section 3 Review

NSES   LS 1a, 1d, 2a, 2b, 3a, 3c, 3d, 5a, 5b, 5c

SECTION VOCABULARY

amniotic egg a type of egg that is surrounded by a membrane, the amnion, and that in reptiles, birds, and egg-laying mammals contains a large amount of yolk and is surrounded by a shell.

1. List What are the four main groups of reptiles alive today?

_____

_____

2. Explain What are the functions of the shell of an amniotic egg?

_____

_____

3. Explain How do reptiles reproduce?

_____

_____

4. Explain How does a reptile embryo get oxygen?

_____

5. Compare Give two ways tuataras differ from lizards.

_____

_____

_____

6. Describe Describe the adaptations reptiles have that allow them to live on land.

_____

_____

_____

7. Apply Concepts Mammals give birth to live young. The embryo develops and is nourished inside the female's body. Which parts of a reptilian amniotic egg could a mammal do without? Explain your answer.

_____

_____

_____

_____

CHAPTER 17 Birds and Mammals

SECTION 1 Characteristics of Birds

National Science
Education Standards
LS 1a, 1d, 2a, 3a, 3b, 3c, 5a, 5b

BEFORE YOU READ

After you read this section, you should be able to answer these questions:

• What are the characteristics of birds?

• How do birds fly?

What Are the Characteristics of Birds?

What do a powerful eagle, a fast-swimming penguin, and a tiny hummingbird have in common? They all have feathers, wings, and beaks. These features make them all birds.

HOW BIRDS AND REPTILES ARE ALIKE

Birds share many characteristics with reptiles. Both birds and reptiles are vertebrates. They both have feet and legs covered with scales. They also have eggs with shells and amniotic sacs.

HOW BIRDS AND REPTILES DIFFER

Birds also have some characteristics that reptiles do not have. Birds have feathers, wings, and beaks. Unlike reptiles, birds are endotherms. They keep their bodies warm from heat produced by chemical reactions in their body cells. Their body temperatures are generally stable. ☑

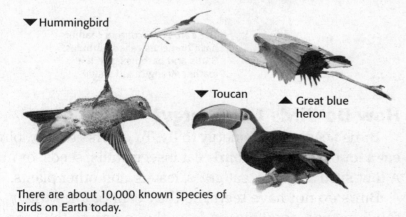

▼Hummingbird

▼ Toucan

▲ Great blue heron

There are about 10,000 known species of birds on Earth today.

STUDY TIP

Outline As you read this section, make an outline describing the characteristics of birds.

READING CHECK

1. Explain How do birds keep their body temperatures stable?

_____

_____

_____

TAKE A LOOK

2. List Name three things that all the animals in this picture have in common.

_____

_____

What Are the Functions of Feathers?

Feathers are one of the most familiar features of birds. They help birds stay dry and warm, attract mates, and fly. Therefore, birds take good care of their feathers.

PREENING AND MOLTING

A bird uses its beak to spread a special oil on its feathers. It gets the oil from a gland near it tail. This process is called **preening**. Preening oil helps waterproof the feathers and keeps them clean. ☑

When feathers wear out, birds shed them and grow new ones. This process is called **molting**. Most birds molt at least once a year.

KINDS OF FEATHERS

Birds have two main kinds of feathers—down feathers and contour feathers. **Down feathers** are fluffy and lie close to a bird's body. These feathers help birds stay warm. When a bird fluffs its down feathers, air gets trapped next to its body. The trapped air keeps heat in, keeping the bird warm.

Contour feathers are stiff and cover a bird's body and wings. These feathers have a stiff shaft with many side branches, called *barbs*. Barbs link together to form a smooth surface. This streamlined surface helps birds fly. Some birds use colorful contour feathers to attract mates.

Shaft
Barbs
Barbules

The barbs of a contour feather have branches called barbules. Barbs and barbules give the feather strength and shape.

How Do Birds Get Energy?

Birds need a lot of energy to fly. To get this energy, birds eat a lot of food. Most birds eat insects, nuts, seeds, or meat. A few, such as geese, eat grass, leaves, and other plants.

Birds do not have teeth, so they cannot chew their food. Instead, food moves from the mouth to the crop. The *crop* stores the food until it moves into the gizzard. The *gizzard* has small stones in it. These stones grind up the food. This grinding action is similar to what happens when we chew our food. The food then moves to the intestines where it is digested.

READING CHECK

3. Identify What are two functions of preening oil?

_____

_____

TAKE A LOOK

4. Complete Feather barbs have branches called

_____ .

Critical Thinking

5. Compare How is a bird's gizzard like our teeth?

_____

_____

_____

_____

_____

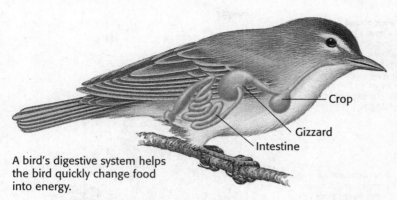

A bird's digestive system helps the bird quickly change food into energy.

A bird's body also needs to break down its food quickly to provide energy. This process creates a lot of heat. Birds cannot sweat to cool off as humans do. Instead, they lay their wings flat and pant like a dog.

How Do Birds Fly?

Most birds can fly. Even flightless birds, such as ostriches, had ancestors that could fly. Birds have many adaptations that make flight possible. They have wings, lightweight bodies, and strong flight muscles. Their hearts beat very fast to bring large amounts of oxygen to the flight muscles. The figure below describes how parts of a bird's body help it fly.

Flight Adaptations of Birds

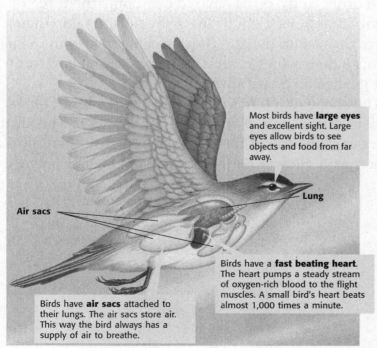

Most birds have **large eyes** and excellent sight. Large eyes allow birds to see objects and food from far away.

Air sacs

Lung

Birds have a **fast beating heart**. The heart pumps a steady stream of oxygen-rich blood to the flight muscles. A small bird's heart beats almost 1,000 times a minute.

Birds have **air sacs** attached to their lungs. The air sacs store air. This way the bird always has a supply of air to breathe.

TAKE A LOOK
6. Identify Circle the organ where food is stored.

Math Focus

7. Calculate When a bird flies long distances, such as during migration, it uses a lot of energy. This causes it to lose weight. If a bird that weighs 325 g loses 40% of its body weight during migration, how much does it weigh?

_____

TAKE A LOOK
8. Identify What is the function of air sacs?

_____

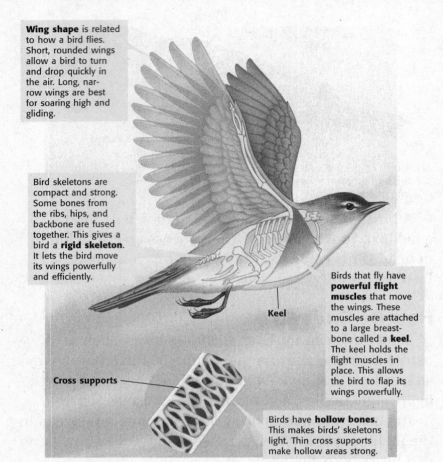

Wing shape is related to how a bird flies. Short, rounded wings allow a bird to turn and drop quickly in the air. Long, narrow wings are best for soaring high and gliding.

Bird skeletons are compact and strong. Some bones from the ribs, hips, and backbone are fused together. This gives a bird a **rigid skeleton**. It lets the bird move its wings powerfully and efficiently.

Birds that fly have **powerful flight muscles** that move the wings. These muscles are attached to a large breastbone called a **keel**. The keel holds the flight muscles in place. This allows the bird to flap its wings powerfully.

Keel

Cross supports

Birds have **hollow bones**. This makes birds' skeletons light. Thin cross supports make hollow areas strong.

Critical Thinking

9. Infer Some birds do not fly. These birds generally do not have large keels. Why are large keels not necessary for flightless birds?

_____

_____

_____

_____

_____

GETTING OFF THE GROUND

In order to fly, birds have to overcome the force of gravity that pulls them to the ground. Birds flap their wings to get into the air. They are able to stay in the air because their wings cause lift. **Lift** is an upward force that pushes on a bird's wings. ☑

The shape of a bird's wing helps create lift. A bird's wing is curved on top and flatter underneath. The air that flows over the top of the wing moves faster than the air underneath. Slower air under the wing pushes upward.

☑ **READING CHECK**

10. Identify What force must birds overcome in order to get off the ground?

_____

Air moving around a bird's wing changes in speed and direction as the bird flies. This creates an upward force that keeps the bird in the air.

Air flow

Lift

TAKE A LOOK

11. Identify What upward force helps a bird overcome the force of gravity?

_____

How Do Birds Reproduce?

Like reptiles, birds reproduce sexually by internal fertilization. They lay amniotic eggs in which embryos grow. However, unlike reptiles, birds must keep their eggs warm so that the embryos can survive. ☑

BROODING

Most birds lay their eggs in nests. They sit on their eggs and use their body heat to keep the eggs warm. This is called **brooding**. Birds sit on the eggs until they hatch. In most species, the female sits on the eggs. In a few species, the males brood the eggs.

This robin's nest is only one example of a bird's nest. Birds build nests of many different shapes and sizes.

PRECOCIAL AND ALTRICIAL

Some chicks, such as chickens and ducks, are active soon after they hatch. These active chicks are called *precocial*. Precocial chicks are covered with downy feathers. They only depend on their parents for warmth and protection. They can walk, swim, and feed themselves.

Other chicks, such as hawks and songbirds, are weak and helpless after hatching. These chicks are called *altricial*. Altricial chicks have no feathers, and their eyes are closed. They cannot walk or fly. Their parents must keep them warm and feed them for several weeks. ☑

Parents of altricial chicks bring food to the nest.

✓ **READING CHECK**

12. Explain What kind of reproduction do birds use?

_____

_____

✓ **READING CHECK**

13. Describe What are the characteristics of newly hatched altricial chicks?

_____

_____

_____

_____

_____

Section 1 Review

NSES   LS 1a, 1d, 2a, 3a, 3b, 3c, 5a, 5b

SECTION VOCABULARY

brooding to sit on and cover eggs to keep them warm until they hatch; to incubate

contour feather one of the most external feathers that cover a bird and that help determine its shape

down feather a soft feather that covers the body of young birds and provides insulation to adult birds

lift an upward force on an object that moves in a fluid

molting the shedding of an exoskeleton, skin, feathers, or hair to be replaced by new parts

preening in birds, the act of grooming and maintaining their feathers

1. Explain How do birds get the energy they need to fly?

_____

_____

2. Compare Complete the Venn Diagram to compare reptiles and birds.

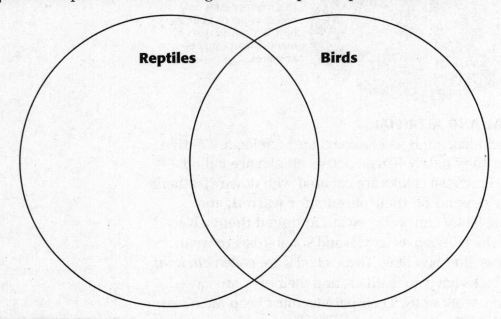

Reptiles   Birds

3. Explain How does a fast-beating heart help a bird fly?

_____

_____

4. Compare How do precocial chicks and altricial chicks differ?

_____

_____

_____

CHAPTER 17 Birds and Mammals

SECTION 2 | # Kinds of Birds

National Science Education Standards
LS 1a, 3a, 5a, 5b

BEFORE YOU READ

After you read this section, you should be able to answer these questions:

• What are the four main groups of birds?

• What adaptations do birds in each group have?

What Are the Different Groups of Birds?

There are about 10,000 species of birds on Earth. Birds come in many different colors, shapes, and sizes. Scientists group living bird species into 28 different orders. However, birds can also be grouped into four nonscientific categories. These categories are flightless birds, water birds, perching birds, and birds of prey. ☑

FLIGHTLESS BIRDS

Although all birds have wings, not all birds can fly. Birds that cannot fly are called *flightless*. Most flightless birds do not have a large keel to anchor strong flight muscles. Even though they cannot fly, flightless birds have evolved other ways to move around. Some have powerful legs for running, while others are excellent swimmers. The figure below shows some flightless birds.

Flightless Birds

▼ Unlike other flightless birds, **penguins** have large keels and strong flight muscles. They use their wings as flippers to "fly" through the water.

◀ **Ostriches** are the largest birds. They can reach a height of 2.5 m and a mass of 125 kg. These birds can run up to 60 km/h.

Kiwis are about the size of chickens. At night, they hunt for worms, caterpillars, and berries. ▶

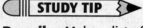

STUDY TIP

Describe Make a list of birds you are familiar with. Decide which of the four groups each bird on your list belongs to.

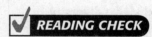

READING CHECK

1. List What are the four main groups of birds?

_____

_____

_____

Say It

Describe In small groups, describe the kinds of birds you have seen around your home or school. What do they look like? What time of year do you see them? Do you know what they eat?

TAKE A LOOK

2. Apply Concepts What characteristic of penguins is generally not seen in other flightless birds?

_____

WATER BIRDS

Some birds that fly can also swim in water. Cranes, ducks, geese, swans, pelicans, and loons are all water birds. Water birds usually have webbed feet for swimming. Some have long legs for wading.

Water birds find food both in the water and on land. Many of them eat plants, invertebrates, or fish. Some water birds have rounded, flat beaks for eating plants and small invertebrates. Others have sharp, long beaks for catching fish.

Water Birds

▼ The **blue-footed booby** is a tropical water bird. These birds attract mates with a courtship dance that includes raising one foot at a time.

▼ Male **wood ducks** have colorful feathers to attract females. Like all ducks, they are strong swimmers and flyers.

◄ The **common loon** can make deep dives when searching for food. It can stay underwater for several minutes.

SECTION 2 Kinds of Birds *continued*

PERCHING BIRDS

Perching birds can sit on branches. Their legs and feet are adapted to let them hold on to branches. Robins, warblers, and sparrows are all perching birds. When a perching bird lands in a tree, its feet close around a branch. The bird's feet will still stay wrapped around the branch, even if the bird falls asleep.

Perching Birds

Parrots have special feet for perching and climbing.

Chickadees are lively little birds. They can hang under a branch by their feet while looking for insects, seeds, or fruits.

Critical Thinking

4. Infer Why don't most ducks sit in trees?

_____

_____

_____

_____

_____

BIRDS OF PREY

Birds that hunt and eat other vertebrates are called *birds of prey*. This group includes owls, eagles, falcons, ospreys, vultures, and hawks. These birds may eat insects, mammals, fish, reptiles, and even other birds. Birds of prey have special adaptations that help them hunt. They have sharp claws and beaks, to help them catch and kill prey. They also have good vision for finding prey. Most birds of prey hunt during the day. However, most owls hunt at night. ☑

Birds of Prey

Owls, such as this **northern spotted owl**, hunt for food at night. They have a strong sense of hearing to help them find prey in the dark.

Ospreys fly over water and catch fish with their claws.

✓ **READING CHECK**

5. List Name three adaptations birds of prey have for catching and killing prey.

_____

_____

_____

Name _____ Class _____ Date _____

Section 2 Review

NSES LS 1a, 3a, 5a, 5b

1. Organize Fill in the chart below to describe the four main groups of birds.

Group of birds	Characteristics	Examples
Flightless birds		
Water birds		
Perching birds		
Birds of prey		

2. Apply Concepts Why would a perching bird *not* be well adapted to live in the water?

_____

_____

_____

3. Explain Into which group would you place a bird that had a small keel and strong legs?

_____

4. Apply Concepts In what type of habitat would you expect to find a bird with long, thin legs? Explain your answer.

_____

_____

5. Infer Penguins have webbed feet and spend much of their time in the water. Why do you think they are not grouped with the water birds?

_____

_____

_____

CHAPTER 17 Birds and Mammals

SECTION
3 **Characteristics of Mammals**

National Science
Education Standards
LS 1a, 1d, 2a, 3a, 3b, 3c, 5a

BEFORE YOU READ

After you read this section, you should be able to answer these questions:

• How did mammals evolve?

• What are the seven characteristics of mammals?

What Are the Characteristics of Mammals?

Like a donkey, a bat, a giraffe, and a whale, you are a mammal. Mammals live in almost every environment on Earth. Though there are almost 5,000 different species of mammals, they all share seven common characteristics.

▲ Mandrill baboon   ▲ Rhinoceros

◀ Beluga whale

Although they look very different, all of these animals are mammals.

SEXUAL REPRODUCTION

All mammals reproduce sexually. Sperm fertilize eggs inside the female's body. Most mammals give birth to live young instead of laying eggs. At least one parent cares for and protects the young until they are grown.

MAKE MILK

Mammary glands are structures that make milk. While all mammals have mammary glands, only mature females that have had offspring can produce milk. Milk is the main source of food for most young mammals.

All milk is made of water, proteins, fats, and sugars. However, different species have different amounts of each nutrient in their milk. For example, cow milk has twice as much fat as human milk. ☑

STUDY TIP

Outline As you read this section, make an outline describing the characteristics of mammals.

 Say It

Describe Before you read the entire section, discuss with your classmates some of the animals you know that are mammals. Make a list of the characteristics you think all mammals share. After you read the section, dicuss whether or not your list of characteristics was correct.

READING CHECK

1. **List** What is milk made of?

_____

_____

SECTION 3 Characteristics of Mammals *continued*

Like all mammals, this calf drinks its mother's milk for its first meals.

ENDOTHERMY

As a mammal's cells use oxygen to break down food, energy is released. Mammals use this energy to keep their bodies warm. Like birds, mammals are *endotherms*. They can keep their body temperatures constant even when outside temperatures change. The ability to stay warm helps many mammals survive in cold areas and stay active in cool weather. ☑

HAIR

Mammals are the only animals that have hair. All mammals—even whales—have hair at some point in their lives. Mammals that live in in cold climates, such as polar bears, usually have thick coats of hair. This is called *fur*. Mammals in warmer climates, such as elephants, do not need warm fur. However, they do have some hair.

Most mammals also have a layer of fat underneath their skin. Fat traps heat in the body. Mammals that live in cold oceans have a very thick layer of fat. This is called *blubber*.

SPECIALIZED TEETH

Unlike most other animals, mammals have teeth with different shapes and sizes for different jobs. For example, humans have three types of teeth. The front of the mouth has cutting teeth called *incisors*. Next to them are stabbing teeth called *canines*. These help grab and hold onto food. In the back are flat teeth that grind called *molars*. ☑

Each kind of tooth helps mammals eat a certain kind of food. Meat-eating mammals have large canines to help them tear prey. Plant-eating mammals have larger incisors and molars to help them bite off plants and chew them up.

☑ **READING CHECK**

2. Identify What are two advantages of being endothermic?

_____

_____

_____

_____

☑ **READING CHECK**

3. List What are the three types of teeth that humans have?

_____

_____

_____

Mountain lions have sharp canine teeth for grabbing their prey.

Horses have sharp incisors in front for cutting plants. They have flat molars in back for grinding plants.

TAKE A LOOK
4. Describe How does a horse's molars help it eat plants?

_____

_____

_____

BREATHE AIR

All animals need oxygen to help their cells break down food. Like birds and reptiles, mammals use lungs to get oxygen from the air. Mammals also have a large muscle called the **diaphragm** that helps them bring air into the lungs. As the diaphragm moves down, air rushes into the lungs. As it moves up, air is pushed out.

LARGE BRAINS

In general, a mammal has a larger brain than a non-mammal of the same size. A large brain lets mammals learn and think quickly. Like many other animals, mammals use vision, hearing, smell, touch, and taste to learn about the world around them. Different senses may be more important to mammals in different environments. For example, mammals that are active at night often depend on their hearing more than their vision.

How Did the First Mammals Evolve?

Scientists have found fossils of mammals from over 225 million years ago. These early mammals were about the size of mice. They were *endotherms*, which means they did not have to depend on their surroundings to stay warm. This allowed them to look for food at night when temperatures were cooler. Looking for food at night helped them avoid being eaten by dinosaurs.

When the dinosaurs died out, there was more food and land for mammals. The mammals were able to spread out to new environments.

Critical Thinking
5. Infer Why do you think the first mammals were active at night but the dinosaurs were not?

_____

_____

_____

_____

_____

_____

_____

Section 3 Review

NSES   LS 1a, 1d, 2a, 3a, 3b, 3c, 5a

SECTION VOCABULARY

diaphragm a dome-shaped muscle that is attached to the lower ribs and that functions as the main muscle in respiration	**mammary gland** in a female mammal, a gland that secretes milk

1. Summarize Complete the organizer below to identify the seven characteristics shared by all mammals.

Characteristics of mammals

2. Explain How is the milk of different mammal species the same and how is it different?

_____

_____

3. List Name three characteristics of mammals that help them stay warm.

_____

_____

4. Apply Concepts A particular mammal skull has large, sharp canine teeth. What does this tell you about the food the mammal ate?

_____

_____

5. Infer A nurse shark and a dolphin are about the same size. Which one would you expect to have a larger brain? Explain your answer.

_____

_____

CHAPTER 17 Birds and Mammals

SECTION 4 Placental Mammals

National Science
Education Standards
LS 1a, 1d, 2a, 3a, 3c, 5a

BEFORE YOU READ

After you read this section, you should be able to answer these questions:

• What is a placental mammal?

• What are some examples of placental mammals?

How Do Most Mammals Develop?

Mammals are classified by how they develop. There are three main groups: placental mammals, monotremes, and marsupials. A **placental mammal** is a mammal whose embryos develop inside the mother's body. The embryo grows in an organ called the *uterus*. Another organ, called the *placenta*, connects the embryo to the uterus. The placenta brings food and oxygen to the embryo. It also carries wastes away from the embryo. ☑

The amount of time that an embryo grows before it is born is called a **gestation period**. Different placental mammals have different gestation periods. For example, the gestation period for humans is 9 months. For elephants, the gestation period is 23 months.

What Are Some Kinds of Placental Mammals?

Placental mammals are divided into groups based on how they evolved and how closely they are related.

ANTEATERS, ARMADILLOS, AND SLOTHS

Anteaters, armadillos, and sloths have backbones like all mammals. However, mammals in this group have extra connections between their vertebrae. These connections strengthen the animals' lower backs and hips. Some members of this group have very small teeth and some have no teeth at all. Many mammals in this group catch insects using long, sticky tongues. ☑

STUDY TIP

Summarize As you read, make a chart that lists the different groups of placental mammals described in this section. In your chart, include the characteristics of each group.

READING CHECK

1. Identify What organ connects the embryo to the uterus?

_____

_____

READING CHECK

2. Explain How do members of this group differ from other mammals?

_____

_____

_____

_____

_____

◀ **Giant anteaters** eat only a few insects from each nest they find.

▲ **Armadillos** eat insects, frogs, mushrooms, and roots.

SECTION 4 Placental Mammals *continued*

MOLES, SHREWS, AND HEDGEHOGS

Most members of this group are small animals with small brains and simple teeth. Many animals in this group rely more on hearing, smell, and touch than on vision. Their long, pointed noses help them smell their food. Members of this group feed mostly on invertebrates, such as insects and worms. Some also eat fish, frogs, lizards, and other small mammals. ☑

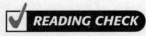

READING CHECK

3. Identify What do most members of the moles, shrews, and hedgehogs group eat?

_____

_____

▲ The **star-nosed mole** has sensitive feelers on its nose. These help the mole find earthworms to eat. Moles have very poor vision.

▲ **Hedgehogs** have spines that keep them safe from most predators.

RODENTS

More than one third of all mammal species are rodents. This group includes squirrels, mice, rats, guinea pigs, and porcupines. Rodents all have one set of incisors in their upper jaws. They chew and gnaw so much that their teeth wear down. However, their incisors grow continuously, so they never wear out completely. Rodents also have sensitive whiskers on their faces. ☑

READING CHECK

4. List What are three characteristics of rodents?

_____

_____

_____

▼ The **capybara** is the largest rodent in the world. Female capybaras can weigh as much as a grown man.

▲ Like all rodents, a **porcupine** has incisors that grow continuously.

SECTION 4 Placental Mammals *continued*

RABBITS, HARES, AND PIKAS

Rabbits, hares, and pikas belong to another group of mammals. Like rodents, these mammals have sharp, gnawing teeth. However, unlike rodents, these mammals have two sets of incisors in their upper jaws. Their tails are also shorter than rodents' tails. The figure below shows some members of this group. ☑

5. Compare How do the teeth of rodents differ from those of rabbits, hares, and pikas?

_____

_____

The **black-tailed jack** rabbit uses its large eyes, ears, and its sensitive nose to detect predators.

Pikas are small animals that live high in the mountains.

FLYING MAMMALS

Bats are the only mammals that can fly. Bats are active at night and sleep during the day. Most bats eat insects or other small animals. Some eat fruit or nectar. A few bats, called *vampire bats*, drink the blood of birds and mammals.

Bats make clicking noises as they fly. The clicks echo off trees, rocks, and insects. The size, shape, and distance of an object affect the echo produced. Bats know what is around them by hearing these echoes. Using echoes to find things is called *echolocation*.

Critical Thinking

6. Infer How do you think bats use echolocation?

_____

_____

_____

Fruit bats, also called *flying foxes*, live in tropical regions. They pollinate plants as they go from plant to plant to find fruit.

The **spotted bat** is found in parts of the southwestern United States. Like most bats, it eats flying insects. It uses its large ears during echolocation.

MAMMALS WITH TEETH FOR SHEARING

Mammals in this group evolved from a species of *carnivore*, or an animal that eats meat. Members of this group include dogs, cats, otters, raccoons, and bears. The teeth of these animals are adapted for shearing, or tearing meat off bone. Although the animals in this group evolved from carnivores, some members, such as pandas, are herbivores. Herbivores are plant eaters. Others, such as black bears, are omnivores. They eat both plants and animals.

Some members of this group live in the oceans. They are called *pinnipeds*. Pinnipeds include seals, sea lions, and walruses.

Word Help: evidence
information showing whether an idea is true or valid

7. Explain Why do some members of this group have shearing teeth, even though they are herbivores?

_____

_____

_____

_____

Coyotes are members of the dog family. They live throughout North America and parts of Central America.

Like all pinnipeds, **walruses** eat in the ocean, and sleep and mate on land. They use their huge canine teeth for defense, to attract mates, and to climb onto ice.

TRUNK-NOSED MAMMALS

Elephants are the only living mammals that have trunks. A trunk is a combination of an upper lip and a nose. An elephant uses its trunk to put food in its mouth. It also uses its trunk to spray water on its back to cool off.

TAKE A LOOK
8. Compare How can you tell the difference between an African elephant and an Indian elephant?

_____

_____

_____

Elephants are social. The females live in herds made up of mothers, daughters, and sisters. These elephants are **African elephants**.

These **Indian elephants** have smaller ears and tusks than African elephants do.

HOOFED MAMMALS

A *hoof* is a thick, hard pad that covers a mammal's toe. A hoof is similar to a toenail or claw, but it covers the entire toe. Horses, pigs, deer, and rhinoceroses all have hoofs. Most hoofed mammals are plant eaters. They have flat molars to help them grind the plants they eat.

Hoofed mammals can have an odd or even number of toes. Odd-toed hoofed mammals have one or three toes. Horses and zebras both have one large hoofed toe on each foot. Rhinoceroses have three toes. Even-toed hoofed mammals have two or four toes on each foot. Pigs, cattle, deer, and giraffes are even-toed.

Critical Thinking

9. Infer Which animals do you think are more closely related to giraffes—deer or rhinoceroses? Explain your answer.

_____

_____

_____

_____

Tapirs are large mammals with an odd number of toes. They live in Central America, South America, and Southeast Asia.

Camels are even-toed mammals. A camel's hump is a large lump of fat. It provides the camel with energy when there is not much food around. Camels can live without drinking water for a long time. This lets them live in dry places.

Giraffes are the tallest living mammals. They have long necks and long legs, and are even-toed.

Say It

Investigate Choose one of the animals from this figure, or one from the text above. Use your school media center to research this animal. Describe this animal to your class. Talk about what it eats, where it lives, and any other interesting facts.

SECTION 4 Placental Mammals *continued*

CETACEANS

Cetaceans are a group of mammals that include whales, dolphins, and porpoises. All cetaceans live in the water. Cetaceans may look more like fish than mammals. However, unlike fish, cetaceans have lungs and nurse their young. ☑

Most cetaceans, such as dolphins and porpoises, have teeth. However, some, such as a humpback whale, have no teeth. Instead, they strain water for tiny organisms.

☑ **READING CHECK**

10. Explain Why are cetaceans mammals, even though they look more like fish?

_____

_____

_____

Spinner dolphins spin like footballs when they leap out of the water. Like all dolphins, they are intelligent and highly social.

Humpback whales do not have teeth. Like all toothless whales, they strain sea water through large, flat plates in their mouths. The plates trap tiny organisms for the whales to eat.

MANATEES AND DUGONGS

Manatees and dugongs are another group of mammals that live in the water. They swim slowly, using their flippers and their tail. They live in the ocean and in rivers. Manatees and dugongs eat mostly seaweed and water plants. To breathe, these mammals lift their noses out of the water.

Critical Thinking

11. Infer Manatees are often killed or seriously hurt by boats. What characteristics of these mammals make injuries likely?

_____

_____

_____

_____

_____

_____

_____

Manatees are also called sea cows.

SECTION 4 Placental Mammals *continued*

PRIMATES

Primates include monkeys, apes, and humans. Members of this group have five fingers on each hand and five toes on each foot. Primates have larger brains than most other mammals. Their eyes face forward. They also have opposable thumbs, which allow them to hold objects.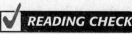

Many primates live in trees. They climb with grasping hands and feet. They have flexible shoulders that let them swing between branches. Most primates eat leaves and fruit. Some hunt for meat.

☑ **READING CHECK**

12. Identify What adaptation have primates evolved that allows them to hold onto objects?

_____

Orangutans and other apes often walk upright. Apes usually have larger brains and bodies than monkeys do.

The **proboscis monkey** has a huge nose! Males have larger noses than females. Some scientists think the male's nose is used to attract females.

Like many monkeys, **spider monkeys** have grasping tails. Their long arms, legs, and tails help them move among the trees.

TAKE A LOOK

13. Identify Which group of primates represented in this figure has the largest brains?

_____

14. Identify What adaptation do many monkeys have for swinging through trees?

_____

Section 4 Review

SECTION VOCABULARY

gestation period in mammals, the length of time between fertilization and birth	**placental mammal** a mammal that nourishes its unborn offspring through a placenta inside its uterus

1. Describe What is the function of the placenta?

_____

_____

2. Explain How do scientists organize placental mammals into groups?

_____

_____

3. Apply Concepts A manatee may look like a pinniped, but they are not classified in the same group. Why do you think scientists put them in different groups?

_____

_____

_____

Use the figure below to answer the questions that follow.

4. Explain How do you know that this animal is not a primate?

_____

_____

5. Apply Concepts With which group of placental mammals would you classify this organism? Explain why it would not belong in any other group described in this section.

_____

_____

_____

_____

CHAPTER 17 Birds and Mammals

SECTION 5 ## Monotremes and Marsupials

National Science Education Standards
LS 1a, 1d, 2a, 3a, 3c, 5a, 5c

BEFORE YOU READ

After you read this section, you should be able to answer these questions:

• What are monotremes?

• What are marsupials?

Do All Mammals Develop Inside Their Mother?

Most mammals are placental. However, not all mammals develop inside their mothers. Some mammals hatch from eggs. These mammals are called monotremes. Other mammals spend the first months of their lives living in their mother's pouch. These mammals are called marsupials.

What Are Monotremes?

A **monotreme** is a mammal that lays eggs. Monotremes, like all mammals, have mammary glands, diaphragms, and hair. They also keep their body temperatures constant. A female monotreme lays eggs and keeps them warm with her body. When the eggs hatch, she nurses her offspring. Monotremes do not have nipples as other mammals do. Baby monotremes lick milk from the skin around the mother's mammary glands. ☑

ECHIDNA

There are only three living species of monotremes. Two of these species are echidnas. *Echidnas* are about the size of a house cat. They have large claws and long snouts. These structures help them dig for ants and termites to eat.

STUDY TIP

List As you read this section, make lists of the characteristics of monotremes and the characteristics of marsupials. Remember to include the characteristics that all mammals share.

READING CHECK

1. Identify Name two characteristics that are unique to monotreme mammals.

_____

_____

Echidnas

The **long-beaked echidna** lives in New Guinea.

The **short-beaked echidna** lives in Australia and New Guinea.

Math Focus

2. Calculate Percentages Only three of the 5,000 known species of mammals are monotremes. What percentage of mammals are monotremes?

_____

_____

PLATYPUS

The other type of monotreme is called a *platypus*. Platypuses live in Australia. They look very different from other mammals. They have webbed feet and flat tails to help them swim. They use their flat bills to search for food. Platypuses have claws on their feet, which they use to dig tunnels in riverbanks. They then lay their eggs in these tunnels.

When underwater, the **duckbill platypus** closes its eyes and ears. It uses its bill to find food.

What Are Marsupials?

Some mammals, such as kangaroos, carry their young in pouches. Mammals with pouches are called **marsupials**. Like all mammals, marsupials have mammary glands, hair, and specialized teeth. Marsupials also give birth to live young. However, the young continue to develop inside their mother's pouch. The young will stay in the pouch for several months. ☑

THE POUCH

Marsupials are not very developed when they are born. For example, a newborn kangaroo is only the size of a bumblebee. Newborn marsupials have no hair and can only use their front limbs. They use these limbs to pull themselves into their mother's pouch. In the pouch, the newborn starts drinking milk from its mother's nipples.

Young kangaroos are called *joeys*. Joeys stay in their mother's pouch for several months. When they first leave the pouch, they do so for only short periods of time.

Word Help: <u>evidence</u> information showing whether an idea is true or valid

3. List Name three characteristics that monotremes share with other mammals.

_____

_____

_____

✓ READING CHECK

4. Identify What is one feature that only marsupials have?

_____

_____

SECTION 5 Monotremes and Marsupials *continued*

KINDS OF MARSUPIALS

You may be familiar with some well known marsupials such as kangaroos. Have you heard of wallabies, bettongs, and numbats? There are over 280 species of marsupials. Most marsupials live in Australia, New Guinea, and South America. The only marsupial that is native to North America is the opossum. ☑

Kinds of Marsupials

Koalas sleep for about 18 hours each day. They eat eucalyptus leaves.

Young **kangaroos** will return to their mother's pouch if there is any sign of danger.

When in danger, an **opossum** will lie perfectly still. It "plays dead" so predators will leave it alone.

5. Identify Where are most marsupials found?

_____

_____

_____

Why Are Many Marsupials Endangered?

The number of living marsupial species is decreasing. At least 22 of Australia's native mammal species have become extinct in the last 400 years. Many more are currently in danger.

Many marsupials have gone extinct or become endangered because of exotic species. Exotic species are organisms that are brought into an area by humans. When Europeans came to Australia in the 1700s and 1800s, they brought animals such as cats, rabbits, and foxes. Many of these animals escaped into the wild. Some of these exotic species now compete with marsupials for food. Others kill marsupials for food.

Exotic species are not the only threat to marsupials. Destruction of habitats has left many maruspials with no place to live and no food. Today, Australia is trying to protect its marsupials.

Critical Thinking

6. Infer Why were cats and rabbits considered exotic species in Australia?

_____

_____

_____

_____

Section 5 Review

NSES LS 1a, 1d, 2a, 3a, 3c, 5a, 5c

SECTION VOCABULARY

marsupial a mammal that carries and nourishes its young in a pouch	**monotreme** a mammal that lays eggs

1. Identify What are the two kinds of monotremes?

_____

2. Compare Fill in the Venn Diagram to compare monotremes and marsupials.

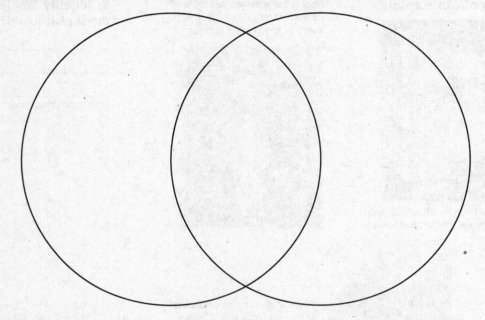

3. Explain How does a platypus use its bill?

_____

4. List Give three examples of marsupials.

_____

_____

5. Describe Describe a newborn marsupial.

_____

_____

6. Explain Why have many of Australia's marsupials become endangered or gone extinct?

_____

_____

_____

CHAPTER 21	Environmental Problems and Solutions

SECTION 1 | Environmental Problems

BEFORE YOU READ

After you read this section, you should be able to answer these questions:

- What is pollution?
- What are some other environmental problems?

National Science Education Standards

LS 3a, 4d

What Is Pollution?

In the late 1700s, people started to depend on machines more and more. This is known as the *Industrial Revolution*. As people used more machines, they put larger amounts of harmful substances into the air, water, and soil. Machines today don't make as many harmful substances as machines many years ago. However, there are now more sources of pollution than there once were.

Pollution is an unwanted change in the environment caused by substances such as wastes, or energy, such as radiation. Anything that causes pollution is called a *pollutant*. Pollutants can harm living things. Natural events such as volcanic eruptions make pollutants. Humans make many other pollutants. ☑

GARBAGE

Americans throw away more trash than people of any other country. Most trash goes into landfills, like the one shown below. Some kinds of trash, such as medical waste and lead paint, are very dangerous. They are called *hazardous wastes*, and include things that can catch fire, eat through metal, explode, or make people sick. ☑

Many industries, such as hospitals, oil refineries, paint manufacturers, power plants, and paper mills, produce hazardous wastes. People need to dispose of hazardous wastes in places set aside for them.

STUDY TIP

Underline As you read, underline any unfamiliar words. Find out what these words mean before you move on to the next section.

READING CHECK

1. Explain Is all pollution caused by humans? Explain your answer.

_____

_____

_____

READING CHECK

2. Identify Give two examples of hazardous wastes.

_____

_____

Every year, Americans throw away 200 million metric tons of garbage. Much of the garbage ends up in landfills.

Type of pollution	Examples or sources	Harmful effects
	nuclear power plants	
Greenhouse gases		

TAKE A LOOK
3. Summarize As you read, complete this chart to describe different types of pollution.

Critical Thinking

4. Infer New refrigerators do not use CFCs. However, CFCs are still being released into the atmosphere. Explain why this is happening.

_____

_____

_____

CHEMICALS

People use chemicals for many things. Some chemicals treat diseases. Others are used to make plastics and to preserve food. Sometimes, the same chemicals that help people may also harm the environment. For example, fertilizers and pesticides can make plants grow bigger and faster. However, they may also pollute the soil and water.

CFCs and PCBs are two examples of chemical pollutants. *CFCs* were once used in spray cans, refrigerators, and plastics. Scientists found that CFCs were destroying the ozone layer. The ozone layer protects Earth by absorbing harmful ultraviolet radiation from the sun. Even though CFCs were banned years ago, they are still found in the atmosphere.

PCBs were once used in appliances and paints. They are poisonous and may cause cancer. PCBs are now banned. However, they are still found all over the Earth.

NUCLEAR WASTES

Nuclear power plants provide electricity. They also produce radioactive wastes. Radioactive wastes are hazardous. They give off radiation, which can cause cancer or radiation poisoning. They may take thousands of years to break down into less harmful materials.

NOISE

Some pollutants affect your senses. These include loud noises, such as airplanes taking off, and even loud music. Noise isn't just annoying. It can affect your ability to think clearly. It can also damage your hearing.

SECTION 1 Environmental Problems *continued*

GREENHOUSE GASES

Earth's atmosphere is made up of a mixture of gases, including carbon dioxide. The atmosphere acts as a blanket. It keeps Earth warm enough for life to exist.

Since the Industrial Revolution, the amount of carbon dioxide in the atmosphere has increased. Carbon dioxide and many pollutants act like a greenhouse, trapping heat around the Earth. Many scientists think the increase in carbon dioxide has caused global temperatures to go up. If temperatures continue to rise, ice at Earth's poles could melt. This would cause the level of the world's oceans to rise and flood many areas of land along coasts.

What Is Resource Depletion?

Resources are depleted when they are used up without being replaced. Some of Earth's resources can be replaced as quickly as they are used. Others, however, can never be replaced.

RENEWABLE RESOURCES

A **renewable resource** is one that can be replaced as quickly as it is used. Solar and wind energy, as well as some kinds of trees, are renewable resources. Fresh water is generally a renewable resource because it is replaced every time it rains. However, some areas are using up water faster than it can replaced. This may cause water to become a nonrenewable resource.

NONRENEWABLE RESOURCES

A **nonrenewable resource** is one that cannot be replaced or can only be replaced over many thousands of years. Minerals and fossil fuels, such as oil, coal, and natural gas, are nonrenewable resources. Nonrenewable resources are depleted as they are used because they cannot be replaced. In addition, removing some resources from Earth may lead to oil spills, loss of habitats, and damage from mining. All are harmful to the environment.

Renewable resources	Nonrenewable resources

Critical Thinking

5. Analyze Ideas Are greenhouse gases always harmful? Explain your answer.

_____

_____

_____

_____

_____

_____

TAKE A LOOK

6. Identify Use the text to complete the chart with examples of both types of resources.

SECTION 1 Environmental Problems *continued*

What Are Exotic Species?

People can carry plant seeds, animal eggs, and adult organisms from one part of the world to another. An animal or plant that is brought into a new environment is an *exotic species*. Sometimes an exotic species cannot survive outside of its natural environment. However, sometimes an exotic species does well in its new home.

Exotic species can cause problems. One reason for this is the organism does not have its natural predators in the new environment. This can allow populations of exotic species to grow out of control. An exotic species may compete with native species for resources. They may also kill the native species. ☑

Northern snakehead fish are an exotic species in the United States. These fish can move across land as they look for water. They can survive out of water for up to four days!

READING CHECK

7. Identify What are two effects exotic species can have on native species?

_____

_____

_____

_____

STANDARDS CHECK

LS 4d The number of organisms an ecosystem can support depends on the resources available and abiotic factors, such as the quantity of light and water, range of temperatures, and soil composition. Given adequate biotic and abiotic resources and no disease or predators, populations (including humans) increase at rapid rates. Lack of resources and other factors, such as predation and climate, limit the growth of populations in specific niches in the ecosystem.

8. Predict What will happen to resources as the human population continues to grow?

_____

_____

_____

_____

_____

Why Is Human Population Growth a Problem?

Advances in medicine, such as immunizations, have helped people live longer. Advances in farming have let farmers grow food to feed more people. Because of this, the number of people on Earth has grown very quickly over the past few hundred years.

Eventually there could be too many people on Earth. **Overpopulation** happens when a population gets so large that individuals cannot get the resources they need. For example, one day there may not be enough food or water on Earth to support the growing human population.

SECTION 1 Environmental Problems *continued*

What Is Habitat Destruction?

An organism's *habitat* is where it lives. Every habitat has its own variety of organisms. This is known as **biodiversity**. If a habitat is damaged or destroyed, biodiversity is lost.

Habitats can be destroyed in different ways. Topsoil may erode, or wash away, when people clear land for crops or buildings. Also, chemicals may pollute streams and rivers. Organisms living in these areas may be left without food and shelter, and may die.

FOREST HABITATS

Trees provide humans with oxygen, wood, food, rubber, and paper. For many of these products trees must be cut down. Sometimes all the trees in a forest are cut down. This is called *deforestation*. People can plant new trees to replace ones that they cut. However, trees take many years to grow. ☑

Tropical rain forests have some of the highest biodiversity on Earth. However, people clear many acres of rainforest for farm land, roads, and lumber. After a forest is cleared, the biodiversity of the area is lost.

Deforestation can lead to soil erosion. This means that soil washes away.

MARINE HABITATS

When people think of pollution in marine habitats, many think of oil spills. An oil spill is an example of *point source pollution*, or pollution that comes from one source.

Unlike oil spills, some pollution comes from many different sources. This is called *nonpoint-source pollution*. For example, chemicals on land wash into rivers, lakes, and oceans. These chemicals can harm or kill organisms that live in marine habitats.

☑ **READING CHECK**

9. Define What is deforestation?

_____

_____

_____

Critical Thinking

10. Apply Concepts Dumping plastics into the oceans is another form of pollution. It can kill many marine animals. Is dumping plastics in oceans an example of point-source or nonpoint-source pollution? Explain your answer.

_____

_____

_____

Section 1 Review

SECTION VOCABULARY

biodiversity the number and variety of organisms in a given area during a specific period of time

nonrenewable resource a resource that forms at a rate that is much slower than the rate at which the resource is consumed

overpopulation the presence of too many individuals in an area for the available resources

pollution an unwanted change in the environment caused by substances or forms of energy

renewable resource a natural resource that can be replaced at the same rate at which the resource is consumed

1. Apply Concepts Use the vocabulary terms above to complete the Concept Map.

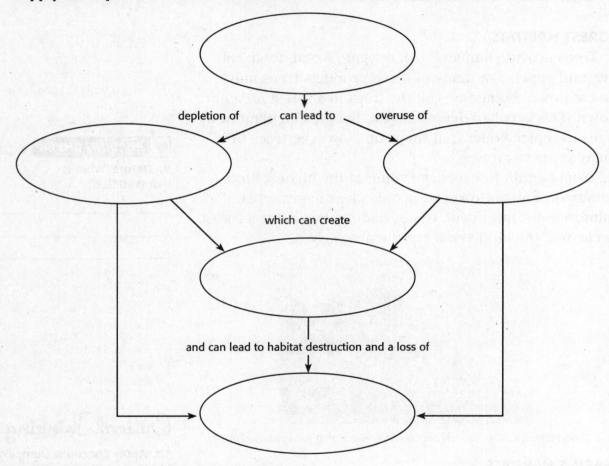

2. Define What is resource depletion?

_____

3. Analyze Ideas Is it possible for a renewable resource to become nonrenewable? Explain your answer and give an example.

_____

_____

_____

CHAPTER 21 Environmental Problems and Solutions

SECTION
2 **Environmental Solutions**

National Science
Education Standards
LS 5c

> **BEFORE YOU READ**
>
> **After you read this section, you should be able to answer these questions:**
>
> • What is conservation?
>
> • What are some things people can do to protect the environment?

How Can People Conserve Resources?

As the human population grows, it will need more resources. People will need food, health care, transportation, and ways to get rid of wastes. All of these needs will affect the Earth. If people don't use resources wisely, people will continue to pollute the air, soil, and water. More natural habitats could be lost and many species could die out. However, there are many things people can do to protect the environment.

Conservation is the protection and wise use of natural resources. When you conserve resources, you use fewer of them. Conservation not only keeps us from using up resources, but also reduces waste, pollution, and habitat destruction. For example, using a bike instead of a car can save fuel and help prevent air pollution.

There are three ways to conserve resources: **R**educe, **R**euse, and **R**ecycle. These are known as the three Rs. ☑

STUDY TIP
Organize As you read, make a Spider Map to show different ways you can help protect the environment.

✓ **READING CHECK**
1. List What are the three Rs of conservation?

_____
_____
_____

TAKE A LOOK
2. Infer How is the girl with the bag reducing her use of resources?

_____
_____
_____
_____

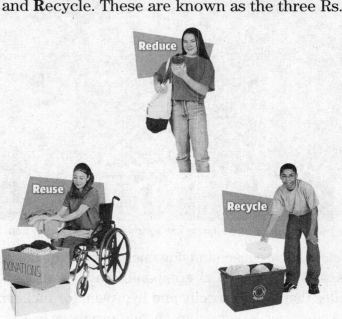

Reduce

Reuse

DONATIONS

Recycle

SECTION 2 Environmental Solutions *continued*

REDUCE

The best way to conserve resources is to use fewer of them. Using fewer resources also helps reduce pollution and the amount of waste we produce. ☑

Almost one third of the waste produced by some countries is packaging material, such as boxes, plastic bags, and paper. Wrapping products in less paper and plastic reduces waste. For example, fast-food restaurants used to serve sandwiches in large plastic containers. Today, many wrap food in thin paper instead. Paper is biodegradable. *Biodegradable* means that living organisms, such as bacteria, can break it down.

THIS BAG IS BIODEGRADABLE

In addition to reducing waste, people need to reduce the amount of nonrenewable resources they use. For example, scientists are looking for sources of energy that can replace fossil fuels, such as oil and gas. One way to use fewer nonrenewable resources is to use renewable resources, such as solar and wind energy.

The people who live in this house use solar panels to get energy from the sun.

Scientists are also studying energy sources such as wind, tides, and waterfalls. Car companies have developed automobiles that use electricity and hydrogen for fuel. Driving these cars uses less gas and oil, and produces less pollution.

✓ READING CHECK

3. Identify What is the best way to conserve resources?

_____

_____

TAKE A LOOK

4. Identify Are the people living in this house using a renewable or nonrenewable resource for energy?

_____

_____

SECTION 2 Environmental Solutions *continued*

REUSE

Every time you reuse a plastic bag, one bag fewer needs to be made. This also means that one bag fewer will end up in a landfill. Reusing products is an important way to conserve resources.

You can reuse many things. For example, clothes can be passed down and worn by someone else. Sports equipment can be repaired instead of being thrown away. Builders can reuse materials such as wood, bricks, and tiles to make new structures. Even old tires can be used again. They can be reused for playground surfaces or even in new homes.

This home is made of reused tires and aluminum cans

American homes use about 100 billion liters of water each day. When you wash your hands or take a shower, most of the water goes down the drain. This is called *wastewater*. No new water is ever made on Earth. Wastewater eventually returns to Earth as rain in the water cycle. However, this takes a very long time. Because of this, many communities are learning how to reuse, or *reclaim*, wastewater. ☑

Reclaiming wastewater allows people to use the same water for more than one thing. One way to do this is to clean the water so that it can be used again. Some organisms can be used to filter water and take out many of the wastes. These organisms include plants and filter-feeding animals, such as clams. The reclaimed water may not be pure enough to drink. However, it can be used to water crops, lawns, and golf courses.

Critical Thinking

5. Identify Relationships How are reducing and reusing related?

_____

_____

_____

_____

_____

✓ **READING CHECK**

6. Explain What does reclaiming wastewater mean?

_____

_____

RECYCLE

Recycling is the recovery of materials from waste. This means that new products can be made from old products. A material that can be recycled is *recyclable*. Some recyclable items, such as paper, are used to make the same kind of product. Other recyclable items are made into different products. For example, yard wastes, such as dead leaves and cut grass, can be recycled into a natural fertilizer.

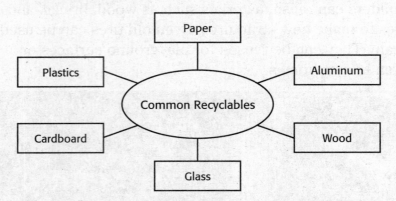

Recycling newspapers could save millions of trees. Recycling aluminum uses 95% less energy than turning raw ore into aluminum. Glass can be recycled many times to make new bottles and jars. This uses less energy than making new glass.

Burning some wastes can produce electricity. Using garbage to make electricity is an example of *resource recovery*. When companies make electricity from their waste products, they save money and conserve resources. However, some people are concerned that burning wastes for electricity pollutes the air. ☑

A waste-to-energy plant can provide electricity for many homes and businesses.

Say It

Investigate Find out where in your neighborhood you can take materials to be recycled. Does your city or town pick up recyclables? What sort of things can you recycle in your community? Share with the class what you learn.

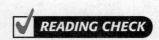
READING CHECK

7. Identify What is one problem with burning garbage to make electricity?

_____

_____

How Can People Help Maintain Biodiversity?

Biodiversity is important because each species has a unique role in an ecosystem. Losing one species could affect the entire ecosystem. Biodiversity also protects against the spread of disease. For example, if a disease spreads in a forest that has only one species, the entire forest may be destroyed. If there are many different species, a disease is not likely to affect them all. ☑

PROTECTING SPECIES

One way to maintain biodiversity is to protect individual species. In the United States, a law called the *Endangered Species Act* was designed to do just that. An endangered species is one that generally has few individuals left. Without protection, an endangered species may become extinct. Scientists identify endangered species and put that species on a special list. The law forbids activities that would harm any species on this list.

The law also requires recovery programs for endangered species. This means that scientists work both to protect existing individuals of an endangered species, and to increase the population. To help some species recover, scientists remove individuals from the wild to breed them. This is known as *captive breeding*. It can help some species produce more offspring than they would in the wild. ☑

Individuals that are bred in captivity are often released back into the wild. However, this is not a solution for all endangered species. Many species are endangered because their habitats have been destroyed. They may have no habitat left to return to. These species can only survive if their habitat is protected as well.

Captive-breeding programs have helped the population of California condors to grow.

READING CHECK

8. Identify Give two reasons that maintaining biodiversity is important.

_____

_____

_____

_____

_____

_____

READING CHECK

9. Explain What is the purpose of a species recovery program?

_____

_____

_____

PROTECTING HABITATS

Scientists want to keep species from becoming endangered. They don't want to wait until a species is almost extinct before they try to protect it.

Plants, animals, and microorganisms depend on each other. Each is part of a huge, interconnected web of organisms. To protect the web, whole habitats need to be protected, not just individual species.

 Say It

Describe Have you ever visited a nature reserve or national park? Tell the class about your visit. If you have never been to a reserve or national park, tell the class about the kind of park you would like to visit.

Nature preserves are large areas of public land set aside for wildlife. They can protect important habitats.

ENVIRONMENTAL STRATEGIES

Laws have been passed to help protect resources and preserve habitats. By following these laws, people can help the environment. People can also use the following environmental strategies.

- **Reduce pollution.** Recycle as much as possible and buy recycled products. Do not dump wastes in forests, lakes, rivers, or oceans. Participate in a local cleanup project.
- **Reduce pesticide use.** Use pesticides that work only on harmful insects. Use natural pesticides whenever possible.
- **Protect habitats.** Preserve entire habitats. Use fewer resources, such as wood and paper, that can destroy habitats.
- **Learn about local issues.** Research how laws or projects will affect your area, and let people know about your concerns.
- **Develop alternative energy sources.** Use fewer nonrenewable resources, such as coal and oil. Use more renewable resources, such as solar and wind power.

Critical Thinking

10. Infer How could recycling help protect habitats?

_____
_____
_____
_____
_____
_____
_____

EPA

The United States Environmental Protection Agency (EPA) is a government organization. Its job is to help protect the environment. The EPA keeps people informed about environmental problems and helps enforce environmental laws.

WHAT YOU CAN DO

Reduce, reuse, and recycle. Protect the Earth. These are jobs for everyone. Children and adults can help clean up the environment. As they improve their environment, they improve their quality of life.

How You Can Help the Environment

1. Volunteer at a local preserve or nature center, and help other people learn about conservation.
2. Give away your old toys.
3. Use recycled paper.
4. Fill up both sides of a sheet of paper.
5. Start an environmental awareness club at your school or in your neighborhood.
6. Recycle glass, plastics, paper, aluminum, and batteries.
7. Don't buy any products made from an endangered plant or animal.
8. Turn off electrical devices when you are not using them.
9. Wear hand-me-downs.
10. Share books with friends, or use the library.
11. Walk, ride a bicycle, or use public transportation.
12. Carry a reusable cloth shopping bag to the store.
13. Use a lunch box, or reuse your paper lunch bags.
14. Turn off the water while you brush your teeth.
15. Buy products made from biodegradable and recycled materials.
16. Use cloth napkins and kitchen towels.
17. Buy things in packages that can be recycled.
18. Use rechargeable batteries.
19. Make a compost heap.

TAKE A LOOK

11. Apply Concepts Next to each item in the figure, write whether the activity is a way to reduce, reuse, or recycle. Some items might have more than one answer.

12. Identify Circle five things in this figure that you could start to do today to help the environment.

Section 2 Review

SECTION VOCABULARY

conservation the preservation and wise use of natural resources	**recycling** the process of recovering valuable or useful materials from waste or scrap

1. Define What does biodegradable mean?

_____

_____

2. Describe Decribe one way that water can be reclaimed.

_____

_____

_____

3. Identify What are two roles of the EPA?

_____

_____

4. Explain How would driving a car that uses hydrogen for fuel be helpful to the environment?

_____

_____

_____

5. List Name six materials that can be recycled in many communities.

_____

_____

6. Explain What is the purpose of the Endangered Species Act?

_____

_____

7. Apply Concepts How is using cloth napkins an example of both reusing and reducing?

_____

_____

_____

CHAPTER 23 Circulation and Respiration

SECTION
2 **Blood**

National Science Education Standards
LS 3a, 3b

What Is Blood?

Your cardiovascular system is made up of your heart, your blood vessels, and blood. **Blood** is a connective tissue made up of plasma, red blood cells, platelets, and white blood cells. Blood travels in blood vessels and carries oxygen and nutrients to all parts of your body. An adult human has only about 5 L of blood. All the blood in your body would not even fill up three 2-L soda bottles! ☑

PLASMA

The fluid part of the blood is called plasma. *Plasma* is made up of water, minerals, nutrients, sugars, proteins, and other substances.

PLATELETS

Platelets are pieces of larger cells found in bone marrow. When you get a cut, you bleed because blood vessels have been opened. Platelets clump together in the damaged area to form a plug. They also give off chemicals that cause fibers to form. The fibers and clumped platelets form a blood clot and stop the bleeding.

STUDY TIP
Ask Questions As you read this section, write down the questions that you have. Then, discuss your questions with a small group.

✓ READING CHECK
1. Define What is blood?

_____
_____
_____
_____

Critical Thinking
2. Infer If a person does not have enough platelets in her blood, what will happen if she gets a cut?

_____
_____
_____
_____
_____

Red blood cell
Platelet

Fibers

Math Focus

3. Calculate One cubic millimeter of blood contains 5 million RBCs and 10,000 WBCs. How many times more RBCs are there than WBCs?

_____

_____

4. Identify Where are most white blood cells made?

_____

_____

STANDARDS CHECK

LS 3b Regulation of an organism's internal environment involves sensing the internal environment and changing physiological activities to keep conditions within the range required to survive.

5. Explain How do wider or narrower blood vessels help your body stay at a constant temperature?

_____

_____

_____

RED BLOOD CELLS

Most blood cells are *red blood cells*, or RBCs. RBCs carry oxygen to all the cells in your body. Cells need oxygen to do their jobs. *Hemoglobin* is the protein in red blood cells that carries the oxygen. It is what makes RBCs look red.

WHITE BLOOD CELLS

A *pathogen* is a virus, bacteria, or other tiny particle that can make you sick. When pathogens get into your body, *white blood cells*, or WBCs, help kill them. WBCs can fight pathogens by:

• leaving blood vessels to destroy pathogens in tissues

• making chemicals called *antibodies* to help destroy pathogens

• destroying body cells that have died or been damaged

Most WBCs are made in bone marrow. Some mature in the lymphatic system. ☑

How Does Blood Control Body Temperature?

Your blood also helps keep your body temperature constant. Your blood vessels can open wider or get narrower to control how much heat is lost through your skin.

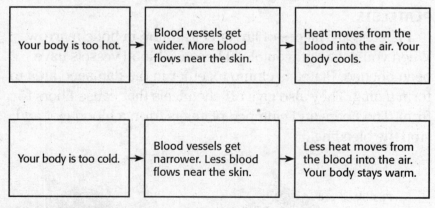

| Your body is too hot. | → | Blood vessels get wider. More blood flows near the skin. | → | Heat moves from the blood into the air. Your body cools. |

| Your body is too cold. | → | Blood vessels get narrower. Less blood flows near the skin. | → | Less heat moves from the blood into the air. Your body stays warm. |

What Is Blood Pressure?

When your heart beats, it pushes blood out of your heart and into your arteries. The force of the blood on the inside walls of the arteries is called **blood pressure**. Blood pressure is measured in millimeters of mercury (mm Hg).

SECTION 2 Blood *continued*

SYSTOLIC AND DIASTOLIC PRESSURE

Blood pressure is given by two numbers, such as 120/80. The first, or top, number is systolic pressure. *Systolic pressure* is the pressure in arteries when the ventricles contract. The rush of blood causes arteries to bulge and produce a pulse. The second, or bottom, number is diastolic pressure. *Diastolic pressure* is the pressure in arteries when the ventricles relax.

For adults, a blood pressure of 120/80 mm Hg or less is healthy. High blood pressure can cause heart or kidney damage.

What Are Blood Types?

Every person has one of four blood types: A, B, AB, or O. Chemicals called *antigens* on the outside of your RBCs determine whch blood type you have. The plasma of different blood types may have different antibodies. *Antibodies* are chemicals that react with antigens of other blood types as if the antigens were pathogens. ☑

| **A** | **B** | **AB** | **O** |

A — A antigen, B antibody
B — B antigen, A antibody
AB — A and B antigens
O — A and B antibodies

This figure shows which antigens and antibodies may be present in each blood type.

IMPORTANCE OF BLOOD TYPES

A person can lose blood from an injury, illness or surgery. To replace lost blood, a person can receive a blood transfusion. A *transfusion* is when a person is given blood from another person.

However, a person cannot receive blood from just anyone. If someone who is type A gets type B blood, the type B antibodies can make the RBCs clump together. The clumps can block blood vessels. A reaction to the wrong blood type can kill you.

Blood type	Can receive blood from:	Can donate blood to:
A	types A and O	types A and AB
B	types B and O	types B and AB
AB	types A, B, AB, and O	type AB only
O	type O only	types A, B, AB, and O

✔ **READING CHECK**

6. Identify What determines your blood type?

_____

_____

TAKE A LOOK
7. Identify What kinds of antigens are found on the RBCs of a person with type AB blood?

_____

_____

TAKE A LOOK
8. Identify Which blood type can receive blood from the most other blood types? Which type can donate blood to the most other types?

_____

_____

Section 2 Review

SECTION VOCABULARY

blood the fluid that carries gases, nutrients, and wastes through the body and that is made up of platelets, white blood cells, red blood cells, and plasma	**blood pressure** the force that blood exerts on the walls of arteries

1. Identify What are two functions of white blood cells?

_____

_____

2. Describe Complete the table to describe the two parts of blood pressure.

Type of pressure	Description	Where it is found in a blood-pressure measurement
systolic		top number
	pressure in the arteries when ventricles relax	

3. List What are three functions of blood?

_____

_____

_____

4. Infer Why does your face get redder when you are hot?

_____

_____

_____

5. Explain Why is it important that a person with type O blood only receive a blood transfusion from another person with type O blood?

_____

_____

_____

6. Predict If a person has a disease that causes hemoglobin to break down, what can happen to his RBCs?

_____

_____

_____

CHAPTER 23 Circulation and Respiration
SECTION 3 The Lymphatic System

National Science Education Standards
LS 1a, 1c, 1d, 1e, 1f

BEFORE YOU READ

After you read this section, you should be able to answer these questions:

• What is the function of the lymphatic system?

• What are the parts of the lymphatic system?

What Does the Lymphatic System Do?

Every time your heart pumps, small amounts of plasma are forced out of the thin walls of the capillaries. What happens to this fluid? Most of it is reabsorbed into your blood through the capillaries. Some of the fluid moves into your lymphatic system.

The **lymphatic system** is the group of vessels, organs, and tissues that collects excess fluid and returns it to the blood. The lymphatic system also helps your body fight pathogens.

What Are the Parts of the Lymphatic System?

Fluid collected by the lymphatic system is carried in vessels. The smallest of these vessels are called lymph capillaries. Larger lymph vessels are called lymphatic vessels. These vessels, along with bone marrow, lymph nodes, the thymus, and the spleen, make up the lymphatic system.

LYMPH CAPILLARIES

Lymph capillaries absorb some of the fluid and particles from between cells in the body. Some of the particles are dead cells or pathogens. These particles are too large to enter blood capillaries. The fluid and particles absorbed into lymph capillaries are called **lymph**.

The white arrows show how lymph moves into lymph capillaries and through lymphatic vessels.

STUDY TIP

Describe Work with a partner to quiz each other on the names and functions of each structure in the lymphatic system.

STANDARDS CHECK

LS 1e The human organism has systems for digestion, reproduction, circulation, excretion, movement, control and coordination, and protection from disease. These systems interact with one another.

1. Identify Relationships How do the lymphatic and circulatory systems work together?

_____

_____

_____

_____

_____

_____

LYMPHATIC VESSELS

Lymph capillaries carry lymph into larger vessels called *lymphatic vessels*. Skeletal muscles and valves help push the lymph through the lymphatic system. Lymphatic vessels drain the lymph into large veins in the neck. This returns the fluid to the cardiovascular system. ☑

The Lymphatic System

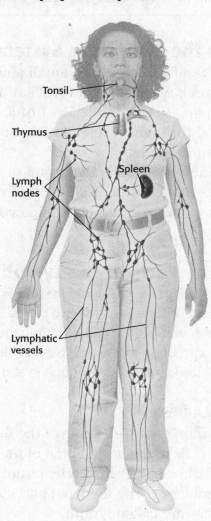

Tonsil

Thymus

Spleen

Lymph nodes

Lymphatic vessels

BONE MARROW

Bone marrow is the soft tissue inside bones that makes red and white blood cells. Recall that platelets, which help blood clot, are made in marrow. White blood cells called *lymphocytes* are part of the lymphatic system. They help fight infection. Killer T cell lymphocytes surround and destroy pathogens. B cell lymphocytes make antibodies that cause pathogens to stick together. This marks them for destruction. ☑

SECTION 3 The Lymphatic System *continued*

LYMPH NODES

As lymph travels through lymphatic vessels, it passes through lymph nodes. **Lymph nodes** are small masses of tissue that remove pathogens and dead cells from the lymph. When bacteria or other pathogens cause an infection, white blood cells multiply and fill the lymph nodes. This may cause lymph nodes to become swollen and painful.

THYMUS

T cells are made in the bone marrow. Before these cells are ready to fight infections, however, they develop further in the **thymus** gland. The thymus is located just above the heart. Mature T cells leave the thymus and travel through the lymphatic system.

SPLEEN

The **spleen** is the largest lymphatic organ. It stores lymphocytes and fights infection. It is a purplish organ located in the upper left side of the abdomen. As blood flows through the spleen, lymphocytes attack or mark pathogens in the blood. The spleen may release lymphocytes into the bloodstream when there is an infection. The spleen also monitors, stores, and destroys old blood cells. ☑

TONSILS

The **tonsils** are lymphatic tissue at the back of the mouth. Tonsils help defend the body against infection by trapping pathogens. Sometimes, however, tonsils can become infected. Infected tonsils may be red, swollen, and sore. They may be covered with patches of white, infected tissue and make swallowing difficult. Tonsils may be removed if there are frequent, severe tonsil infections that make breathing difficult.

Critical Thinking

5. Infer Sometimes you can easily feel your lymph nodes when they are swollen. If you had swollen lymph nodes, what could you infer?

_____

_____

READING CHECK

6. List Name three functions of the spleen.

_____

_____

_____

_____

Inflamed tonsils

Tonsils help protect your throat and lungs from infection by trapping pathogens.

Section 3 Review

NSES LS 1a, 1c, 1d, 1e, 1f

SECTION VOCABULARY

lymph the fluid that is collected by the lymphatic vessels and nodes	**spleen** the largest lymphatic organ in the body; serves as a blood reservoir, disintegrates old red blood cells, and produces lymphocytes and plasmids
lymph node an organ that filters lymph and that is found along the lymphatic vessels	**thymus** the main gland of the lymphatic system; it releases mature T lymphocytes
lymphatic system a collection of organs whose primary function is to collect extracellular fluid and return it to the blood; the organs in this system include lymph nodes and the lymphatic vessels	**tonsils** organs that are small, rounded masses of lymphatic tissue located in the pharynx and in the passage from the mouth to the pharynx

1. Describe How does the lymphatic system fight infection?

_____

_____

_____

2. Summarize Complete the Process Chart below to show how fluid travels between the cardiovascular system and the lymphatic system.

Plasma is pushed out of capillaries.

3. List What are three things that can be found in lymph?

_____

4. Analyze Why is it important that lymphatic tissue is spread throughout the body?

_____

_____

CHAPTER 23 | Circulation and Respiration

SECTION 4 | The Respiratory System

BEFORE YOU READ

After you read this section, you should be able to answer these questions:

• What is the respiratory system?
• What are some respiratory disorders?

What Is the Respiratory System?

Breathing: you do it all the time. You're doing it right now. You probably don't think about it unless you can't breathe. Then, it becomes very clear that you have to breathe in order to live. Why is breathing important? Breathing helps your body get oxygen. Your body needs oxygen in order to get energy from the foods you eat.

The words *breathing* and *respiration* are often used to mean the same thing. However, breathing is only one part of respiration. **Respiration** is the way the body gains and uses oxygen and gets rid of carbon dioxide. ☑

Respiration is divided into two parts. The first part involves inhaling and exhaling, or breathing. The second part is cellular respiration. *Cellular respiration* involves the chemical reactions that let you get energy from food.

The **respiratory system** is the group of organs and structures that take in oxygen and get rid of carbon dioxide. The nose, throat, lungs, and passageways that lead to the lungs make up the respiratory system.

 STUDY TIP

Compare Make a chart showing the features of the different parts of the respiratory system.

☑ **READING CHECK**

1. Define What is respiration?

_____
_____
_____
_____

Parts of the Respiratory System

Nose
Pharynx
Larynx
Trachea
Bronchus
Lung
Diaphragm

TAKE A LOOK

2. List What are the parts of the respiratory system?

_____
_____
_____
_____

SECTION 4 The Respiratory System *continued*

THE NOSE, PHARYNX, LARYNX, AND TRACHEA

Your *nose* is the main passageway into and out of the respiratory system. You breathe air in through your nose. You also breathe air out of your nose. Air can also enter and leave through your mouth. ☑

From the nose or mouth, air flows through the **pharynx**, or throat. Food and drink also move through the pharynx on the way to the stomach. The pharynx branches into two tubes. One tube, the *esophagus*, leads to the stomach. The other tube leads to the lungs. The larynx sits at the start of this tube.

The **larynx** is the part of the throat that contains the vocal cords. The *vocal cords* are bands of tissue that stretch across the larynx. Muscles connected to the larynx control how much the vocal cords are stretched. When air flows between the vocal cords, the cords vibrate. These vibrations make sound.

The larynx guards the entrance to a large tube called the **trachea**, or windpipe. The trachea is the passageway for air traveling from the larynx to the lungs. ☑

THE BRONCHI AND ALVEOLI

Inside your chest, the trachea splits into two branches called **bronchi** (singular, *bronchus*). One bronchus connects to each lung. Each bronchus branches into smaller and smaller tubes. These branches form a smaller series of airways called *bronchioles*. In the lungs, each bronchiole branches to form tiny sacs that are called **alveoli** (singular, *alveolus*).

> **READING CHECK**
>
> **3. Describe** What is the main function of the nose?
>
> _____
>
> _____
>
> _____

> **READING CHECK**
>
> **4. Identify** What is the trachea?
>
> _____
>
> _____

TAKE A LOOK

5. Infer Which do you have the most of in your lungs: bronchi, bronchioles, or alveoli?

_____

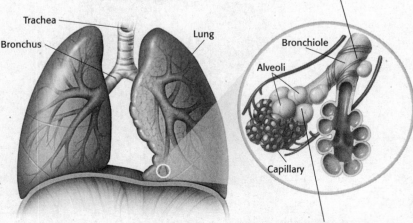

Inside your lungs, the bronchi branch into bronchioles.

Trachea
Bronchus
Lung
Bronchiole
Alveoli
Capillary

The bronchioles branch into tiny sacs called alveoli. Gases can move between the alveoli and the blood that is in the capillaries.

SECTION 4 The Respiratory System *continued*

How Does Breathing Work?

Your lungs have no muscles of their own. Instead, your diaphragm and rib muscles do the work that helps you breathe. The *diaphragm* is a dome-shaped muscle underneath the lungs. When the diaphragm contracts and moves down, you inhale. At the same time, some of your rib muscles contract and lift your rib cage. The volume of your chest gets larger. As a result, air is sucked in.

Exhaling is this process in reverse. Your diaphragm relaxes, your rib muscles relax, and air moves out.

BREATHING AND CELLULAR RESPIRATION

In cellular respiration, cells use oxygen to release the energy that is stored in molecules of a sugar. This sugar is called *glucose*. When cells break down glucose, they give off carbon dioxide.

Oxygen moves into your blood. Your red blood cells carry the oxygen to other parts of your body.

Alveoli

Blood

CO_2 enters the blood. The blood carries the carbon dioxide back to the lungs.

Carbon dioxide gas can move from your blood into your lungs to be exhaled.

Capillary

Tissues and cells pick up O_2 from the blood.

When you breathe in, air enters your lungs. The air contains oxygen gas. When you breathe out, air moves out of your lungs. The air carries carbon dioxide out of your body.

Critical Thinking

6. Predict Consequences What would happen to a person whose diaphragm could not contract?

_____

_____

TAKE A LOOK

7. Explain How does oxygen gas get from the air into the cells in your body?

_____

_____

_____

_____

_____

What Are Some Respiratory Disorders?

People who have *respiratory disorders* have trouble getting the oxygen they need. Their cells cannot release all the energy they need from the food they eat. Therefore, these people may feel tired all the time. They may also have problems getting rid of carbon dioxide. The carbon dioxide can build up in their cells and make them sick.

Respiratory Disorder	What it is
Asthma	A disorder that causes bronchioles to narrow, making it hard to breathe.
Emphysema	A disorder caused when alveoli are damaged.
Severe Acute Respiratory Syndrome (SARS)	A disorder caused by a virus that makes it hard to breathe.

Section 4 Review

SECTION VOCABULARY

alveolus any of the tiny air sacs of the lungs where oxygen and carbon dioxide are exchanged	**respiration** the exchange of oxygen and carbon dioxide between living cells and their environment; includes breathing and cellular respiration
bronchus one of the two tubes that connect the lungs with the trachea	**respiratory system** a collection of organs whose primary function is to take in oxygen and expel carbon dioxide; the organs of this system include the lungs, the throat, and the passageways that lead to the lungs
larynx the area of the throat that contains the vocal cords and produces vocal sounds	
pharynx in flatworms, the muscular tube that leads from the mouth to the gastrovascualr cavity; in animals with a digestive tract, the passage from the mouth to the larynx and esophagus	**trachea** in insects, myriapods, and spiders, one of the network of air tubes; in vertebrates, the tube that connects the larynx to the lungs

1. **List** What are three respiratory disorders?

_____

2. **Define** What is cellular respiration?

_____

_____

3. **Compare** How is respiration different from breathing?

_____

_____

4. **Explain** The nose is the main way for air to get into and out of your body. How can a person still breathe if his or her nose is blocked?

_____

5. **Describe** How do vocal cords produce sound?

_____

_____

6. **Explain** What are two ways that a respiratory disorder can make a person sick?

_____

_____

_____

CHAPTER 24 The Digestive and Urinary Systems

SECTION 1

The Digestive System

National Science Education Standards
LS 1a, 1d, 1e, 1f, 3b

BEFORE YOU READ

After you read this section, you should be able to answer these questions:

- What are the parts of the digestive system?
- How does each part of the digestive system work?

What Are the Parts of the Digestive System?

The **digestive system** is a group of organs that break down, or digest, food so your body can get nutrients. The main organs of the digestive system make one long tube through the body. This tube is called the *digestive tract*. The digestive tract includes the mouth, pharynx, esophagus, stomach, small intestine, and large intestine.

The digestive system has several organs that are not part of the digestive tract. The liver, gallbladder, pancreas, and salivary glands add materials to the digestive tract to help break down food. However, food does not go into these organs. ☑

The Digestive System

- Teeth
- Mouth
- Salivary glands
- Pharynx
- Esophagus
- Liver
- Stomach
- Gallbladder
- Pancreas
- Small intestine
- Large intestine
- Rectum
- Anus

STUDY TIP

Organize As you read, make combination notes about each digestive organ. Write the function of the organ in the left column of the notes. Draw or describe the structure in the right column.

✓ READING CHECK

1. Identify What is the name of the tube that food passes through?

_____
_____

TAKE A LOOK

2. Color Use a colored pencil to shade all of the digestive organs that food passes through.

SECTION 1 The Digestive System *continued*

3. Infer How does the circulatory system work with the digestive system?

_____
_____
_____
_____
_____

Critical Thinking

4. Infer Why do you think you should chew your food well before you swallow it?

_____
_____
_____
_____
_____

Math Focus

5. Compute Ratios Young children get a first set of 20 teeth called *baby teeth*. These teeth usually fall out and are replaced by 32 permanent teeth. What is the ratio of baby teeth to permanent teeth?

_____
_____

How Is Food Broken Down?

The sandwich you eat for lunch has to be broken into tiny pieces to be absorbed into your blood. First, food is crushed and mashed into smaller pieces. This is called *mechanical digestion*. However, the food is still too large to enter your blood. Next, the small pieces of food are broken into their chemical parts, or molecules. This is called *chemical digestion*. The molecules can now be taken in and used by the body's cells.

Most food is made up of three types of nutrients: carbohydrates, proteins, and fats. The digestive system uses proteins called *enzymes* to break your food into molecules. Enzymes act as chemical scissors to cut food into smaller particles that the body can use.

What Happens to Food in the Mouth and Stomach?

MOUTH

Digestion begins in the mouth where food is chewed. You use your teeth to mash and grind food. Chewing creates small, slippery pieces of food that are easy to swallow. As you chew, the food mixes with a liquid called *saliva*. Saliva is made in salivary glands in the mouth. Saliva has enzymes that start breaking down starches into simple sugars.

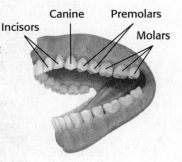

Most adults have 32 permanent teeth. Each type of permanent tooth has a different role in breaking up food.

Incisors   Canine   Premolars   Molars

ESOPHAGUS

Once the food has been chewed to a soft mush, it can be swallowed. The tongue pushes the food into the *pharynx*. The *pharynx* is the part of the throat that makes food go to the esophagus and air go to the lungs. The **esophagus** is a long, straight tube that leads from the pharynx to the stomach. Muscle contractions, called *peristalsis*, squeeze food in the esophagus down to the stomach.

SECTION 1 The Digestive System *continued*

STOMACH

The stomach is a muscular, saclike organ. The stomach uses its muscles to continue mechanical digestion. It squeezes and mashes food into smaller and smaller pieces.

The stomach also has glands that make enzymes and acid. These chemicals help break down food into nutrients. Stomach acid also kills most bacteria in the food. After a few hours of chemical and mechanical digestion, the food is a soupy mixture called *chyme.* ☑

✔ **READING CHECK**

6. Identify What kinds of digestion occur in the stomach?

_____

_____

The stomach squeezes and mixes food for hours before it releases the mixture into the small intestine.

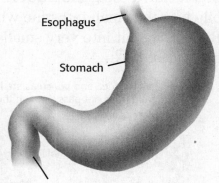

Esophagus

Stomach

Part of small intestine

What Happens to Food in the Small and Large Intestines?

Most chemical digestion takes place after food leaves the stomach. Chyme slowly leaves the stomach and enters the small intestine. The pancreas, liver, and gallbladder add enzymes and other fluids to the small intestine to help finish digestion. The large intestine absorbs water and gets rid of waste.

PANCREAS

The **pancreas** is an organ located between the stomach and small intestine. Food does not enter the pancreas. Instead, the pancreas makes a fluid that flows into the small intestine. The chart below shows the chemicals that make up this pancreatic fluid, and the function of each.

TAKE A LOOK

7. Identify What is the role of enzymes in pancreatic fluid?

_____

_____

_____

Chemical in pancreatic fluid	Function
sodium bicarbonate	to protect the small intestine from acid in the chyme
enzymes	to chemically digest chyme
hormones	to control blood sugar levels

LIVER

The **liver** is a large, reddish brown organ found on the right side of the body under the ribs. The liver helps with digestion in the following ways.

- It makes bile.
- It stores extra nutrients.
- It breaks down toxins, such as alcohol.

GALLBLADDER

Bile is made in the liver, and stored in a small, saclike organ called the **gallbladder**. The gallbladder squeezes bile into the small intestine when there is food to digest. Bile breaks fat into very small droplets so that enzymes can digest it. ☑

The liver, gall bladder, and pancreas are linked to the small intestine. However, food does not pass through these organs.

Liver
Stomach
Gallbladder
Pancreas
Part of the small intestine

SMALL INTESTINE

The **small intestine** is a long, thin, muscular tube where nutrients are absorbed. If you stretched out your small intestine, it would be much longer than you are tall—about 6 m! If you flattened out the surfaces of the small intestine, it would be larger than a tennis court.

The inside wall of the small intestine is covered with many small folds. The folds are covered with cells called *villi*. Villi absorb nutrients. The large number of folds and villi increase the surface area of the small intestine. A large surface area helps the body get as many nutrients from food as possible. ☑

READING CHECK

8. Identify What is the function of bile?

_____

_____

_____

TAKE A LOOK

9. Identify Which organs in this diagram does food pass through?

_____

_____

_____

READING CHECK

10. Explain Why is a large surface area in the small intestine important?

_____

_____

_____

_____

The inside of the small intestine is folded.
The folds are covered with finger-like
structures called **villi**.

Villi are covered
with cells that
absorb nutrients and
pass them to the
bloodstream.

TAKE A LOOK
11. Explain How do
nutrients get into the
bloodstream?

_____

_____

_____

_____

Most nutrient molecules are taken into the blood from
the small intestine. However, the body can't use everything you eat. The soupy mixture of water and food that
cannot be absorbed moves into the large intestine.

LARGE INTESTINE

The **large intestine** is the last part of the digestive
tract. It stores, compacts, and rids the body of waste.
The large intestine is wider than the small intestine, but
shorter. It takes most of the water out of the mixture
from the small intestine. By removing water, the large
intestine changes the liquid into mostly solid waste called
feces, or *stool*.

The *rectum* is the last part of the large intestine. The
rectum stores feces until your body can get rid of them.
Feces leave the body through an opening called the *anus*.
It takes about 24 hours for food to make the trip from
your mouth to the end of the large intestine.

You can help keep your digestive system healthy by
eating whole grains, fruits, and vegetables. These foods
contain a carbohydrate called *cellulose*, or *fiber*. Humans
cannot digest fiber. However, fiber keeps the stool soft and
keeps materials moving well through the large intestine.

 Say It

Name With a partner, name
as many foods as you can
that are sources of fiber.

Section 1 Review

NSES LS 1a, 1d, 1e, 1f, 3b

SECTION VOCABULARY

digestive system the organs that break down food so that it can be used by the body	**pancreas** the organ that lies behind the stomach and that makes digestive enzymes and hormones that regulate sugar levels
esophagus a long, straight tube that connects the pharynx to the stomach	**small intestine** the organ between the stomach and the large intestine where most of the breakdown of food happens and most of the nutrients from food are absorbed
gallbladder a sac-shaped organ that stores bile produced by the liver	
large intestine the wider and shorter portion of the intestine that removes water from mostly digested food and that turns the waste into semisolid feces, or stool	**stomach** the saclike, digestive organ between the esophagus and the small intestine and that breaks down food by the action of muscles, enzymes, and acids
liver the largest organ in the body; it makes bile, stores and filters blood, and stores excess sugars as glycogen	

1. List What organs in the digestive system are not part of the digestive tract?

_____

_____

2. Describe What is the function of saliva?

_____

_____

3. Compare How is chemical digestion different from mechanical digestion?

_____

_____

_____

4. List Name three places in the digestive tract where chemical digestion takes place.

_____

5. Explain How does the structure of the small intestine help it absorb nutrients?

_____

_____

6. Apply Concepts How would digestion change if the liver didn't make bile?

_____

_____

_____

_____

CHAPTER 24 The Digestive and Urinary Systems

SECTION
2 **The Urinary System**

BEFORE YOU READ

After you read this section, you should be able to answer these questions:

• What is the function of the urinary system?

• How do the kidneys filter the blood?

• What are common problems with the urinary system?

National Science Education Standards
LS 1a, 1c, 1d, 1e, 1f, 3a, 3b

What Does the Urinary System Do?

As your cells break down food for energy, they produce waste. Your body must get rid of this waste or it could poison you! As blood moves through the body and drops off oxygen, it picks up the waste from cells. The **urinary system** is made of organs that take wastes from the blood and send them out of the body.

The chart below describes the main organs of the urinary system.

STUDY TIP

Underline As you read, underline any unfamiliar words. Use the glossary or a dictionary to find out what these words mean. Write the definitions in the margins of the text.

Organ	What it looks like	Function
Kidneys	a pair of organs	to clean the blood and produce urine
Ureters	pair of thin tubes leading from the kidneys to the bladder	to carry urine from the kidneys to the bladder
Urinary bladder	a sac	to store urine
Urethra	tube leading from the bladder to outside your body	to carry urine out of the body

TAKE A LOOK
1. Identify Which organs clean the blood?

_____

The Urinary System

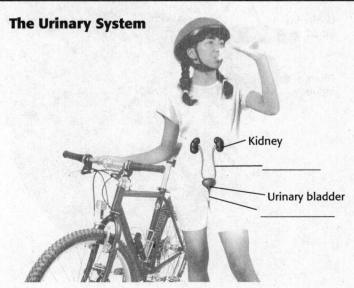

Kidney

_____

Urinary bladder

_____

TAKE A LOOK
2. Identify Use the chart above to help you label the organs of the urinary system.

SECTION 2 The Urinary System *continued*

Math Focus

3. Calculate Your kidneys filter about 2,000 L of blood each day. Your body has about 5.6 L of blood. About how many times does your blood cycle through your kidneys each day?

_____

How Do the Kidneys Clean the Blood?

The **kidneys** are a pair of organs that clean the blood. Each kidney is made of many small filters called **nephrons**. Nephrons remove waste from the blood. One of the most important substances that nephrons remove is urea. *Urea* is formed when your cells use protein for energy. The figure below shows how kidneys clean the blood.

How the Kidneys Filter Blood

❶ Blood enters the kidney through an artery and moves into nephrons.

❷ Water, sugar, salts, urea, and other waste products move out of the blood and into the nephron.

❸ The nephron returns most of the water and nutrients to the blood. The wastes are left in the nephron.

❹ The cleaned blood leaves the kidney and goes back to the body.

❺ The waste left in the nephron is a yellow fluid called *urine*. Urine leaves the kidneys through tubes called *ureters*.

❻ The urine is stored in the bladder. Urine leaves the body through the urethra.

Nephron

Artery

Unfiltered blood

Filtered blood

Vein

Ureter

Urine

TAKE A LOOK

4. Explain What happens to blood after it is cleaned in the kidneys?

_____

_____

_____

5. Identify What structures carry urine from the kidneys?

_____

How Does the Urinary System Control Water?

You lose water every day in sweat and urine, and you replace water when you drink. You need to get rid of as much water as you drink. If you don't, your body will swell up. Chemical messengers called *hormones* help control this balance.

One of these hormones is called *antidiuretic hormone* (ADH). ADH keeps your body from losing too much water. When there is not much water in your blood, ADH tells the nephrons to put water back in the blood. The body then makes less urine. If there is too much water in your blood, your body releases less ADH.

Drinking water when you exercise helps replace the water you lose when you sweat.

Some drinks contain caffeine, which is a diuretic. *Diuretics* cause kidneys to make more urine. This means that a drink with caffeine can actually cause you to lose water.

What Problems Can Happen in the Urinary System?

The chart below shows some common problems of the urinary system.

Problem	Description	Treatment
Bacterial infections	Bacteria can infect the urinary system and cause pain or permanent damage.	Antibiotics
Kidney stones	Wastes can be trapped in the kidney and form small stones. They can stop urine flow and cause pain.	Most can pass out of the body on their own. Some may need to be removed by a doctor.
Kidney disease	Damage to the nephrons can stop the kidneys from working.	A kidney machine can be used to filter the blood.

Critical Thinking

6. Infer What do you think happens when your body releases less ADH?

_____

_____

_____

_____

_____

TAKE A LOOK
7. Explain What problems do kidney stones cause?

_____

_____

_____

Section 2 Review

SECTION VOCABULARY

kidney one of the pair of organs that filter water and wastes from the blood and that excrete products as urine **nephron** the unit in the kidney that filters blood	**urinary system** the organs that make, store, and eliminate urine.

1. List What are the main organs that make up the urinary system?

_____

2. Summarize Complete the process chart to show how blood is filtered.

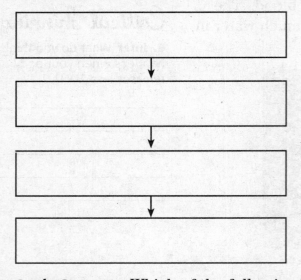

    a. Water is put back in the blood.

    b. Blood goes into the kidney.

    c. Water and waste go into the nephron.

    d. Nephrons separate water and waste.

3. Apply Concepts Which of the following has more water: the blood going into the kidney, or the blood leaving it? Explain your answer.

_____

_____

_____

4. Explain How does the urinary system control the amount of water in the body?

_____

_____

_____

5. Infer Is it a good idea to drink beverages with caffeine when you are exercising? Explain your answer.

_____

_____

_____

CHAPTER 25 Communication and Control

SECTION 1 The Nervous System

National Science
Education Standards
LS 1a, 1d, 1e, 3b, 3c

BEFORE YOU READ

After you read this section, you should be able to answer these questions:

• What does the nervous system do?

• What is the structure of the nervous system?

What Are the Two Main Parts of the Nervous System?

What is one thing that you have done today that did not involve your nervous system? This is a trick question! Your nervous system controls almost everything you do.

The nervous system has two basic functions. First, it collects information and decides what the information means. This information comes from inside your body and from the world outside your body. Second, the nervous system responds to the information it has collected.

The nervous system has two parts: the central nervous system and the peripheral nervous system. The **central nervous system** (CNS) includes the brain and the spinal cord. The CNS takes in and responds to information from the peripheral nervous system. ☑

The **peripheral nervous system** (PNS) includes all the parts of the nervous system except the brain and the spinal cord. The PNS connects all parts of the body to the CNS. Special structures called nerves in the PNS carry information between the body and the CNS.

Part of the nervous system	What it includes	What it does
Central nervous system (CNS)		takes in and responds to messages from the PNS
Peripheral nervous system (PNS)		

STUDY TIP

Organize As you read, make a chart that describes different structures in the nervous system.

READING CHECK

1. Identify What are the two main parts of the nervous system?

_____

_____

_____

_____

TAKE A LOOK

2. Summarize Complete the chart to describe the main parts of the nervous system.

SECTION 1 The Nervous System *continued*

Math Focus

3. Calculate To calculate how long an impulse takes to travel a certain distance, you can use the following equation:

$$time = \frac{distance}{speed}$$

If an impulse travels 100 m/s, about how long will it take the impulse to travel 10 meters?

_____

TAKE A LOOK

4. Identify Add an arrow to the diagram that shows the direction of impulses at the dendrites.

 Say It

Identify In a small group, discuss what you think sensory receptors in your eyes, nose, ears, and finger tips respond to.

How Does Information Move Through the Nervous System?

Special cells called **neurons** carry the information that travels through your nervous system. Neurons carry information in the form of electrical energy. These electrical messages are called *impulses*. Impulses may travel up to 150 m/s!

Like any other cell in your body, a neuron has a nucleus and organelles. The nucleus and organelles are found in the *cell body* of the neuron. However, neurons also have structures called dendrites and axons that are not found in other kinds of cells.

Dendrites are parts of the neuron that branch from the cell body. Most dendrites are very short compared to the rest of the neuron. A single neuron may have many dendrites. Dendrites bring messages from other cells to the cell body.

Axons are longer than dendrites. Some axons can be as long as 1 m! Axons carry information away from the cell body to other cells. The end of an axon is called an *axon terminal*.

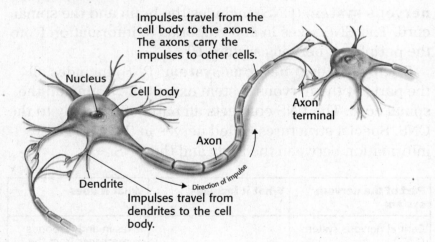

Impulses travel from the cell body to the axons. The axons carry the impulses to other cells.

Nucleus

Cell body

Axon terminal

Axon

Dendrite

Direction of impulse

Impulses travel from dendrites to the cell body.

SENSORY NEURONS

Some neurons are sensory neurons. *Sensory neurons* carry information about what is happening in and around your body. Some sensory neurons are called receptors. *Receptors* can detect changes inside and outside your body. For example, receptors in your eyes can sense light. Sensory neurons carry information from the receptors to the CNS.

MOTOR NEURONS

Motor neurons carry impulses from the CNS to other parts of your body. Most motor neurons carry impulses to muscle cells. When muscles cells receive impulses from motor neurons, the muscle cells contract. Some motor neurons carry impulses to glands, such as sweat glands. These messages tell sweat glands when to make sweat.

NERVES

In many parts of your body, groups of axons are wrapped together with blood vessels and connective tissue to form bundles. These bundles are called **nerves**. Your central nervous system is connected to the rest of your body by nerves.

Nerves are found everywhere in your PNS. Most nerves contain axons from both sensory neurons and motor neurons. Many nerves carry impulses from your CNS to your PNS. Other nerves carry impulses from your PNS to your CNS.

Spinal cord

An impulse from the brain travels down the spinal cord. Then, it travels along the axon of a motor neuron inside a nerve. The axon connects to a muscle. The impulse makes the muscle contract.

Nerve

Muscle fiber

Axon terminal

Axon

What Are the Parts of the Peripheral Nervous System?

Recall that the PNS connects the CNS to the rest of the body. Sensory neurons and motor neurons are both found in the PNS. Sensory neurons carry information to the CNS. Motor neurons carry information from the CNS to the PNS. The motor neurons in the PNS make up two groups: the somatic nervous system and the autonomic nervous system. ☑

STANDARDS CHECK

LS 1d Specialized cells perform specialized functions in multicellular organisms. Groups of specialized cells cooperate to form a tissue, such as a muscle. Different tissues are in turn grouped together and form larger functional units called organs. Each type of cell, tissue, and organ has a distinct <u>structure</u> and set of <u>functions</u> that serve the organism as a whole.

Word Help: <u>structure</u>
a whole that is built or put together from parts

Word Help: <u>function</u>
use or purpose

5. Predict What would happen if your nerves stopped working?

_____
_____
_____
_____
_____

✓ **READING CHECK**

6. Identify What are the two main groups of motor neurons in the PNS?

_____
_____
_____
_____

THE SOMATIC NERVOUS SYSTEM

The *somatic nervous* system is made up of motor neurons that you can control. These neurons are connected to skeletal muscles. They control voluntary movements, or movements that you have to think about. These movements include walking, writing, and talking.

THE AUTONOMIC NERVOUS SYSTEM

The *autonomic nervous system* controls body functions that you do not have to think about. These include digestion and the beating of your heart. The main job of the autonomic nervous system is to keep all of the body's functions in balance.

The autonomic nervous system has two divisions: the *sympathetic nervous system* and the *parasympathetic nervous system*. These two divisions work together to maintain a stable state inside your body. This stable state is called *homeostasis*. The table below shows how the sympathetic and parasympathetic nervous systems work together. ☑

Critical Thinking

7. Explain How does eating a piece of pizza involve both the somatic and autonomic nervous systems?

_____

_____

_____

_____

_____

✓ **READING CHECK**

8. Identify What are the two divisions of the autonomic nervous system?

_____

_____

Organ	Effect of sympathetic nervous system	Effect of parasympathetic nervous system
Eye	makes pupils larger to let in more light	returns pupils to normal size
Heart	raises heart rate to increase blood flow	lowers heart rate to decrease blood flow
Lungs	makes bronchioles larger to get more oxygen into the blood	returns bronchioles to normal size
Blood vessels	makes blood vessels smaller to increase blood pressure	has little or no effect
Intestines	reduces blood flow to stomach and intestines to slow digestion	returns digestion to normal pace

What Are the Parts of the Central Nervous System?

The central nervous system receives information from sensory neurons. It responds by sending messages to the body through motor neurons. The CNS is made of two important organs: the brain and the spinal cord.

The **brain** is the control center of the nervous system. It is also the largest organ in the nervous system. Many processes that the brain controls are involuntary. However, the brain also controls many voluntary processes. The brain has three main parts: the cerebrum, the cerebellum, and the medulla. Each part of the brain has its own job.

THE CEREBRUM

The *cerebrum* is the largest part of your brain. This dome-shaped area is where you think and where most memories are kept. The cerebrum controls voluntary movements. It also lets you sense touch, light, sound, odors, tastes, pain, heat, and cold. ☑

The cerebrum is made up of two halves called *hemispheres*. The left hemisphere controls most movements on the right side of the body. The right hemisphere controls most movements on the left side of the body. The two hemispheres also control different types of activities, as shown in the figure below. However, most brain activities use both hemispheres.

✔ **READING CHECK**

9. Identify What kind of movements does the cerebrum control?

_____

_____

TAKE A LOOK

10. Explain Which hemisphere of your brain are you mainly using as you read this book? Explain your answer.

_____

_____

_____

_____

_____

_____

The **left hemisphere** mainly controls activities such as speaking, reading, writing, and solving problems.

The **right hemisphere** mainly controls activities such as processing music and interpreting emotions.

Top of Brain

THE CEREBELLUM

The *cerebellum* is found beneath the cerebrum. The cerebellum receives and processes information from your body, such as from your skeletal muscles and joints. This information lets the brain keep track of your body's position. For example, your cerebellum lets you know when you are upside-down. Your cerebellum also sends messages to your muscles to help you keep your balance. ☑

THE MEDULLA

The *medulla* is the part of your brain that connects to your spinal cord. It is only about 3 cm long, but you cannot live without it. It controls involuntary processes, such as breathing and regulating heart rate.

Your medulla is always receiving sensory impulses from receptors in your blood vessels. It uses this information to control your blood pressure. If your blood pressure gets too low, your medulla sends impulses that cause blood vessels to tighten. This makes your blood pressure rise. The medulla also sends impulses to the heart to make it beat faster or slower.

READING CHECK

11. Identify What are two functions of the cerebellum?

_____

_____

_____

_____

TAKE A LOOK

12. Identify Which part of the brain controls breathing?

_____

13. Identify Which part of the brain senses smells?

_____

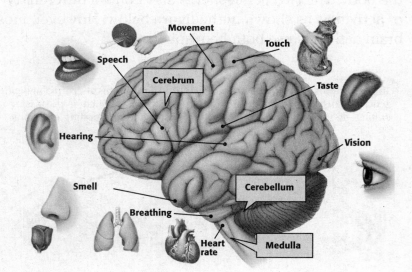

SECTION 1 The Nervous System *continued*

THE SPINAL CORD

Your spinal cord is part of your central nervous system. It is made up of neurons and bundles of axons that send impulses to and from the brain. The spinal cord is surrounded by bones called *vertebrae* (singular, *vertebra*) to protect it.

The axons in your spinal cord let your brain communicate with your PNS. The axons of sensory neurons carry impulses from your skin and muscles to your spinal cord. The impulses travel through the spinal cord to your brain. The brain then processes the impulses and sends signals back through the spinal cord. The impulses travel from the spinal cord to motor neurons. The axons of motor neurons carry the signals to your body.

Critical Thinking

14. Explain What is one way your nervous system and skeletal system work together?

_____

_____

_____

_____

_____

Spinal cord

Vertebra

Motor information

Sensory information

The spinal cord carries information to and from the brain. Vertebrae protect the spinal cord.

SPINAL CORD INJURIES

A spinal cord injury may block the messages to and from the brain. For example, a spinal cord injury might block signals to and from the feet and legs. People with such an injury cannot sense pain, touch, or temperature in their feet or legs. They may not be able to move their legs.

Each year, thousands of people are paralyzed by spinal cord injuries. Most spinal cord injuries in young people happen during sports. You can help prevent such injuries by using proper safety equipment. ☑

✓ READING CHECK

15. Identify How can you help prevent spinal cord injuries while playing sports?

_____

_____

_____

Section 1 Review

SECTION VOCABULARY

brain the mass of nerve tissue that is the main control center of the nervous system	**neuron** a nerve cell that is specialized to receive and conduct electrical impulses
central nervous system the brain and the spinal cord	**peripheral nervous system** all of the parts of the nervous system except for the brain and the spinal cord
nerve a collection of nerve fibers through which impulses travel between the central nervous system and other parts of the body	

1. Compare How do the functions of the CNS and the PNS differ?

_____

_____

_____

2. Summarize Complete the diagram below to show the structure of the nervous system.

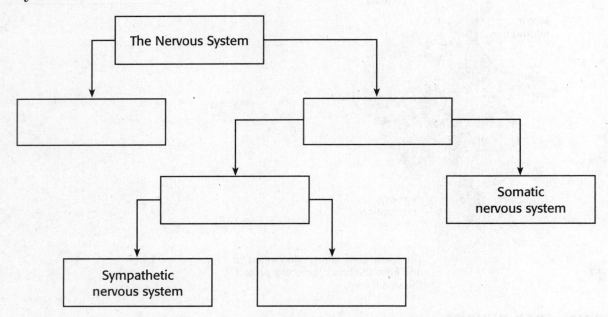

3. Compare How do the functions of dendrites and axons differ?

_____

_____

4. Explain What can happen to someone with a spinal cord injury?

_____

_____

_____

CHAPTER 25 Communication and Control

SECTION 2 Responding to the Environment

National Science
Education Standards
LS 1a, 1d, 1e, 3a

BEFORE YOU READ

After you read this section, you should be able to answer these questions:

• How do the integumentary system and nervous system work together?

• What is a feedback mechanism?

• How do your five senses work?

How Does Your Sense of Touch Work?

When a friend taps you on the shoulder or when you feel a breeze, how does your brain know what has happened? Receptors throughout your body gather information about the environment and send this information to your brain.

You skin is part of the integumentary system. The **integumentary system** is an organ system that protects the body. This system also includes hair and nails. Your skin is the main organ that helps you sense touch. It has many different *sensory receptors* that are part of the nervous system. Each kind of receptor responds mainly to one kind of stimulation. For example, *thermoreceptors* respond to temperature changes.

Sensory receptors detect a stimulus and create impulses. These impulses travel to your brain. In your brain, the impulses produce a sensation. A *sensation* is the awareness of a stimulus.

STUDY TIP

List As you read, make a list of the five senses. In your list, include the type of receptors used by those senses.

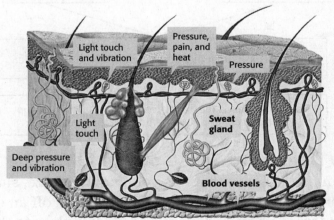

Your skin is made of several layers of tissues and contains many structures. Different kinds of receptors in your skin can sense different things.

TAKE A LOOK

1. List What are three types of sensations that your skin can detect?

_____

_____

_____

REFLEXES

When you step on something sharp, pain receptors in your foot send messages to your spinal cord. The spinal cord sends a message back to move your foot. This immediate reaction that you can't control is a **reflex**. Messages that cause reflexes do not travel all the way to your brain. If you had to wait for your brain to act, you could be badly hurt.

FEEDBACK MECHANISMS

Most of the time, the brain decides what to do with the messages from the skin receptors. Your brain helps to control many of your body's functions by using feedback mechanisms. A **feedback mechanism** is a cycle of events in which one step controls or affects another step. In the example below, your brain senses a change in temperature. It tells your sweat glands and blood vessels to react. ☑

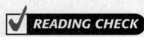

Say It

Discuss With a partner, name some other examples of reflexes. What part of the body is involved? When does the reflex happen? How does the reflex protect your body?

✓ READING CHECK

2. Complete Feedback mechanisms in your nervous system are controlled by the

_____.

On a hot day, heat receptors in your skin detect a change in temperature.

↓

Your brain sends messages to your sweat glands to make sweat, and it tells blood vessels to expand.

Sweat glands make sweat → Your body cools.

Blood vessels expand. → Heat leaves the blood.

Receptors in skin detect that the body has gotten cooler.

↓

Your brain sends messages to tell sweat glands to stop making sweat and to tell blood vessels to constrict.

How Does Your Sense of Sight Work?

Sight is the sense that lets you know the size, shape, motion, and color of objects. Light bounces off an object and enters your eyes. Your eyes send impulses to the brain that produce the sensation of sight.

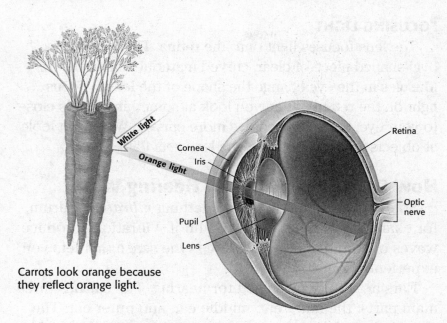

Carrots look orange because they reflect orange light.

Eyes are complex sensory organs. A clear membrane called the *cornea* protects the eye but lets light through. Light enters an opening called the *pupil*. The light then travels through the lens and hits the retina at the back of the eye.

The **retina** contains neurons called *photoreceptors* that sense light. When light hits a photoreceptor, it sends electrical impulses to the brain. The brain interprets these impulses as light.

The retina has two kinds of photoreceptors: rods and cones. *Rods* are very sensitive to dim light. They are important for night vision and for seeing in black and white. *Cones* are very sensitive to bright light. They let you see colors and fine details. ☑

The impulses from rods and cones travel along axons. The axons form the optic nerve that carries the impulses to your brain.

READING CHECK
4. Identify What are the two kinds of photoreceptors in the retina?

_____

_____

REACTING TO LIGHT
Your pupil looks like a black dot in the center of your eye. Actually, it is an opening that lets light enter the eye. Around the pupil is a ring of muscle called the *iris*. The iris controls how much light enters your eye. It also gives your eye its color. ☑

READING CHECK
5. Identify What is the function of the iris?

_____

_____

_____

In bright light the iris contracts. This makes the pupil smaller.

In dim light the iris relaxes. This makes the pupil dilate, or get larger

SECTION 2 **Responding to the Environment** *continued*

FOCUSING LIGHT

The lens focuses light onto the retina. The *lens* is an oval-shaped piece of clear, curved material behind the iris. Muscles in the eye change the shape of the lens to focus light on the retina. When you look at something that is close to your eye, the lens becomes more curved. When you look at objects that are far away, the lens gets flatter. ☑

How Does Your Sense of Hearing Work?

Sound is produced when something *vibrates*. A drum, for example, vibrates when you hit it. Vibrations produce waves of sound energy. Hearing is the sense that lets you experience sound energy.

Ears are the organs used for hearing. The ear has three main parts: the inner ear, middle ear, and outer ear. The chart below shows the structures and functions of each.

Part of ear	Main structures	Function
Outer ear	ear canal	funnels sound waves into the middle ear
Middle ear	eardrum; three ear bones	sends vibrations to the inner ear
Inner ear	cochlea and auditory nerve	sends impulses to the brain

A sound wave travels through the air into the outer ear. The wave produces vibrations in the middle ear and inner ear. These vibrations produce impulses in the cochlear nerve that travel to the brain

READING CHECK

6. Identify What is the function of the lens?

_____

_____

TAKE A LOOK

7. Identify Use colored pencils to color the outer ear blue, the middle ear green, and the inner ear red.

SECTION 2 **Responding to the Environment** *continued*

SENDING SOUND ENERGY TO YOUR BRAIN

Sound waves create vibrations throughout your ear that your brain can interpret as sound. The outer ear funnels sound waves to the middle ear. Sound waves hit the eardrum and make it vibrate. These vibrations make tiny ear bones vibrate. One of these bones vibrates against the **cochlea**, an organ filled with fluid. The vibrations make waves in the fluid. This causes neurons in the cochlea to send impulses along the auditory nerve to the brain. ☑

How Does Your Sense of Taste Work?

Taste is the sense that lets you detect chemicals and tell one flavor from another flavor. Your tongue is covered with tiny bumps called *papillae* (singular, *papilla*) that contain taste buds. Taste buds have receptors called taste cells that respond to dissolved food molecules in your mouth. Taste cells react to four basic tastes: sweet, sour, salty, and bitter.

How Does Your Sense of Smell Work?

Neurons called *olfactory cells* are located in the nose and have receptors for smell. Your brain combines the information from taste buds and olfactory cells to let you sense flavor.

Molecules that you inhale dissolve in the moist lining of the nasal cavity and trigger an impulse. The brain interprets the impulse as the sensation of smell.

✔ **READING CHECK**

8. Explain What does your brain interpret as sound?

_____

_____

Critical Thinking

9. Apply Concepts Why do you have a hard time tasting things when you have a cold?

_____

_____

_____

_____

_____

_____

Section 2 Review

NSES LS 1a, 1d, 1e, 3a

SECTION VOCABULARY

cochlea a coiled tube that is found in the inner ear and that is essential to hearing	**reflex** an involuntary and almost immediate movement in response to a stimulus
feedback mechanism a cycle of events in which information from one step controls or affects a previous step	**retina** the light-sensitive inner layer of the eye that receives images formed by the lens and transmits them through the optic nerve to the brain
integumentary system the organ system that forms a protective covering on the outside of the body	

1. List What are the five senses?

_____

2. Explain How do the integumentary system and nervous system work together?

_____

_____

_____

3. Explain What are reflexes and why are they important for the body?

_____

_____

_____

4. Explain Why is important for your eyes to have both rods and cones?

_____

_____

_____

5. Summarize Complete the chart to summarize the major senses and sense receptors.

Sense	Receptors	What the receptors respond to
Touch	many different kinds	
Sight		
	neurons in the cochlea	
Taste		dissolved molecules
	olfactory cells	

CHAPTER 25 Communication and Control

SECTION 3 The Endocrine System

- Why is the endocrine system important?
- How do feedback systems work?
- What are common hormone imbalances?

National Science Education Standards
LS 1a, 1d, 1e

What Is the Endocrine System?

The **endocrine system** controls body functions using chemicals made by endocrine glands. A **gland** is a group of cells that makes special chemicals for your body. The chemicals made by endocrine glands are called hormones. A **hormone** is a chemical messenger. It is made in one cell or tissue and causes a change in another cell or tissue. Hormones flow through the bloodstream to all parts of the body. ☑

STUDY TIP

Describe As you read, fill in the chart at the end of the section to name the major endocrine glands and what each one does.

READING CHECK

1. Explain How do hormones move from one part of the body to another?

_____

_____

_____

Glands and Organs of the Endocrine System

The **pituitary gland** makes hormones that affect other glands and organs.

The **parathyroid gland** controls calcium levels in the blood.

The **adrenal glands** help the body respond to danger.

The **pancreas** controls glucose levels in the blood.

The **ovaries** (in females) produce hormones needed for reproduction.

The **thyroid gland** increases the rate at which you use energy.

The **thymus gland** helps control your immune system, which helps your body fight disease.

The **testes** (in males) produce hormones needed for reproduction.

TAKE A LOOK
2. Identify What two structures produce hormones needed for reproduction?

_____

_____

3. Identify Which gland makes hormones that affect organs and other glands?

_____

ADRENAL GLANDS

Endocrine glands may affect many organs at one time. For example, the adrenal glands release the hormone *epinephrine*, sometimes called *adrenaline*. Epinephrine increases your heartbeat and breathing rate. This response is called the fight-or-flight response. When you are scared, angry, or excited, the fight-or-flight response prepares you either to fight the danger or to run from it.

How Do Feedback Systems Work?

Recall how feedback mechanisms work in the nervous system. Feedback mechanisms are cycles in which information from one step controls another step in the cycle. In the endocrine system, endocrine glands control similar feedback mechanisms.

The pancreas has specialized cells that make two different hormones, *insulin* and *glucagon*. These two hormones control the level of glucose in the blood.

Critical Thinking

4. Infer Why do you think increasing your breathing rate helps prepare you to fight or run away?

_____

_____

_____

_____

_____

_____

1 Glucose is fuel for your body. Glucose is absorbed into the bloodstream from the small intestine.

2 When the glucose level in the blood is high, such as after a meal, the pancreas releases the hormone insulin into the blood.

5 Glucagon tells the liver to break down glycogen and release glucose into the blood.

Pancreas

Pancreas

4 When the blood-glucose level is too low, the pancreas releases the hormone glucagon instead of insulin.

3 Insulin signals the liver to take glucose from the blood and store it in the liver as glycogen.

Liver

TAKE A LOOK

5. Explain How could you raise your blood-glucose level without involving hormones?

_____

_____

6. Identify Which hormone tells the liver to release glucose into the blood?

_____

_____

SECTION 3 The Endocrine System *continued*

What Is a Hormone Imbalance?

Sometimes, an endocrine gland makes too much or not enough of a hormone. For example, a person's body may not make enough insulin or be able use it properly. This is a condition called *diabetes mellitus*. A person who has diabetes may need daily injections of insulin. These injections help keep his or her blood-glucose levels within safe limits. Some patients get their insulin automatically from a small machine worn on the body. ☑

This woman has diabetes. She is wearing a device that delivers insulin to her body.

✓ **READING CHECK**
7. Define What is a hormone inbalance?
_____
_____
_____
_____

Another hormone imbalance is when a child's pituitary gland doesn't make enough growth hormone. As a result, the child does not grow as quickly or as much as he or she should. If the problem is found early in childhood, a doctor can prescribe growth hormone.

In some cases, the pituitary gland may make too much growth hormone. This may cause a child to grow taller than expected.

Endocrine gland	Function
Pituitary	
	increases the rate at which you use energy

TAKE A LOOK
8. Summarize Use this chart to help you summarize the major endocrine glands and their functions.

Section 3 Review

SECTION VOCABULARY

endocrine system a collection of glands and groups of cells that secrete hormones that regulate growth, development, and homeostasis; includes the pituitary, thyroid, parathyroid, and adrenal glands, the hypothalamus, the pineal body, and the gonads	**gland** a group of cells that make special chemicals for the body **hormone** a substance that is made in one cell or tissue and that causes a change in another cell or tissue in a different part of the body

1. Explain What is the function of the endocrine system?

_____

2. Compare How are the thymus and thyroid gland similar? How are they different?

_____

_____

_____

3. Identify Relationships How do the circulatory system and the endocrine system work together?

_____

_____

4. Explain What does insulin do?

_____

_____

5. Apply Concepts Many organs in the body are part of more than one organ system. List three examples from this section of organs that are part of both the endocrine system and another organ system.

_____

_____

_____

6. Infer Glucose is a source of energy. Epinephrine quickly raises your blood-glucose level when you are excited or scared. Why is epinephrine important during these times?

_____

_____

_____

CHAPTER 26 Reproduction and Development

SECTION 1 **Animal Reproduction**

BEFORE YOU READ

After you read this section, you should be able to answer these questions:

• What is asexual reproduction?

• What is sexual reproduction?

• What is the difference between external and internal fertilization?

Why Do Organisms Reproduce?

Organisms live for different amounts of time. For example, a fruit fly lives for about 40 days. Some pine trees can live for almost 5,000 years. However, all living things will die. For a species to surivive, its members must reproduce.

How Are Offspring Made with One Parent?

Some animals reproduce asexually. In **asexual reproduction**, one parent has offspring. These offspring are genetically identical to the parent.

Asexual reproduction can occur through budding, fragmentation, or regeneration. *Budding* happens when the offspring buds or grows out from the parent's body. The new organism then pinches off. *Fragmentation* occurs when part of an organism breaks off and then develops into a new organism. *Regeneration* occurs when part of the organism's body is lost and the organism regrows it. The lost body part can also develop into an offspring. ☑

The hydra bud will separate from its parent. Buds from other organisms, such as some coral, stay attached to the parent.

◀ The largest arm on this sea star was lost from another sea star. A new sea star has grown from this arm.

STUDY TIP

Describe As you read, make a chart describing characteristics and types of asexual and sexual reproduction.

READING CHECK

1. List What are three types of asexual reproduction?

_____

_____

_____

TAKE A LOOK

2. Identify What kind of asexual reproduction does this sea star in this picture show?

_____

SECTION 1 Animal Reproduction *continued*

What Is Sexual Reproduction?

Most animals reproduce sexually. In **sexual reproduction**, offspring form when sex cells from more than one parent combine. The offspring will share traits from both parents. Sexual reproduction usually requires two parents—a male and a female. The female makes sex cells called **eggs**. The male makes sex cells called **sperm**. When a sperm and an egg join together, a fertilized egg, or *zygote* is made. This process is called *fertilization.* ☑

Almost all human cells have 46 chromosomes. However, egg and sperm cells only have 23 chromosomes. These sex cells are formed by a process called *meiosis.* In humans, meiosis occurs when one cell with 46 chromosomes divides to make sex cells with 23 chromosomes. This way, when a sperm and egg join, the zygote will have the typical number of chromosomes.

☑ **READING CHECK**

3. Define What is fertilization?

_____
_____
_____

How Do Offspring Get Their Parent's Traits?

Genetic information is carried by *genes.* Genes are located on *chromosomes.* At fertilization in humans, the egg and sperm both give 23 chromosomes to the zygote. This zygote will then develop into an organism that has traits from both parents. The figure below shows how genes are passed from parent to offspring.

TAKE A LOOK
4. Identify What fraction of your genes did you inherit from each grandparent?

_____

Eggs and sperm contain chromosomes. You inherited half of your chromosomes from each parent.

How Does Fertilization Occur?

Fertilization can occur outside or inside the female's body. **External fertilization** occurs when the sperm fertilizes the eggs outside the female's body. Some fish and amphibians, such as frogs, use external fertilization. The female releases her eggs and the male releases his sperm over the eggs. External fertilization generally takes place in wet environments so that the new zygotes do not dry out.

Internal fertilization occurs when an egg and sperm join inside a female's body. This allows the female to protect the developing zygote inside her body. Reptiles, birds, mammals, and some fishes use internal fertilization. Many mammals give birth to well-developed young. However, other animals, such as chickens, use internal fertilization to lay fertilized eggs.

Critical Thinking
5. Infer Name some environments where animals could use external fertilization.

_____

_____

_____

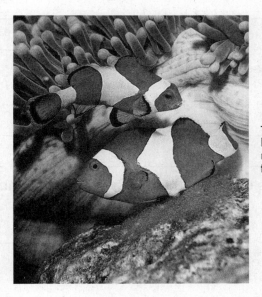

The female clownfish has laid her eggs on the rock. The male will then fertilize them.

TAKE A LOOK
6. Identify Is this an example of internal or external fertlization?

_____

_____

How Do Mammals Reproduce?

All mammals reproduce sexually by internal fertilization. They also feed their young with milk. Mammals reproduce in one of the following ways. ☑

- *Monotremes* lay eggs. A platypus is a monotreme.

- *Marsupials* give birth to young that are not well developed. After birth, the young crawl into their mother's pouch to develop. A kangaroo is a marsupial.

- *Placental mammals* are fed and protected inside their mother's body before birth. These mammals are born well developed. Humans are placental mammals.

READING CHECK
7. Identify Name two ways that all mammals are alike.

_____

_____

_____

Name _____ Class _____ Date _____

Section 1 Review

SECTION VOCABULARY

asexual reproduction reproduction that does not involve the union of sex cells and in which a single parent produces offspring that are genetically identical to the parent	**internal fertilization** fertilization of an egg by sperm that occurs inside the body of a female
egg a sex cell produced by a female	**sexual reproduction** reproduction in which the sex cells from two parents unite to produce offspring that share traits from both parents
external fertilization the union of sex cells outside the bodies of the parents	**sperm** the male sex cell

1. Compare How is fragmentation different from budding?

_____

_____

2. Infer Why is reproduction as important to a bristlecone pine as it is to a fruit fly?

_____

_____

3. Apply Concepts Why is meiosis important in sexual reproduction?

_____

_____

_____

4. Identify What type of reproduction produces offspring that are genetically identical to the parent?

_____

5. Compare What is the difference between external and internal fertilization?

_____

_____

6. Identify What is one advantage of internal fertilization?

_____

_____

7. List What are three groups of animals that use internal fertilization?

_____

CHAPTER 26 Reproduction and Development

SECTION 2 Human Reproduction

National Science
Education Standards
LS 1d, 1f

> ## BEFORE YOU READ
>
> After you read this section, you should be able to answer these questions:
> - How are sperm and eggs made?
> - How does fertilization occur?
> - What problems can happen in the reproductive system?

What Happens in the Male Reproductive System?

The male reproductive system has two functions:

- to make sperm
- to deliver sperm to the female reproductive system

To perform these functions, organs in the male reproductive system make sperm, hormones, and fluids. The **testes** (singular, *testis*) are a pair of organs that hang outside the body covered by a skin sac called the *scrotum*. They make sperm and *testosterone*, the main male sex hormone.

A male can make millions of sperm each day. Immature sperm cells divide and change shape as they travel through the testes and epididymis. The *epididymis* is a tube attached to the testes that stores sperm as they mature. ☑

Mature sperm pass into the *vas deferens*, which connects the epididymis and urethra. The *urethra* is a tube that runs from the bladder through the penis. The **penis** is the male organ that delivers sperm to the female. Before leaving the body, sperm mixes with a fluid mixture to form *semen*.

STUDY TIP

Summarize As you read, create two Process Charts. In the first, describe the path an egg takes from ovulation to fertilization. In the second, describe the path of an egg that does not get fertilized.

READING CHECK

1. Identify How many sperm can a male make in one day?

_____

The Male Reproductive System

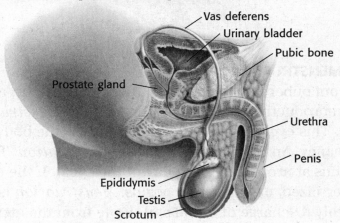

- Vas deferens
- Urinary bladder
- Pubic bone
- Prostate gland
- Urethra
- Penis
- Epididymis
- Testis
- Scrotum

TAKE A LOOK

2. Identify On the diagram, draw an arrow pointing to the structure that makes sperm.

What Happens in the Female Reproductive System?

The female reproductive system has three functions: to produce eggs, to protect and nourish developing offspring, and to give birth. Unlike males, who produce new sperm throughout their lives, females have all their eggs when they are born.

Eggs are produced in an **ovary**. Ovaries also release the main female sex hormones: estrogen and progesterone. These hormones control the release of eggs from the ovaries and the development of female characteristics. Females generally have two ovaries.

THE EGG'S JOURNEY

During *ovulation* an ovary releases an egg. The egg passes into a *fallopian tube*. The fallopian tube leads from the ovary to the uterus. If sperm are present, fertilization usually takes place in the fallopian tube.

After fertilization, the embryo moves to the uterus and may embed in the thick lining. An embyo develops into a fetus in the **uterus**. When the baby is born, it passes from the uterus and through the vagina. The **vagina** is the canal between the outside of the body and the uterus.

The Female Reproductive System

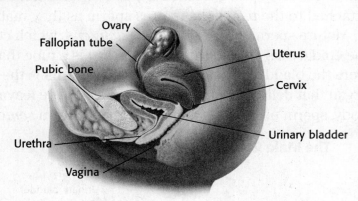

Ovary
Fallopian tube
Pubic bone
Urethra
Vagina
Uterus
Cervix
Urinary bladder

THE MENSTRUAL CYCLE

From puberty through her late 40s or early 50s, a woman's reproductive system goes through the *menstrual cycle*. This cycle of about 28 days prepares the body for pregnancy. An ovary releases an egg at *ovulation*. This happens at around the 14th day of the cycle. If the egg is not fertilized, menstruation begins. *Menstruation* is the monthly discharge of blood and tissue from the uterus.

Math Focus

3. Calculate The average woman ovulates each month from about the age of 12 to about the age of 50. How many mature eggs does she release from age 18 to age 50? Assume that she has never been pregnant.

TAKE A LOOK

4. Identify On the diagram, put a circle around the structure that produces eggs. Put a square around the structure where an embryo develops.

What Problems Can Happen in the Reproductive System?

Problems such as disease can cause the reproductive system to fail. When couples cannot have children, they are considered *infertile*. Men are infertile if they do not make enough healthy sperm. Women are infertile if they do not ovulate normally. Reproductive problems are often caused by sexually transmitted diseases and cancers.

SEXUALLY TRANSMITTED DISEASES

A *sexually transmitted disease* (STD) is a disease that can pass from one person to another during sexual contact. STDs are also called *sexually transmitted infections* (STIs). Sexually-active young people have the highest risk for STDs.

One example of an STD is human immunodeficiency virus (HIV), the virus that leads to AIDS. HIV destroys the immune system of the infected person. People with AIDS generally die from infections that are not fatal to people with healthy immune systems. Below is a table showing the most common STDs and how fast they are spreading in the United States.

STD	Approximate number of new cases each year
Chlamydia	3 to 10 million
Genital HPV (human papilloma virus)	5.5 million
Genital herpes	1 million
Gonorrhea	650,000
Syphilis	70,000
HIV/AIDS	40,000 to 50,000

CANCER

Sometimes cancer happens in reproductive organs. *Cancer* is a disease in which cells grow at an uncontrolled rate. In men, the two most common cancers of the reproductive system happen in the testes and prostate gland. In women, two common reproductive cancers are cancer of the cervix and cancer of the ovaries.

STANDARDS CHECK

LS 1f Disease is the breakdown in structures or functions of an organism. Some diseases are the result of intrinsic failures of the system. Others are the result of damage by infection by other organisms.

5. Identify What are two common causes of reproductive problems?

_____

_____

Critical Thinking

6. Infer In women, some untreated STDs can block the fallopian tubes. How would this affect fertilization?

_____

_____

_____

_____

_____

 Say It

Research Use your school library or the internet to research one of the STDs in the chart. What organism or virus causes it? How does it affect the body? What treatments are available? Present your findings to the class.

Section 2 Review

NSES LS 1d, 1f

SECTION VOCABULARY

ovary an organ in the female reproductive system of animals that produces eggs	**uterus** in female placental mammals, the hollow, muscular organ in which an embryo embeds itself and develops into a fetus
penis the male organ that transfers sperm to a female and that carries urine out of the body	**vagina** the female reproductive organ that connects the outside of the body to the uterus
testes the primary male reproductive organs which produce sperm and testosterone (singular, *testis*)	

1. Explain What is the purpose of the menstrual cycle?

_____

_____

2. Organize Complete the chart below to describe the functions or characteristics of structures in the female reproductive system.

Structure	Characteristic or function
	produces eggs; releases female sex hormones
uterus	
fallopian tube	
	canal that connects uterus to the outside

3. Explain What is fertilization and where does it occur?

_____

_____

4. Apply Concepts Fraternal twins are created when two sperm fertilize two different eggs. Paternal, or identical, twins are created when a single egg divides after fertilization. Why are fraternal twins not identical?

_____

_____

_____

_____

CHAPTER 26 Reproduction and Development

SECTION 3 Growth and Development

National Science
Education Standards
LS 1a, 1c, 1d, 1e, 2b

BEFORE YOU READ

After you read this section, you should be able to answer these questions:

• What happens after an egg is fertilized?

• How does a fetus develop?

• How does a person develop after birth?

How Does Fertilization Occur?

A man can release millions of sperm at once. However, only one sperm can fertilize an egg. Why are so many sperm needed?

Only a few hundred sperm survive the journey from the vagina to the uterus and into a fallopian tube. In the fallopian tube only a few sperm find and cover the egg. Once one sperm enters, or *penetrates*, the egg, it causes the egg's covering to change. This change keeps other sperm from entering the egg. When the nuclei of the sperm and egg join, the egg is fertilized.

Fertilization and Implantation

b The egg is fertilized in the fallopian tube by a sperm.

a The egg is released from the ovary.

c The embryo implants itself in the wall of the uterus.

What Stages Does a Fertilized Egg Go Through?

At fertilization, the egg is only a single cell. At this stage, the fertilized egg is called a *zygote*. As the zygote becomes an embryo it moves down the fallopian tube, and divides many times. After about a week, the **embryo** is a ball of cells. This ball of cells implants in the uterus. ☑

As the cells of the embryo continue to divide, some cells start to *differentiate*. They develop special structures for certain jobs in the body. After week 10 of the pregnanacy, the embryo is called a **fetus**.

STUDY TIP

Summarize As you read, make a a timeline that shows the stages of human development from fertilized egg to adulthood.

Critical Thinking

1. Form Hypothesis Why do you think millions of sperm are released to fertilize one egg?

_____

_____

_____

_____

_____

TAKE A LOOK

2. Identify Where does fertilization usually take place?

_____

_____

READING CHECK

3. Identify What is the egg called right after fertilization?

_____

_____

SECTION 3 Growth and Development *continued*

TAKE A LOOK
4. List List the three stages a fertilized egg goes through as it develops.

_____
_____
_____

| The fertilized egg, called a *zygote*, divides and becomes a ball of cells | → | The ball of cells, called an *embryo*, implants in the uterus | → | The cells of the embryo divide and differentiate; the embryo becomes a *fetus* |

How Does an Embryo Develop?

WEEKS 1 AND 2

A woman's pregnancy starts when an egg is fertilized, and ends at birth. Pregnancy is measured from the starting date of a woman's last menstruation. This is easier than trying to determine the exact date fertilization took place. Fertilization takes place at about the end of week 2. ☑

READING CHECK
5. Explain Why is pregnancy measured from the starting date of the woman's last period?

_____
_____
_____

WEEKS 3 AND 4

In week 3, the embryo moves to the uterus. As the embryo travels, it divides many times. It becomes a ball of cells that implants itself in the wall of the uterus.

WEEKS 5 TO 8

After an embryo implants in the uterus, the placenta forms. The **placenta** is an organ used by the embryo to exchange materials with the mother. The placenta has many blood vessels that carry nutrients and oxygen from the mother to the embryo. They also carry wastes from the embryo to the mother.

In week 5 of pregnancy, the **umbilical cord** forms. It connects the embryo to the placenta. A thin membrane called the amnion develops. The *amnion* surrounds the embryo and is filled with fluid. This fluid cushions and protects the embryo. ☑

READING CHECK
6. Explain What is the function of the umbilical cord?

_____
_____
_____

WEEKS 9 TO 16

At week 9, the embryo may start to make tiny movements. The fetus grows very quickly during this stage. It doubles, then triples in size within a month. In about week 13, the fetus's face begins to look more human. During this stage the fetus's muscles also grow stronger. It can even make a fist.

SECTION 3 Growth and Development *continued*

WEEKS 17 TO 24

By week 17 the fetus can make faces. By week 18 the fetus starts to make movements that its mother can feel. It can also hear sounds through the mother's uterus. By week 23 the fetus makes a lot of movements. A baby born during week 24 might survive, but it would need a lot of help.

Placenta

Umbilical cord

Amnion

Uterus

Cervix

The placenta, amnion, and umbilical cord are the life support system for the fetus. This fetus is about 20 to 22 weeks old.

TAKE A LOOK
7. Identify What structure surrounds the fetus?

_____

_____

WEEKS 25 TO 36

At about 25 or 26 weeks, the fetus's lungs are well-developed. However, they are not fully mature. The fetus still gets oxygen from its mother through the placenta. The fetus will not take its first breath of air until it is born.

By the 32nd week, the fetus can open and close its eyes. Studies show that the fetus responds to light. Some scientists think fetuses at this stage show brain activity and eye movements like sleeping children or adults. These scientists think a sleeping fetus may dream. After 36 weeks, the fetus is almost ready to be born.

BIRTH

At weeks 37 to 38 the fetus is fully developed. A full pregnancy is usually 40 weeks. As birth begins, the muscles of the uterus begin to squeeze, or contract. This is called *labor*. These contractions push the fetus out of the mother's body through the vagina. ☑

Once the baby is born, the umbilical cord is tied and cut. The navel is all that will remain of the point where the umbilical cord was attached. Once the mother's body has pushed out the placenta, labor is complete.

✓ **READING CHECK**

8. Define What is labor?

_____

_____

_____

SECTION 3 Growth and Development *continued*

Pregnancy Timeline

Week

Fertilization takes place.

2 ——————————————• The fertilized egg becomes a ball of hundreds of cells.

4 ———————————• Implantation is complete.

6 — The spinal cord and brain begin to form.

8 ——————————————• Well-defined tiny fingers and toes become apparent.

————————————• The embryo may make tiny movements that may be detected by ultrasound.

10 —

———————• The embryo is now called a *fetus*.

12 —

—

14 —

————————————————• Bones and bone marrow continue to form.

16 —

18 —

—

20 —

—

22 —

A layer of fat begins to form under the skin.

24 —

The fetus's lungs are almost ready to breathe air.

The fetus is developing taste buds, and its brain is growing rapidly.

26 —

——————————————————• The fetus practices breathing and has brain wave activity.

28 —

——————• The eyes of the fetus are open, and the fetus may turn toward a bright light.

30 —

—

32 —

————————————————• The fetus's skin turns from red to pink.

34 —

36 ——————• The fetus's skull has hardened.

38 —

——————• The baby is born.

40 —

TAKE A LOOK

9. Identify By what week has the brain of the embryo started to form?

_____

10. Identify At around what week does the fetus start to develop taste buds?

_____

SECTION 3 Growth and Development *continued*

How Does a Person Grow and Change?

The human body goes through several stages of development. One noticeable difference is the change in body proportion.

Body Proportions During Stages of Human Development

Infant	**4 years**	**7 years**	**11 years**	**Adult**

The chart below lists the different stages of life and the characteristics of that stage.

Stage	Ages	Characteristics
Infancy	birth to age 2	• Baby teeth appear. • Nervous system and muscles develop. • Coordination improves.
Childhood	age 2 to puberty	• Permanent teeth grow. • Nerve pathways mature, and child can learn new skills. • Muscle coordination increases.
Adolescence	in females, puberty takes place between the ages of 9 and 14	**Females:** • Breasts enlarge. • Body hair appears. • Menstruation begins.
	in males, puberty takes place between the ages of 11 and 16	**Males:** • Body grows more muscular. • Voice deepens. • Facial and body hair appear.
	puberty to adulthood	• Reproductive system matures (puberty).
Adulthood	age 20+	• From ages 20 to 40, physical development is at its peak. • After age 40, hair may turn gray, skin may wrinkle, athletic ability may decrease.

TAKE A LOOK
11. Identify At which stage or age is the head largest in proportion to the rest of the body?

_____

Math Focus
12. Calculate Alice is 80 years old. She started puberty at age 12. Calculate the percentage of her life that she has spent in each stage of development.

_____

_____

_____

_____

TAKE A LOOK
13. Identify Which stage of development are you in?

_____

Name _____ Class _____ Date _____

Section 3 Review

NSES LS 1a, 1c, 1d, 1e, 2b

SECTION VOCABULARY

embryo in humans, a developing individual from first division after fertilization through the 10th week of pregnancy	**placenta** the partly fetal and partly maternal organ by which materials are exchanged between a fetus and the mother
fetus a developing human from the end of the 10th week of pregnancy until birth	**umbilical cord** the ropelike structure through which blood vessels pass and by which a developing mammal is connected to the placenta

1. Define What is fertilization?

_____

_____

2. Explain Why can only one sperm enter an egg?

_____

_____

_____

3. Explain What does it mean that cells differentiate?

_____

_____

4. Identify What is the function of the amnion?

_____

5. Explain Why is the placenta important to a developing embryo?

_____

_____

_____

_____

6. Explain Why is it necessary for cells in an embryo to differentiate?

_____

_____

7. List What are the four stages of human development after birth?

_____

_____

8. Identify What is the main characteristic of adolescence?

_____

CHAPTER 27 Body Defenses and Disease

SECTION
1 **Disease**

BEFORE YOU READ

After you read this section, you should be able to answer these questions:

• What causes disease?

• How can we protect ourselves from disease?

What Causes Disease?

All your life, you've probably had adults tell you to wash your hands or to cover your mouth when you sneeze. What is all the fuss about? They tell you to do these things to stop the spread of *disease*. When you have a disease, your body cannot function the way that it should.

INFECTIOUS DISEASE

Many diseases, such as a cold, or the flu, can be passed from one living thing to another. This called an **infectious disease**. In other words, you can "catch" an infectious disease. Infectious diseases are caused by **pathogens**. Pathogens can be bacteria, fungi, worms, proteins, or viruses. *Viruses* are tiny particles that depend on living things to reproduce. ☑

This virus causes rabies.

These bacteria, called *Streptococcus*, can cause strep throat.

NONINFECTIOUS DISEASE

Some diseases, such as cancer or heart disease, cannot be passed from person to person. These are called **noninfectious diseases**. Some noninfectious diseases are caused by genes. Others can be caused by lifestyle choices, such as smoking, lack of exercise, and a high-fat diet. Avoiding harmful habits may help you avoid noninfectious diseases.

National Science Education Standards
LS 1f

 STUDY TIP

Outline As you read, make an outline of this section. Be sure to answer the questions asked in each heading and define unfamiliar terms.

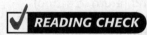 **READING CHECK**

1. Identify What cause infectious diseases?

_____

STANDARDS CHECK

LS 1b Disease is the breakdown in structures or functions of an organism. Some diseases are the result of intrinsic failures of the system. Others are the result of damage by infection by other organisms.

2. Compare How are infectious diseases different from noninfectious diseases?

_____

_____

_____

_____

_____

_____

_____

_____

SECTION 1 Disease *continued*

How Do Pathogens Move Between People?

Pathogens can pass from one person to another in many different ways. Being aware of how pathogens are passed can help you stay healthy.

AIR

Some pathogens travel through the air. A single sneeze can release thousands of droplets of moisture. These droplets can carry pathogens.

A sneeze can force thousands of droplets carrying pathogens out of your body at up to 160 km/hr. That's more than the speed limit on most highways!

OBJECTS

You probably already know that if you drink from a glass used by sick person, you can become infected too. Pathogens can also be carried on objects such as doorknobs, keyboards, combs, or towels. A sick person may leave pathogens on anything he or she touches.

PERSON TO PERSON

People can transfer pathogens directly. You can become infected by kissing, shaking hands, or touching sores on an infected person.

ANIMALS

Some pathogens are carried by animals. For example, people can get a fungus called ringworm by touching an infected cat or dog. Ticks carry bacteria that cause Lyme's disease and Rocky Mountain spotted fever.

FOOD AND WATER

Food and water can contain pathogens. Most drinking water in the United States is safe. However, pathogens can enter the public water supply.

Foods such as meat, fish, and eggs that are not cooked enough can contain harmful bacteria or parasites. Because pathogens grow in food, it is important to wash all cooking surfaces and tools well.

Critical Thinking

3. Infer Why do you think it is important to cover your mouth and nose when you cough or sneeze?

_____

_____

_____

Math Focus

4. Calculate You catch a cold and return to school sick. Your friends don't have immunity to the virus. On the first day, you expose five people to the virus. The next day, each of those friends passes on the virus to five more people. If this same pattern continues, how many people will be infected after 5 days?

Say It

Discuss When was the last time you were sick? How do you think you got sick? Were your friends, siblings, or other people in your class sick at the same time? Talk about these questions with a partner.

How Can We Protect Ourselves From Disease?

Pathogens such as bacteria and viruses are everywhere. So how can we protect ourselves from them?

PASTEURIZATION

Milk and other dairy products can carry certain types of pathogens. To destroy pathogens, dairy products and other foods are treated by a process called *pasteurization*. This method was invented by the French scientist Louis Pasteur. It uses heat to kill bacteria. ☑

Juices, shellfish, and dairy products, such as milk, are all pasteurized to kill pathogens.

VACCINES

A *vaccine* is a substance that helps your body to resist a disease. The ability to resist an infectious disease is called **immunity**. Vaccines contain pathogens that have been killed or treated so they can't make you very sick. The vaccine is enough like the pathogen to help your body develop a defense against the disease.

ANTIBIOTICS

Doctors can treat bacterial infections, such as strep throat, with antibiotics. An *antibiotic* is a substance that kills bacteria or slows their growth.

Antibiotics do not affect viruses. This is because antibiotics only kill living things. Viruses are not considered to be alive because they cannot reproduce on their own. Although antibiotics do not destroy viruses, scientists are working to develop antiviral medications.

☑ **READING CHECK**

5. Complete In pasteurization, bacteria are killed with

_____.

TAKE A LOOK

6. List Name three types of foods that are pasteurized.

_____

_____

_____

Critical Thinking

7. Compare What is the difference between a vaccine and an antibiotic?

_____

_____

_____

_____

_____

Name _____ Class _____ Date _____

Section 1 Review

SECTION VOCABULARY

immunity the ability to resist an infectious disease	**noninfectious disease** a disease that cannot spread from one individual to another
infectious disease a disease that is caused by a pathogen and that can be spread from one individual to another	**pathogen** a microorganism, another organism, a virus, or a protein that causes disease

1. Explain Why are food products, such as milk, pasteurized?

_____

_____

2. Compare Complete the table below to compare infectious and noninfectious diseases.

Type of disease	What causes it?	Can it be passed from person to person?
Infectious		
Non-infectious		

3. Apply Concepts Can you get a vaccine for a noninfectious disease? Explain your answer.

_____

_____

_____

4. List Name five ways that you could come into contact with a pathogen.

_____

_____

_____

5. Apply Concepts The common cold is caused by a virus. Should your doctor give you an antibiotic to help you fight a cold? Explain your answer.

_____

_____

_____

Copyright © by Holt, Rinehart and Winston. All rights reserved.
Interactive Textbook   **428**   Body Defenses and Disease

CHAPTER 27 Body Defenses and Disease

SECTION
2 **Your Body's Defenses**

National Science Education Standards
LS 1b, 1d, 1e, 1f, 3a, 3b

BEFORE YOU READ

After you read this section, you should be able to answer these questions:

• How does your body keep pathogens out?

• How does your immune system destroy pathogens that do get into your body?

How Does Your Body Keep Pathogens out?

Bacteria and viruses are all around us in the air, in water, and on surfaces. Your body must constantly protect itself against these pathogens. Luckily, your body has its own built-in defense system.

Keeping pathogens from entering the body is an important defense against infection. Your body has several barriers that keep pathogens from entering. These include your skin and special secretions in your eyes, nose, and throat. ☑

Your skin is made of many layers of flat cells. The outer layers are dead. Many pathogens that land on your skin cannot find a live cell to infect. These dead cells drop off your body as new skin cells grow beneath them. When the dead skin cells fall off, they carry viruses, bacteria, and other pathogens with them. Your skin also has glands that produce oil to cover the skin's surface. The oil contains chemicals that kill many pathogens.

Your body loses and replaces about 1 million skin cells every 40 minutes. As skin cells fall off, pathogens fall off with them.

Pathogens also try to enter your body through your eyes, nose, or mouth. These pathogens are destroyed by chemicals called *enzymes*. Some pathogens that enter your nose are washed down your throat by a slippery fluid called *mucus*. Mucus carries pathogens to your stomach, where they are digested.

STUDY TIP

Underline As you read, underline the different defenses your body has against disease.

READING CHECK

1. List What are two of your body's barriers against infection?

_____

_____

_____

_____

Math Focus

2. Calculate About how many skin cells does your body lose and replace in 24 hours?

_____

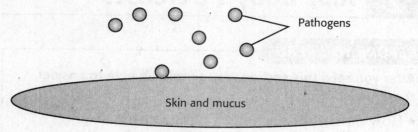

Defense Level 1: Barriers keep most pathogens from getting into your body.

3. Identify Relationships Your skin is part of the integumentary system. How do your integumentary system and immune system work together?

_____

_____

_____

_____

_____

_____

_____

What Happens If Pathogens Do Get into Your Body?

Some pathogens may get past your body's barriers. For example, pathogens can enter the body if the skin is cut or punctured. The body reacts quickly to keep more pathogens out. Blood flow to the injured area increases. Particles in the blood called *platelets* help seal the wound so no more pathogens can enter.

Blood also brings cells that belong to the immune system. The **immune system** is the body system that fights pathogens. It is not found in one specific place in your body, and it is not controlled by one organ. Instead, the immune system is a team of cells, tissues, and organs that work together to protect you from pathogens.

How Does Your Body Know a Pathogen Is an Invader?

For your body to fight pathogens, it must be able to recognize that they are invaders. How can it do this? The cells of your body have special proteins on their surfaces. Your proteins are different from everyone else's. Your proteins tell your body which cells are yours. Pathogens also have proteins on their surfaces. When pathogens get into your body, their surface proteins tell your body that the particles do not belong to you. ☑

✓ READING CHECK

4. Explain How does your body know a pathogen does not belong in your body?

_____

_____

_____

_____

What Kind of Cells Attack Pathogens First?

Immune system cells called **macrophages** can surround and destroy many pathogens that enter your body. Generally, macrophages will attack any invader. If only a few pathogens enter your body at one time, macrophages can usually destroy them.

Defense Level 2: Macrophages attack most invaders.

If too many pathogens enter your body at once, the macrophages may not be able to stop all of them. Some pathogens will invade your body cells. Once this happens, another group of cells goes to work. This is known as the *immune response.* ☑

Defense Level 3: If too many pathogens enter the body, the macrophages cannot stop all of them. The pathogens will infect body cells. Other types of immune cells go to work.

What Is the Immune Response?

In the immune response, immune cells work to destroy any body cells that have been infected by a pathogen. This helps keep the pathogen from infecting more body cells.

Recall that pathogens have proteins on their surfaces that tell your body the particle does not belong to you. These proteins trigger the immune response. Anything that starts the immune response is called an *antigen.* When a pathogen invades a body cell, the pathogen's proteins are also displayed on the surface of the body cell.

T CELLS AND B CELLS

Two general kinds of immune systems cells go to work in response to antigens: T cells and B cells. While macrophages will generally attack any invader, T cells and B cells work together to attack specific invaders. These cells recognize specific invaders by their antigens. **T cells** attack infected body cells and tell other immune cells to respond to an invader. **B cells** make antibodies. ☑

READING CHECK

5. Explain What happens when too many pathogens enter your body at one time?

_____
_____
_____
_____

READING CHECK

6. Identify What kind of immune cells produce antibodies?

_____

SECTION 2 Your Body's Defenses *continued*

ANTIBODIES

An **antibody** is a protein that attaches to a specific antigen. Antibodies tag a pathogen so that other cells can destroy it. When antibodies attach to antigens, they make the pathogens clump together. Macrophages can find these clumps easily and destroy them.

Your body can make billions of different kinds of antibodies. The shape of an antibody is very specialized. It matches an antigen like a key fits a lock. Each antibody usually attaches to just one type of antigen.

Pathogen

Antibodies

B cell

Antigen

An antibody's shape is very specialized. It matches an antigen like a key fits a lock.

How Does the Immune System Fight a Virus?

The figures below show what happens when a pathogen, such as a virus, enters the body. When virus particles enter the body, one of two things may happen. Some viruses enter body cells and start to make copies of themselves. Others are attacked by macrophages.

1 When viruses invade the body, two things can happen.

Some virus particles that enter the body are engulfed, or eaten, by macrophages. These macrophages then display the viral antigens. This is the start of the immune response.

Viral antigen

Virus

Some virus particles may infect body cells. Infected body cells display viral antigens.

Viral antigen

Macrophage

Body cell

TAKE A LOOK

7. Identify What two things can happen to a virus that enters your body?

_____

_____

_____

_____

8. Explain What happens to a macrophage after it engulfs a virus particle?

_____

_____

_____

2 **Two Responses** Helper T cells have receptor proteins that recognize the shape of the viral antigen on the macrophages. These helper T cells begin two responses: a T cell response and a B cell response.

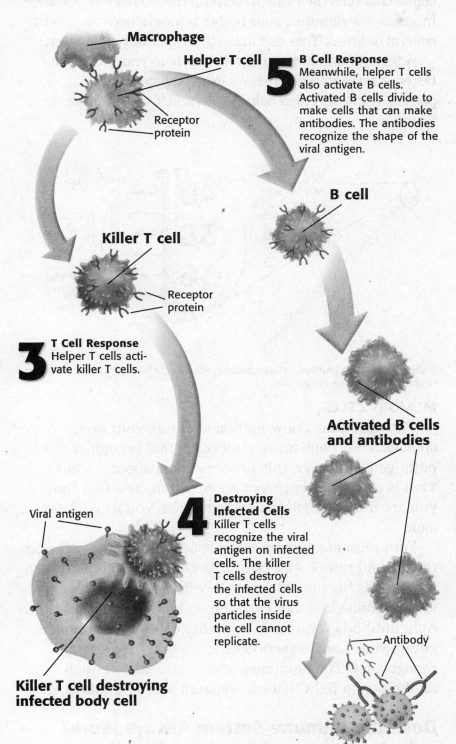

Macrophage

Helper T cell

Receptor protein

Killer T cell

Receptor protein

3 **T Cell Response** Helper T cells activate killer T cells.

Viral antigen

4 **Destroying Infected Cells** Killer T cells recognize the viral antigen on infected cells. The killer T cells destroy the infected cells so that the virus particles inside the cell cannot replicate.

Killer T cell destroying infected body cell

5 **B Cell Response** Meanwhile, helper T cells also activate B cells. Activated B cells divide to make cells that can make antibodies. The antibodies recognize the shape of the viral antigen.

B cell

Activated B cells and antibodies

Antibody

6 **Destroying Viruses** Antibodies bind to the viral antigen on the viruses. The antibodies bound to the viruses cause the viruses to clump together. Clumping marks the virus particles for destruction.

TAKE A LOOK
9. Identify What structures on helper T cells recognize viral antigens?

_____

10. Explain What two things happen when a helper T cell recognizes a viral antigen?

_____

_____

_____

11. Identify What is the role of killer T cells?

_____

_____

FEVERS

When macrophages activate helper T cells, they send a signal that tells the brain to turn up the body's temperature. In just a few minutes, your body's temperature can rise by several degrees. This rise in body temperature is a *fever*.

A fever of one or two degrees can help you get better faster. A moderate fever slows down the growth of pathogens. Fevers also help B cells and T cells reproduce faster.

Critical Thinking
12. Infer Why is it not a good idea to use medicines that stop a moderate fever?

_____
_____
_____
_____
_____
_____

TAKE A LOOK
13. Explain What kind of fever can become dangerous?

_____
_____
_____

A slight fever helps immune cells reproduce. However, a fever of more than a few degrees can become dangerous.

MEMORY CELLS

The first time a new pathogen enters your body, specialized B cells make antibodies that recognize the pathogen. However, this process takes about 2 weeks. That is too long to prevent an infection. The first time you are infected with a new pathogen, you usually get sick.

Your immune system can respond faster to a pathogen the second time it enters your body. After an infection, a few B cells become memory B cells. A **memory B cell** is an immune cell that can "remember" how to make the right antibody for a specific pathogen. If that pathogen enters your body a second time, memory B cells can recognize it. The immune system can make enough antibodies to fight that pathogen in just 3 or 4 days. ☑

Does the Immune System Always Work?

The immune system is not perfect. Sometimes, it can't prevent diseases. There also are conditions in which the immune system attacks the wrong cells.

READING CHECK
14. Define What is the role of a memory B cell?

_____
_____
_____
_____

SECTION 2 Your Body's Defenses *continued*

ALLERGIES

Sometimes the immune system overreacts to antigens that are not harmful to the body. This inappropriate reaction is an **allergy**. Many things, including foods, medicines, plant pollen, and animals, can cause allergies.

AUTOIMMUNE DISEASES

An **autoimmune disease** happens when the immune system attacks the body's own cells. In this type of disease, immune system cells mistake body cells for pathogens. Rheumatoid arthritis, multiple sclerosis, and type 1 diabetes are all autoimmune diseases. ☑

In rheumatoid arthritis, immune-system cells cause joint tissues to swell. This can cause joint deformities.

✔ **READING CHECK**

15. Explain What happens in an autoimmune disease?

_____

_____

_____

_____

CANCER

Healthy cells divide at a regulated rate. Sometimes, a cell doesn't respond to the body's regulation, and it divides uncontrollably. Killer T cells normally kill this type of cell. But sometimes, the immune system cannot control these cells. **Cancer** is a condition in which some of the body's cells divide at an uncontrolled rate.

AIDS

The *human immunodeficiency virus* (HIV) causes *acquired immune deficiency syndrome* (AIDS). HIV is different from most viruses, which infect cells in the nose, mouth, lungs, or intestines. HIV infects the immune system itself. It uses helper T cells to make more viruses. The helper T cells are destroyed in the process. ☑

Without helper T cells, there is nothing to activate B cells and killer T cells. The immune system cannot attack HIV or any other pathogens. In fact, most people with AIDS don't die of AIDS itself. Instead, they die because their immune systems cannot fight off other diseases.

✔ **READING CHECK**

16. Identify Name one way HIV is different from most other viruses.

_____

_____

_____

_____

_____

Name _____ Class _____ Date _____

Section 2 Review

NSES LS 1b, 1d, 1e, 1f, 3a, 3b

SECTION VOCABULARY

allergy a reaction to a harmless or common substance by the body's immune system

antibody a protein made by B cells that binds to a specific antigen

autoimmune disease a disease in which the immune system attacks the organism's own cells

B cell a white blood cell that makes antibodies

cancer a tumor in which the cells begin dividing at an uncontrolled rate and become invasive

immune system the cells and tissues that recognize and attack foreign substances in the body

macrophage an immune system cell that engulfs pathogens and other materials

memory B cell a B cell that responds to an antigen more strongly when the body is reinfected with an antigen than it does during its first encounter with an antigen

T cell an immune system cell that coordinates the immune system and attacks many infected cells

1. List What are the three main kinds of cells in the immune system?

_____

2. Summarize Complete the process chart to show what happens when a pathogen, such as a virus, enters the body.

Receptor proteins on helper T cells recognize viral antigens on a macrophage

Killer T cells recognize viral antigens on infected body cells

Antibodies bind to viral proteins and mark the virus for destruction

3. Apply Concepts Why do you think that most people only get a disease such as chickenpox once?

_____

_____

_____

CHAPTER 28 | Staying Healthy

SECTION 1 | **Good Nutrition**

After you read this section, you should be able to answer these questions:

• What are nutrients?

• What are several practices for good nutrition?

• What causes malnutrition?

What Are Nutrients?

Have you ever heard someone say "You are what you eat"? This doesn't mean that you are pizza! However, the substances in pizza and other foods help build your body. These substances are called nutrients.

Nutrients provide the materials your body needs to grow and maintain itself. They are grouped into six classes: carbohydrates, proteins, fats, water, vitamins, and minerals. Carbohydrates, proteins, and fats provide energy for the body in units called *Calories* (Cal). To stay healthy, you need to take in each class of nutrients daily. ☑

CARBOHYDRATES

Carbohydrates are your body's main source of energy. A **carbohydrate** is a compound made up of sugar molecules. There are two types of carbohydrates: simple and complex. Simple carbohydrates are made of one or a few sugar molecules linked together. You can digest them easily for quick energy.

Complex carbohydrates are made of many sugar molecules linked together. You digest complex carbohydrates more slowly than simple carbohydrates. Complex carbohydrates give you long-lasting energy.

Some complex carbohydrates are good sources of fiber. Fiber is a part of a healthy diet and is found in whole-grain foods, such as brown rice and whole-wheat bread. Many fruits and vegetables also contain fiber.

STUDY TIP

List As you read, make a list of the nutrients you need for good health.

READING CHECK

1. Complete Energy for the body is measured in units

called _____.

Critical Thinking

2. Apply Concepts If you wanted to have more fiber in your diet, would you choose to eat simple carbohydrates or complex carbohydrates? Explain your answer.

_____

_____

_____

_____

_____

SECTION 1 Good Nutrition *continued*

Say It

Discuss Think about what you eat in a typical day. What foods do you eat that contain protein? Talk with a partner to see if you eat the same kinds of proteins.

Math Focus

3. Calculate Percentages If you eat 2,500 Cal per day and 20% are from fat, 30% are from protein, and 50% are from carbohydrates, how many Calories of each nutrient do you eat?

_____

_____

_____

TAKE A LOOK

4. Identify Use colored pencils to circle the foods that contain carbohydrates, fats, and proteins. Use red for carbohydrates, blue for fats, and green for proteins. You may circle a food more than once.

PROTEINS

Proteins are nutrients your body uses to build and repair itself. Your body can make the proteins it needs. However, it must get building blocks called *amino acids* from the proteins you eat. Foods such as poultry, fish, milk, eggs, nuts, and beans are good sources of protein.

FATS

Fats are nutrients that store energy. Your body also uses fats to store vitamins and make hormones. Fats help keep your skin healthy and insulate your body.

There are two types of fats: saturated and unsaturated. *Saturated fats* are found in meat, dairy products, coconut oil, and palm oil. Saturated fats raise blood cholesterol levels. Although *cholesterol* is found naturally in the body, high levels can increase the risk of heart disease.

Unsaturated fats and foods high in fiber may help reduce blood cholesterol levels. Your body cannot make unsaturated fats. They come from foods such as vegetable oils and fish.

Pasta · Chicken · Watermelon · Cheese · Butter · Green Beans

WATER

We could not live without water. Water moves substances through our bodies, keeps our temperatures stable, and keeps body tissues moist.

You cannot survive for more than a few days without water. In fact, your body is about 70% water. Many health professionals think you should drink at least eight glasses of water a day. You also get water from other liquids you drink and the foods you eat. Fresh fruits and vegetables, juices, soups, and milk are good sources of water.

SECTION 1 Good Nutrition *continued*

VITAMINS AND MINERALS

Vitamins are compounds that your body needs to control many body functions. Some of these functions are listed in the table below. Your body cannot make most vitamins, so you need to get them from food.

Vitamin	What it does	Where you get it
A	keeps skin and eyes healthy; builds strong teeth and bones	yellow and orange fruits and vegetables, leafy greens, meats, and milk
B	helps body use carbohydrates; helps blood, nerves, and heart function	meats, whole grains, beans, peas, nuts, and seafood
C	strengthens tissues; helps the body absorb iron and fight disease	citrus fruits, leafy greens, broccoli, peppers, and cabbage
D	builds strong bones and teeth; helps the body use calcium and phosphorus	sunlight, enriched milk and soymilk, eggs, and fish
E	protects red blood cells from destruction; keeps skin healthy	oils, fats, eggs, whole grains, wheat germ, liver, and leafy greens
K	helps your blood to clot	leafy greens, tomatoes, and potatoes

Minerals are chemical elements that are essential for good health. You need six minerals in large amounts: calcium, chloride, magnesium, phosphorus, potassium, and sodium. Your body needs other minerals, such as fluorine, iodine, iron, and zinc, in small amounts. Some minerals and their functions are listed in the table below.

Mineral	What it does
Calcium	makes teeth and bones strong
Magnesium and sodium	help the body use proteins
Potassium	helps regulate heartbeat and makes muscles move
Iron	helps make blood cells

How Can You Get All the Nutrients You Need?

For good health, you need a variety of nutrients from different foods. The next figure can help you find out how much of each type of food you should eat every day. The six stripes represent five food groups. The width of each stripe shows how much food from that group you should eat.

TAKE A LOOK
5. Identify Which vitamins can you get from leafy greens?

_____

6. List Which foods could you eat to help give you strong bones and teeth?

_____

TAKE A LOOK
7. Identify Which mineral do you need to make your muscles move?

_____

SECTION 1 Good Nutrition *continued*

TAKE A LOOK

8. Identify Which food group should you eat the most foods from each day?

_____

9. Apply Ideas Design a healthy lunch that includes one food from each group. What would you eat?

_____

_____

_____

MyPyramid
STEPS TO A HEALTHIER YOU

GRAINS	VEGETABLES	FRUITS	MILK	MEAT & BEANS
Make half your grains whole.	Vary your veggies.	Focus on fruit. Go easy on juices.	Get your calcium-rich foods.	Go lean with protein. Choose more fish, beans, peas, nuts, and seeds.

Find your balance between food and physical activity. Children and teens should be active for 60 minutes on most days.

Know your limits on fats, sugars, and salt. Get most of your fat from vegetable oils, nuts, and fish. Choose foods and drinks low in added sugar.

Critical Thinking

10. Infer How could eating only junk food, such as candy and fast food, cause malnutrition?

_____

_____

_____

_____

✓ **READING CHECK**

11. List What are three problems that both anorexia and bulimia can cause?

_____

_____

_____

What Happens If You Do Not Get the Nutrients You Need?

Malnutrition occurs when someone does not eat enough of the nutrients the body needs. It can happen when you do not eat enough food. It can also happen when you eat too much food that is high in fat and low in other nutrients. Malnutrition can affect how you look. It can also keep your body from fighting illness or repairing itself quickly.

EATING DISORDERS

Conditions called *eating disorders* can cause malnutrition. People with *anorexia nervosa* starve themselves by not eating. They have a strong fear of gaining weight. People with *bulimia nervosa* eat very large amounts of food at once. They will then try to get rid of the food quickly. They may do this by vomiting or using diuretics and laxatives.

Anorexia can lead to severe malnutrition. Bulimia can damage the teeth and nervous system. Both anorexia and bulimia can cause problems such as weak bones, low blood pressure, and heart problems. They can even lead to death. ☑

SECTION 1 Good Nutrition *continued*

OBESITY

Obesity is having a high percentage of body fat. Obesity increases the risk of certain health problems. These include high blood pressure, heart disease, and diabetes. People suffering from obesity may not be eating foods that give them the correct balance of nutrients. Exercising very little can also lead to obesity.

Eating a balanced diet and exercising regularly can help reduce obesity. However, obesity can be caused by other things. For example, people who are obese often have obese parents. Scientists are studying the link between obesity and heredity. ☑

What Do Food Labels Tell You?

Reading food labels can help you make healthy eating choices. Nutrition facts show how much of each nutrient is in one serving of a food. Packaged foods, such as cereal, peanut butter, and pasta, all have these labels. The label below is from a can of chicken noodle soup.

READING CHECK

12. Identify Name two things that can help reduce obesity.

_____

_____

Nutrition Facts

Serving Size 1/2 cup (120 ml) — **Serving information**
Servings per Container 2.5

Amount per Serving	Prepared	
Calories	70	**Number of Calories per serving**
Calories from Fat	25	

	% Daily Value
Total Fat 2.5 g	4%
Saturated Fat 1 g	5%
Trans Fat 0 g	
Cholesterol 15 mg	5%
Sodium 960 mg	40%
Total Carbohydrate 8 g	3%
Dietary Fiber less than 1 g	4%
Sugars 1 g	
Protein 3 g	
Vitamin A	15%
Vitamin C	0%
Calcium	0%
Iron	4%

Percentage of daily values

*Percent Daily Values are based on a 2,000 Calorie diet. Your daily values may be higher or lower depending on your Calorie needs:

	Calories	2,000	2,500
Total Fat	Less than	65g	80g
Sat Fat	Less than	20g	25g
Cholesterol	Less than	300mg	300mg
Sodium	Less than	2,400mg	2,400mg
Total Carbohydrate		300g	375g
Dietary Fiber		25g	30g
Protein		50g	60g

Math Focus

13. Calculate How many Calories are in the entire can of soup?

_____

_____

TAKE A LOOK

14. Evaluate Is this soup a good source of vitamin C? Explain your answer.

_____

_____

_____

Section 1 Review

SECTION VOCABULARY

carbohydrate a class of energy-giving nutrients that includes sugars, starches, and fiber

fat an energy-storage nutrient that helps the body store some vitamins

malnutrition a disorder of nutrition that results when a person does not consume enough of each of the nutrients that are needed by the human body.

mineral a class of nutrients that are chemical elements that are needed for certain body processes

nutrient a substance in food that provides energy or helps form body tissues and that is necessary for life and growth

protein a molecule that is made up of amino acids and that is needed build and repair body structures and to regulate processes in the body

vitamin a class of nutrients that contain carbon and that are needed in small amounts to maintain health and allow growth

1. **Apply Concepts** Name some of the nutrients that can be found in a glass of milk.

_____

2. **Infer** Which type of fats are healthier—saturated or unsaturated?

_____

_____

3. **Compare** How do anorexia nervosa and bulimia nervosa differ?

_____

_____

_____

4. **Infer** Is it possible for someone to suffer from both obesity and malnutrition? Explain your answer.

_____

_____

_____

5. **Explain** How would you use a Nutrition Facts label to choose a food that is high in calcium?

_____

_____

_____

6. **List** What are the five main food groups?

_____

_____

CHAPTER 28 Staying Healthy

SECTION 2 **Risks of Alcohol and Other Drugs**

BEFORE YOU READ

After you read this section, you should be able to answer these questions:

- What is a drug?
- What are some of the problems caused by drug abuse?

What Is a Drug?

Sometimes when people talk about drugs, they are talking about helpful substances, such as medicines. Other times, we hear about illegal drugs and their dangers. So what is a drug?

A **drug** is any chemical substance that causes a physical or psychological change in your body. Some drugs enter the body through the skin. Other drugs are swallowed, inhaled, or injected.

All of these products contain drugs.

You can buy some drugs at the grocery store, while others must be prescribed by a doctor. Some drugs are illegal to buy, sell, or have. When used correctly, legal drugs can help your body heal. When used improperly, however, even legal drugs can be harmful.

How Can Drugs Be Harmful?

Addiction is dependence on a substance. Many drugs cause addiction. They are *addictive*. A person with an addiction finds it very hard to stop taking a drug.

The body can form a *physical dependence*, or need for a drug. If the body doesn't get a drug that it is physically dependent on, it can show withdrawal symptoms. These can include nausea, vomiting, pain, and tremors or shakes.

Some people also form *psychological dependence* on a drug. This means they have strong cravings for the drug. ☑

STUDY

Underline This section may have many words that are unfamiliar. As you read, underline these words and find out what they mean. Write their definitions in the margin.

Say It

Discuss Does it surprise you that all of the items in the figure contain drugs? What kinds of things do you usually think about when you hear the word "drug"? Share your ideas in small groups.

READING CHECK

1. Explain Why does a person experience withdrawal symptoms?

_____

_____

_____

_____

SECTION 2 Risks of Alcohol and Other Drugs *continued*

What Are Some Types of Drugs?
HERBAL MEDICINES

Some types of plants called *herbs* contain chemicals with healing properties. Information about these *herbal medicines* has been handed down for centuries. Even though they come from plants, herbs are drugs and should be used carefully. The United States Food and Drug Administration (FDA) does not regulate herbal medicines or teas. This means it cannot guarantee that these products are safe to use. ☑

PRESCRIPTION AND OVER-THE-COUNTER DRUGS

Many drugs need a prescription from a doctor. A *prescription* describes the drug, how to use it, and how much to take. Below are some important drug safety tips you should always follow.

Drug Safety Tips

- Never take another person's prescription medicine.
- Read the label before each use. Always follow the instructions on the label and those provided by your doctor or pharmacist.
- Do not take more or less medication than prescribed.
- Consult a doctor if you have any side effects.
- Throw away leftover and out-of-date medicines.

Some drugs, such as aspirin, can be bought without a prescription. These are called *over-the-counter (OTC) drugs*. You should still read and follow directions carefully for OTC drugs. Both prescription and OTC drugs can cause side effects. *Side effects* are uncomfortable symptoms, such as headache, nausea, or sleepiness.

TOBACCO

Cigarettes contain tobacco. They are addictive, and smoking has serious health effects. Tobacco contains a chemical called nicotine. **Nicotine** increases heart rate and blood pressure, and it is extremely addictive.

Smoking increases the chances of lung cancer. It has also been linked to other cancers, bronchitis, and heart disease. Experts estimate that there are more than 430,000 deaths related to smoking each year in the United States. Secondhand smoke also can be harmful.

☑ **READING CHECK**

2. Explain What does it mean that the FDA doesn't regulate herbal medicines?

_____

_____

_____

Critical Thinking

3. Infer Why can someone become addicted to cigarettes?

_____

_____

_____

_____

Effects of Smoking

▼ Healthy lung tissue of a nonsmoker   ▼ Damaged lung tissue of a smoker

Cilia in your lungs clean the air you breathe and keep debris out of your lungs. Smoking damages the cilia so that they cannot do their job.

Smokeless, or chewing, tobacco is also addictive and can cause health problems. Nicotine is absorbed through the lining of the mouth. Smokeless tobacco increases the risk of several cancers, including mouth and throat cancer. It also causes gum disease and yellowing of the teeth.

ALCOHOL

In most of the United States, using alcohol is illegal for people under age 21. Alcohol slows down the central nervous system and can cause memory loss. Excessive use of alcohol can damage the liver, pancreas, brain, nerves, and cardiovascular system. It can even cause death. ☑

Alcohol affects decision-making and can lead you to take unhealthy risks. Some people suffer from **alcoholism**, which means that they are physically and psychologically dependent on alcohol. Alcoholism is considered a disease. Scientists think certain genes can make some people more likely to develop alcoholism.

MARIJUANA

Marijuana is a drug that comes from a plant called hemp. It is illegal in most places. Marijuana affects different people in different ways. It may increase anxiety or cause feelings of paranoia. Marijuana slows down your ability to react, clouds your thinking, and makes you less coordinated. ☑

COCAINE

Cocaine and its purified form, crack, are made from the coca plant. Both drugs are illegal and highly addictive. Users can become addicted to them in a very short time. Cocaine can make a person feel very excited, but later it can make them feel anxious and depressed. Both drugs increase heart rate and blood pressure and can cause heart attacks.

TAKE A LOOK
4. Identify What is the function of cilia in your lungs?

_____

_____

_____

✓ **READING CHECK**
5. Identify What is the legal age for using alcohol in most of the United States?

_____

✓ **READING CHECK**
6. List What are three effects of marijuana?

_____

_____

_____

_____

SECTION 2 Risks of Alcohol and Other Drugs *continued*

NARCOTICS AND DESIGNER DRUGS

Drugs made from the opium plant are called **narcotics**. Some narcotics are used to treat severe pain. These narcotics are illegal unless a doctor prescribes them.

Some narcotics, such as heroin, are always illegal. Users usually inject heroin, and they might share needles. This puts heroin users at a high risk of diseases such as hepatitis and AIDS. Heroin users can also die of an overdose. ☑

Other kinds of illegal drugs include inhalants, barbiturates, amphetamines, and designer drugs. Designer drugs are made by making small changes to other drugs. Ecstasy, or "X," is a designer drug. Over time, the drug can cause lesions or holes to develop in a user's brain. Ecstasy users are also more likely to develop depression.

HALLUCINOGENS

Users of hallucinogens have *hallucinations*. This means that they see and hear things that are not real. Drugs such as LSD and PCP are powerful, illegal hallucinogens. Sniffing glue or solvents, such as paint thinner, can also cause hallucinations and serious brain damage. ☑

✔ **READING CHECK**

7. Explain Why are heroin users at a high risk for developing diseases such as hepatitis and AIDS?

_____

_____

_____

_____

✔ **READING CHECK**

8. Define What is a hallucination?

_____

_____

_____

TAKE A LOOK

9. Complete Use the text to complete the chart on the harmful effects of certain drugs.

Type of drug	Legal or illegal?	Harmful effects
Herbal medicines		not fully known
Prescription	legal when used properly	
Tobacco	legal over age 18 in most of U.S.	
Alcohol		
Marijuana		
Cocaine		
Narcotics		
Hallucinogens		

What Is Drug Abuse?

Drug use and drug abuse are not the same thing. Someone can use drugs to prevent or help a medical problem. The drug user gets these drugs legally and uses them properly. People who abuse drugs usually do not take the drugs for a medical problem. Instead, they may take drugs to help them feel good, escape from problems, or fit in. Drug abusers often get drugs illegally. ☑

How Does Drug Abuse Start, and How Can It Stop?

Young people often start to use drugs because of peer pressure. Teenagers may drink, smoke, or try marijuana to make friends. Many teenagers begin using illegal drugs to feel like part of a group. However, drug abuse can lead to many problems with friends, family, school, and money. These problems often lead to depression and social isolation.

Many people who start using drugs do not recognize the dangers. Incorrect information about drugs can be found in many places. Some of the most common myths about drugs are shown below.

Drug Myths

Myth **"It's only alcohol, not drugs."**
Reality Alcohol is a mood-altering and mind-altering drug. It affects the central nervous system and is addictive.

Myth **"I won't get hooked on one or two cigarettes a day."**
Reality Addiction is not related to the amount of a drug used. Some people become addicted after using a drug once or twice.

Myth **"I can quit any time I want."**
Reality Addicts may quit and return to drug usage many times. Their inability to stay drug-free shows how powerful the addiction is.

READING CHECK
10. **List** Give three reasons a person may abuse drugs.
_____
_____
_____
_____

TAKE A LOOK
11. **Explain** Can someone become addicted to a drug only after using a lot of it or using it for a long time? Explain your answer.
_____
_____
_____
_____

The first step to quitting drugs is to admit to drug abuse and to decide to stop. The addicted person should get proper medical treatment. Getting off drugs can be very difficult. However, people who stop abusing drugs lead happier and healthier lives.

Name _____ Class _____ Date _____

Section 2 Review

SECTION VOCABULARY

addiction a dependence on a substance, such as alcohol or another drug

alcoholism a disorder in which a person repeatedly drinks alcoholic beverages in an amount that interferes with the person's health and activities

drug any substance that causes a change in a person's physical or psychological state

narcotic a drug that is derived from opium and that relieves pain and induces sleep

nicotine a toxic, addictive chemical that is found in tobacco and that is one of the major contributors to the harmful effects of smoking

1. Compare What is the difference between physical and psychological dependence?

_____
_____
_____

2. Explain Can prescription and over-the-counter drugs be harmful? Explain your answer.

_____
_____
_____

3. Define What are side effects? Give several examples.

_____
_____
_____
_____

4. Analyze Is smokeless tobacco safer to use than cigarettes? Explain your answer.

_____
_____
_____
_____

5. List Name five drugs that are always illegal.

_____

6. Explain Why are drug use and drug abuse not the same thing?

_____
_____
_____
_____
_____

CHAPTER 28 Staying Healthy

SECTION
3 # Healthy Habits

BEFORE YOU READ

After you read this section, you should be able to answer these questions:

• What are some habits you can practice to stay healthy?

• What are some ways to prevent accidents and injuries?

Why Should You Take Care of Your Health?

Do you like playing sports or acting in plays? How does your health affect your favorite activities? The better your health is, the better you can perform. To keep yourself healthy, you need to practice healthy habits every day.

What Is Hygiene?

Hygiene is the science of preserving and protecting your health. Practicing good hygiene is not hard. One of the easiest things you can do to stay healthy is to wash your hands. This helps prevent the spread of disease. You should always wash your hands after using the bathroom and before and after handling food. Taking care of your skin, hair, and teeth is also important for good hygiene. ☑

Why Is Posture Important?

Standing up straight not only makes you look better, but it can make you feel better. Posture is important to your health. Bad posture strains your muscles and makes breathing difficult. To have good posture, imagine a line passing through your ear, shoulder, hip, knee, and ankle when you stand. You can have good posture at a desk by pulling your chair forward and keeping your feet on the floor. ☑

STUDY TIP

Underline As you read this section, underline all the things you can do to take care of your health.

READING CHECK

1. Identify What is one of the easiest things you can do to prevent the spread of disease?

_____

_____

READING CHECK

2. Identify What problems can bad posture cause?

_____

_____

_____

When you have good posture, your ear, shoulder, hip, knee, and ankle are in a straight line.

Bad posture strains your muscles and ligaments and can make breathing difficult.

Why Is Exercise Important?

Aerobic exercise at least three times a week is essential to good health. **Aerobic exercise** is vigorous, constant exercise of the whole body for 20 minutes or more. ☑

Types of aerobic exercise include:

- walking
- dancing
- running
- swimming
- biking
- playing sports, such as soccer, basketball, or tennis

Aerobic exercise increases your heart rate. This helps your body take in more oxygen. Aerobic exercise protects your physical and mental health in the following ways:

- strengthens the heart, bones, and lungs
- burns Calories
- helps your body conserve some nutrients
- helps your digestive system work well
- gives you more energy and stamina

How Much Sleep Do You Need?

Believe it or not, teenagers actually need more sleep than younger children. Do you ever fall asleep in class, like the girl in the figure below? If so, you may not be getting enough sleep. Scientists say teenagers need about 9.5 hours of sleep each night. At night, the body goes through several cycles of deeper and deeper sleep. If you do not sleep long enough, you will not enter the deepest, most restful period of sleep. ☑

READING CHECK

3. Identify How long should aerobic exercise last?

_____

Say It

Discuss Do you play any sports, or perform other aerobic activities? How do you feel after you exercise? Tell the class about your favorite form of exercise.

READING CHECK

4. Identify About how many hours of sleep each night do scientists say teenagers need?

_____

If you fall asleep easily during the day, you are probably not getting enough sleep.

What Is Stress?

Have you ever been excited about your team's upcoming soccer game? Have you ever been upset or angry because you got a bad grade on a test? The game and the test were causing you stress. **Stress** is the physical and mental response to pressure, such as being worried, anxious, or excited.

Some stress is a normal part of life. Stress tells your body to prepare for difficult or dangerous situations. However, sometimes you may have no outlet for the stress, and it builds up. Too much stress can be harmful to your health. It can also make it hard for you to do everything you need to do each day.

Some signs of too much stress include:

- headaches
- upset stomach
- inability to fall asleep at night
- nervous habits, such as nail biting
- becoming irritable or resentful

 Say It

Describe Have you ever felt stressed? What do you think caused your stress? How did it make you feel? Describe this to a partner.

Critical Thinking

5. Analyze How can stress be both good and bad?

_____

_____

_____

_____

_____

TAKE A LOOK

6. Identify Circle all the things in this picture that could cause stress.

What Are Some Ways to Cope with Stress?

Different things stress different people. Once you learn what things cause you stress, you can find ways to deal with it. If you cannot remove the cause of stress, here are some ideas for handling stress. ☑

- Share your problems. Talk them over with a parent, friend, teacher, or school counselor.
- Make a list of all the things you would like to get done. Rank these things in order of how important they are. Do the most important thing first.
- Exercise regularly.
- Get enough sleep
- Pet or play with a friendly animal.
- Spend some quiet time alone.
- Practice deep breathing or other relaxation techniques.

What Are Some Ways to Prevent Injuries?

Practicing healthy habits includes preventing injuries. Accidents can happen any time. It is impossible to prevent all accidents. However, you can decrease your risk of injury by following some basic safety rules.

OUTDOOR SAFETY

If you enjoy outdoor activities, such as biking, hiking, or boating, some rules you should follow are:

- never hike or camp alone
- dress for the weather
- tell someone where you are going and when you will return
- learn how to swim, and never swim alone
- wear a life jacket when you are in a boat
- if a storm approaches, get out of the water and seek shelter
- always wear a helmet when you are biking, and obey the rules of the road

You should practice other common sense habits as well. For example, you should always wear a seat belt in a moving vehicle. Never ride in a car with someone who has been drinking alcohol or using illegal drugs.

☑ **READING CHECK**

7. Explain What do you need to do before you can deal with stress?

_____

_____

Critical Thinking

8. Infer Why do you think it is important to tell somone where you are going and when you will return?

_____

_____

_____

_____

_____

SECTION 3 Healthy Habits *continued*

SAFETY AT HOME

Many accidents can be avoided. The figure below shows ways you can help prevent accidents in your home.

Bathroom
• Never touch electrical switches or appliances while touching water.
• Use nonslip mats in the shower and tub.
• Use a night light.

• Have a parent install smoke detectors on every floor.

Kitchen
• Clean up spills quickly.
• Do not allow pot handles to extend over the edge of the stove.
• Use a stool to reach high shelves.
• Keep grease and drippings away from open flames.

Entrance and Stairs
• Use a railing.
• Never leave objects on stairs.

Living Room
• Keep electrical cords out of walkways.
• Do not plug too many electrical devices into one outlet.

TAKE A LOOK
9. Apply Concepts List three things from this picture that you can do to protect your home from fires.

_____
_____
_____
_____
_____

What Should You Do If an Accident Happens?

Accidents can happen, so you should be prepared. If you see someone in danger, such as a person choking, you should call for medical help right away. In most communities, you can dial 911 on the telephone. This will connect you with emergency personnel who will send help. Once you dial 911, you should:

• stay calm
• speak slowly and clearly
• give the complete address, phone number, and description of where you are
• describe the accident and tell how many people are injured and what kind of injuries they have
• ask what to do and listen carefully to the instructions
• let the other person hang up the phone first to be sure there are no more questions or instructions for you ☑

✓ READING CHECK

10. Explain When you make a 911 call, why should you let the other person hang up first?

_____
_____
_____
_____

Name _____ Class _____ Date _____

Section 3 Review

SECTION VOCABULARY

aerobic exercise physical exercise intended to increase the activity of the heart and lungs to promote the body's use of oxygen	**hygiene** the science of health and ways to preserve health
	stress a physical or mental response to pressure

1. List Name four ways aerobic exercise can help you stay healthy.

_____

_____

2. Summarize Complete the organizer below to identify some healthy habits.

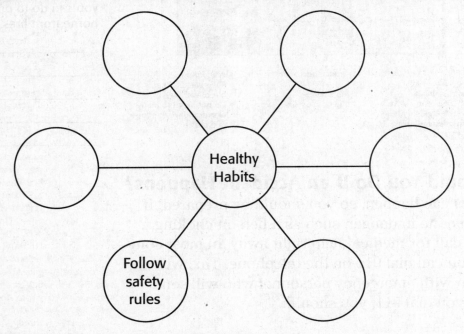

3. List Give three symptoms of too much stress.

_____

_____

4. Explain Why do you miss the most restful hours of sleep if you don't sleep long enough?

_____

_____

5. Describe How can you have good posture while sitting at a desk?

_____

_____

Photo Credits

Abbreviations used: c-center, b-bottom, t-top, l-left, r-right, bkgd-background.

Page 1 Sam Dudgeon/HRW; 2 Hank Morgan/Photo Researchers; 3 (t) NASA; (c) Gerry Gropp; (b) Chip Simons Photography; 6 Sam Dudgeon/HRW; 7 Sam Dudgeon/HRW; 11 Sam Dudgeon/HRW; 13 Royalty Free/CORBIS; 17 (c) CENCO; (inset) Robert Brons/Biological Photo Service; 18 (tl) Sinclair Stammers/Science Photo Library/Photo Researchers; (inset) Microworks/Phototake; (tr) Pascal Goetgheluck/Photo Researchers; (inset) Visuals Unlimited/Karl Aufderheide; 23 (l) Wolfgang Kaehler/Liaison International/Getty News Images; (inset) Visuals Unlimited; 24 (tl) David M. Dennis/Tom Stack and Associates; (tr) David M. Dennis/Tom Stack and Associates; 25 (tl) James M. McCann/Photo Researchers; (tr) Visuals Unlimited/Stanley Flegler ; 27 Wolfgang Bayer; 28 Alex Kerstitch/Visuals Unlimited; 29 (tl) William J. Hebert/Getty Images; (tr) SuperStock; (b) Kevin Schafer/Peter Arnold; 33 (l) Kevin Collins/Visuals Unlimited; (inset) Leonard Lessin/Peter Arnold; 34 (tl) M.I. Walker/Photo Researchers; (tr) Steve Allen/Photo Researchers; (bl) Michael Abbey/Visuals Unlimited; (br) Biodisc/Visuals Unlimited; 37 (t) Wolfgang Baumeister/Science Photo Library/Photo Researchers; (b) Biophoto Associates/Photo Researchers; 51 (bl) Sam Dudgeon/HRW; (br) Sam Dudgeon/HRW; 56 (br) John Langford/HRW; 59 (b) CNRI/Science Photo Library/Photo Researchers ; 60 Biophoto Associates/Photo Researchers; 61 (tl) Ed Reschke/Peter Arnold; (tr) Ed Reschke/Peter Arnold; (cl) Ed Reschke/Peter Arnold; (cr) Ed Reschke/Peter Arnold; (bl) Biology Media/Photo Researchers; (br) Biology Media/Photo Researchers; (b) Visuals Unlimited; 63 (b) National Geographic Image Collection/Ned M. Seidler; 69 (b) Joe McDonald/Visuals Unlimited; 75 (b) CNRI/Phototake NYC; (inset) Biophoto Associates/Photo Researchers; 80 (t) Rob vanNostrand; 87 (inset) J.R. Paulson & U.K. Laemmli/University of Geneva; 89 (c) David M. Phillips/Visuals Unlimited; 93 (tr) Jackie Lewin/Royal Free Hospital/Science Photo Library/Photo Researchers; (br) Jackie Lewin/Royal Free Hospital/Science Photo Library/Photo Researchers; 95 (l) James Beveridge/Visuals Unlimited; (c) Doug Wechsler/Animals Animals; (r) Gail Shumway/Getty Images; 96 (bl) Ken Lucas; (br) John Cancalosi/ Tom Stack & Associates; 98 (t) Courtesy of Research Casting International and Dr. J. G. M. Thewissen; (tc) Courtesy of Research Casting International and Dr. J. G. M. Thewissen; (bc) Philip Gingerich/Courtesy of the Museum of Paleontology, The University of Michigan; (b) Courtesy of Betsy Webb, Pratt Museum, Homer, Alaska, 99 (camel) Ron Kimball/Ron Kimball Stock; (pig) Carol & Ann Purcell/CORBIS; (bison) SuperStock; (hippo) Martin B. Withers/CORBIS; (whale) Martin Ruegner/Alamy Photos; (whale) James D. Watt/Alamy Photos; 103 (b) Carolyn A. McKeone/Photo Researchers; 107 (b) Getty Images; 123 (br) Daniel J. Cox/Getty Images; 125 John Reader/Science Photo Library/Photo Researchers; 126 John Gurche; 127 Volker Steger/Nordstar-4 Million Years, of Man/Science Photo Library/Photo Researchers; 135 Biophoto Associates/Photo Researchers; 136 (t) Dr. Tony Brian & David Parker/Science Photo Library/Photo Researchers; (b) Sherrie Jones/Photo Researchers; 138 (t) Phil A. Dotson/Photo Researchers; (b) © Royalty Free/CORBIS; 139 (t) © Royalty-Free/CORBIS; 143 (tl) Andrew Syred/Photo Researchers; (tr) David M. Phillips/Visuals Unlimited; (b) CNRI/Science Photo Library/Photo Researchers; 144 (c) David M. Phillips/Visuals Unlimited; (inset) SuperStock; 145 (c) SuperStock; (inset) Dr. Kari Lounatmaa/

Science Photo Library/Photo Researchers; 148 Peter Van Steen/HRW; 149 (t) Carmela Leszczynski/Animals Animals/Earth Scenes; (b) Aaron Haupt/Photo Researchers; 151 E.O.S./Gelderblom/Photo Researchers; 152 (tl) Hans Gelderblom/Visuals Unlimited; (tr) K.G. Murti/Visuals Unlimited; (bl) Dr. O. Bradfute/Peter Arnold; (br) Oliver Meckes/MPI-Tubingen/Photo Researchers; 155 (tl) David Phillips/Visuals Unlimited; (tr) Matt Meadows/Peter Arnold; (bl) Breck P. Kent; (br) Michael Abbey/Photo Researchers; 156 Dr. Hilda Canter-Lund; 157 (t) Eric Grave/Science Source/Photo Researchers; 159 Robert Brons/Biological Photo Service; 160 Manfred Kage/Peter Arnold; 163 (t) P. Parks/OSF/Animals Animals; (b) Manfred Kage/Peter Arnold; 165 Matt Meadows/Peter Arnold; 167 (l) Runk/Schoenberger/Grant Heilman; (r) Stan Flegler/Visuals Unlimited; 169 A. Davies/Bruce Coleman; 170 (t) Andrew Syred/Science Photo Library/Photo Researchers; (b) J. Forsdyke/Gene Cox/Science Photo Library/Photo Researchers; 171 (t) Bill Beatty; (b) Michael Fogden/DRK; 172 (t) David M. Dennis/Tom Stack; (b) Walter H. Hodge/Peter Arnold; 173 (tl,tr) Stephen & Sylvia Duran Sharnoff/National Geographic Society Image Collection; (bl) Stan Osolinski; 177 (l) Bruce Coleman; (r) Runk/Schoenberger/Grant Heilman; 187 T. Branch/Photo Researchers; 189 (tl) Dwight R. Kuhn; (tr) Runk/Schoenberger/Grant Heilman; (b) Nigel Cattlin/Holt Studios International/Photo Researchers; 191 (br) Stephen J. Krasemann/Photo Researchers; 192 Tom Bean; 193 Everett Johnson/Jupiterimages; 195 George Bernard/Science Photo Library/Photo Researchers; 203 (bl) Jerome Wexler/Photo Researchers; (bc) Paul Hein/Unicorn Stock Photos; (br) George Bernard/Earth Scenes; 205 (b) Cathlyn Melloan/Getty Images; 206 (l) R. F. Evert; (r) R. F. Evert; 209 (cl) David B. Fleetham/Getty Images; 210 (cl) Visuals Unlimited/Fred Hossler; 213 (cl) Michael & Patricia Fogden/CORBIS; 214 Tim Davis/Getty Images; 215 Gerard Lacz/Peter Arnold; 216 Ralph A. Clevenger/CORBIS; 217 Brian Kenney; 219 Peter Weimann/Animals Animals/Earth Scenes; 220 Johnny Johnson/Animals Animals/Earth Scenes; 221 (t) © Ron Kimball/Ron Kimball Stock; (b) Richard R. Hansen/Photo Researchers; 227 (tl) Biophoto Associates/Science Source/Photo Researchers; (tr) Lee Foster/Getty Images; (bl) David Fleetham/Getty Images; (br) Randy Morse/Tom Stack & Associates; 228 CNRI/Science Photo Library/Photo Researchers; 229 (t) Visuals Unlimited/R. Calentine; (b) Visuals Unlimited/A. M. Siegelman; 231 (inset) Nigel Cattlin/Holt Studios International/Photo Researchers; (b) Visuals Unlimited/David M. Phillips; 233 Milton Rand/Tom Stack & Associates; 235 Leroy Simon/Visuals Unlimited; 236 (t) M.H. Sharp/Photo Researchers; (b) CNRI/Science Photo Library/Photo Researchers; 237 (tl) Visuals Unlimited/A. Kerstitch; (tr) Dr. E. R. Degginger/Color-Pic; (b) Daniel Gotshall/Visuals Unlimited; (inset) M.I. Walker/Photo Researchers; 238 Leroy Simon/Visuals Unlimited; 241 (l) Cabisco/Visuals Unlimited; (r) Paul McCormick/Getty Images; 243 (tl) Andrew J. Martinez/Photo Researchers; (tr) Robert Dunne/Photo Researchers; (cl) Flip Nicklin/Minden Pictures; (cr) Marty Snyderman/Visuals Unlimited; (bl) Chesher/Photo Researchers; (br) Daniel W. Gotshall/Visuals Unlimited; 245 (tl) Randy Morse/Tom Stack; (tr) G.I. Bernard OSF/Animals Animals; 247 James Watt/Animals Animals/Earth Scenes; 249 (t) Steinhart Aquarium/Photo Researchers; (c) Hans Reinhard/Bruce Coleman; (bl) Norbert Wu; (br) Martin Barraud/Getty Images; (bc) Index Stock Imagery; 250 (l) Steinhart Aquarium/Tom McHugh/Photo Researchers; (r) Ron & Valerie Taylor/Bruce Coleman; (b) Bruce Coleman; 253 David M. Dennis/Tom Stack & Associates; 255 M.P.L. Fogden/Bruce Coleman; 256 (tl) Richard Thom/Visuals

Unlimited; (tr) Stephen Dalton/NHPA; (bl) Leonard Lee Rue/Photo Researchers; (br) Breck P. Kent; 257 Felix Labhardt/Getty Images; 259 Danilo B. Donadoni/Bruce Coleman; 260 (l) Stanley Breeden/DRK Photo; (r) Visuals Unlimited/Joe McDonald; 261 (l) Mike Severns/Getty Images; (r) Dr. Carl H. Ernst; 262 (tl) Wayne Lynch/DRK Photo; (tr) Kevin Schafer/Peter Arnold; (bl) Animals Animals/Earth Scenes; (br) Uhlenhut, Klaus/Animals Animals/Earth Scenes; 263 Kevin Schafer/CORBIS; 269 (t) D. Cavagnaro/DRK Photo; (b) Hal H. Harrison/Grant Heilman; 271 (l) Kevin Schafer/Getty Images; (c) Gavriel Jecan/Getty Images; (r) APL/J. Carnemolla/Westlight; 272 (t) Tui De Roy/Minden Pictures; (c) S. Nielsen/DRK Photo; (b) Wayne Lankinen/Bruce Coleman; 273 (tr) Stephen J. Krasemann/DRK Photo; (tl) Frans Lanting/Minden Pictures; (bl) Greg Vaughn/Getty Images; (br) Fritz Polking/Bruce Coleman; 275 (tl) Gerard Lacz/Animals Animals; (tr) Nigel Dennis/Photo Researchers; (b) Tim Davis/Photo Researchers; 276 Hans Reinhard/Bruce Coleman; 277 (l) Tom Tietz/Getty Images; (r) Sylvain Cordier/Photo Researchers; 279 (l) Wayne Lynch/DRK Photo; (r) John D. Cunningham/Visuals Unlimited; 280 (tl) D. R. Kuhn/Bruce Coleman; (tr) Gail Shumway/Getty Images; (bl) Gerry Ellis/Minden Pictures; (br) Frans Lanting/Minden Pictures; 281 (tl) David Cavagnaro/Peter Arnold; (tr) John Cancalosi; (bl) Art Wolfe/Getty Images; (br) Merlin D. Tuttle/Bat Conservation International; 282 (tl) Gail Shumway/Getty Images; (tr) Arthur C. Smith III/Grant Heilman; (bl) Art Wolfe/Getty Images; (br) Manoj Shah/Getty Images; 283 (tl) Gail Shumway; (tr) Roberto Arakaki/International Stock/ImageState; (b) Scott Daniel Peterson/Liaison/Getty News Images; 284 (tl) Flip Nicklin/Minden Pictures; (tr) Pete Atkinson/NHPA; (b) Tom & Therisa Stack; 285 (t) Inga Spence/Tom Stack; (bl) J. & P. Wegner/Animals Animals; (r) Martin Harvey/NHPA; 286 Joe McDonald/Bruce Coleman; 287 Pavel German/NHPA; (r) Edwin & Peggy Bauer/Bruce Coleman; 288 Dave Watts/Nature Picture Library; 289 (tl) Art Wolfe/Getty Images; (tr) Jean-Paul Ferrero/AUSCAPE; (b) Hans Reinhard/Bruce Coleman; 301 Ross Hamilton/Getty Images; 302 (t) Jack Wilburn/Animals Animals/Earth Scenes; (b) Art Wolfe; 303 Stanley Breeden/DRK Photo; 304 (t) Tom J. Ulrich/Visuals Unlimited; (b) Jeff Lepore/Photo Researchers; 305 Thomas Kitchin/Natural Selection; 306 (t) Robert & Linda Mitchell Photography; (b) Ed Robinson/Tom Stack & Associates; 307 (t) Gay Bumgarner/Getty Images; (b) Rick & Nora Bowers/Visuals Unlimited; 313 (l) Diana L. Stratton/Tom Stack & Associates; (r) Stan Osolinski; 326 (c) Stuart Westmorland/Getty Images; (inset) Manfred Kage/Peter Arnold; 329 Jeff Hunter/Getty Images; 335 Larry Lefever/Grant Heilman Photography; 338 REUTERS/Jonathan Searle /NewsCom; 339 Rex Ziak/Getty Images; 341 (l) Peter Van Steen/HRW; (r) Peter Van Steen/HRW; (c) Peter Van Steen/HRW; 342 (t) Stephen J. Krasemann/DRK Photo; (b) Photo Disc/Getty Images; 343 (c) Novopix / Luc Novovitch; (inset) Singeli Agnew/Taos News; 344 Martin Bond/Science Photo Library/Photo Researchers; 345 K. W. Fink/Bruce Coleman; 346 Stephen J. Krasemann/DRK Photo; 408 Sam Dudgeon/HRW; 409 Will & Deni McIntyre/Photo Researchers; 411 (r) Cabisco/Visuals Unlimited; (l) Innerspace Visions Photography; 413 Getty Images; 422 (tr) David Phillips/Photo Researchers; (tl) Petit Format/Nestle/Science Source/Photo Researchers; (c) Photo Lennart Nilsson/Albert Bonniers Forlag AB, A Child Is Born, Dell Publishing Company; (b) Keith/Custom Medical Stock Photo; 423 Peter Van Steen/HRW; 425 (l) Tektoff-RM/CNRI/Science Photo Library/Photo Researchers; (r) CNRI/Science Photo Library/Photo Researchers; 426 Kent Wood/Photo Researchers; 427 Peter Van Steen/HRW; 429 Peter Van Steen/HRW; 435 Clinical Radiology Dept., Salisbury District Hospital/Science Photo Library/Photo Researchers; 438 (cl) Sam Dudgeon/HRW; (cl) Peter Van Steen/HRW; 445 (l) E. Dirksen/Photo Researchers; (r) Dr. Andrew P. Evans/Indiana University; 449 Sam Dudgeon/HRW; 450 Peter Van Steen/HRW; 451 Sam Dudgeon/HRW.